THE HOWARD FACTOR

THE HOWARD FACTOR

A Decade that Transformed the Nation

Edited by NICK CATER

THE AUSTRALIAN

MELBOURNE
UNIVERSITY
PRESS

MELBOURNE UNIVERSITY PRESS
An imprint of Melbourne University Publishing Limited
187 Grattan Street, Carlton, Victoria 3053, Australia
mup-info@unimelb.edu.au
www.mup.com.au

Published in association with
♠ THE AUSTRALIAN

First published 2006
Text © The Australian, 2006
Design and typography © Melbourne University Publishing Ltd, 2006

Designed by Phil Campbell Design
Typeset in New Baskerville 10.25/13.6 point by J&M Typesetting
Printed by Griffin Press, Netley, S.A.

National Library of Australia Cataloguing-in-Publication entry

The Howard factor : a decade that transformed the nation.

ISBN 0 522 85284 X.

ISBN 978 0 52285 284 4.

1. Howard, John, 1939 — Political and social views. 2.
Liberal Party of Australia. 3. Political leadership —
Australia. 4. Prime ministers — Australia. 5. Australia —
Politics and government — 1996– . I. Cater, Nick.

320.994

CONTENTS

THE CONTRIBUTORS

Nick Cater has been a senior editorial executive at *The Australian* since September 2004. He is a former deputy editor at *The Sunday Telegraph* and assistant editor at *The Daily Telegraph*. He has worked in the Canberra press gallery as a News Limited bureau chief and in Hong Kong as the group's Asia correspondent. He worked in the UK as a journalist with BBC TV.

Roy Eccleston was Washington correspondent for *The Australian* from 2000 to 2005, covering the September 11 attacks, the Washington perspective of the Afghanistan and Iraq wars and the re-election of President Bush in 2004. He has been the paper's foreign affairs writer in Canberra and Brisbane bureau chief and is now based in Adelaide for *The Weekend Australian Magazine*.

Paul Kelly is editor-at-large of *The Australian*. He was previously editor-in-chief (1991–96). He writes on Australian and international issues and is a regular commentator on television. He is the author of *The Unmaking of Gough* (1976), *The Hawke Ascendancy* (1984), *The End of Certainty* (1992), *November 1975* (1995), *Paradise Divided* (2000) and *100 Years— The Australian Story* (2001). He has been Graham Perkins Journalist of the Year, a Walkley Award Winner, a visiting fellow at Harvard University and is a fellow of the Academy of the Social Sciences.

Bill Leak suffered his first attack of culture shock in 1956 when, having fully expected to be born in Madrid, his birth took place in Adelaide. Predictably, he drifted into cartooning and painting. He has been drawing for *The Australian* since 1994. He has won eight Walkley Awards, 19 Stanley Awards and no Archibald Prizes. A collection of his cartoons, *Moments of Truth*, was published in 2005, as was his first novel, *Heart Cancer*.

Kate Legge is a Melbourne-based writer for *The Australian* who has covered federal politics out of Canberra and US presidential elections in Washington DC. She was the Graham Perkin Australian Journalist of the Year in 1994 and a Walkley Award winner in 2003.

Steve Lewis is chief political reporter of *The Australian*. He has worked in the Canberra parliamentary press gallery since 1992 and previously worked in Sydney, where he reported on banking and finance. He has co-authored a series of books on finance and higher education and was a joint Walkley Award winner in 1993.

Samantha Maiden has covered national politics from the Canberra press gallery since 1998. She reported for the Seven Network and the ABC before covering state and federal politics for the 10 Network and *The Advertiser*. She joined *The Australian* in 2003.

George Megalogenis spent 11 years in the Canberra press gallery between 1988 and 1999 before moving to Melbourne as a senior writer with *The Australian*. He is the author of *Faultlines: Race, Work and the Politics of Changing Australia* (2003). His new book is *The Longest Decade* (2006).

Glenn Milne has covered federal politics for 20 years, including stints as political editor of *The Australian* and political editor of the Seven Network. He now writes a syndicated column for News Limited's Sunday newspapers and a weekly column for *The Australian*. In 1997 Glenn won a Walkley Award for journalism.

Brad Norington is a senior writer with *The Australian* who specialises in industrial relations. He is a former industrial editor at *The Sydney Morning Herald* where he also reported on politics from Canberra and Sydney's Macquarie Street. Norington is the author of *Jennie George* (1998), a biography of the former ACTU president, and *Sky Pirates: The Pilots' Strike that Grounded Australia* (1990).

Caroline Overington joined *The Australian* in 2005 after three years as New York correspondent for *The Sydney Morning Herald* and *The Age*. In 2004, she won a Walkley Award for her work on the hoax author Norma Khouri. She won the Prime Ministerial Women and Sport Award for sports writing in 1998. Her first book, about life in New York, will be published in 2006.

Christopher Pearson is a columnist for *The Australian*. He was founding editor of *The Adelaide Review* and the *Sydney Review*. He served for two terms as a member of the Australia Council and is currently on the boards of the National Museum of Australia and SBS Corporation. He is a former speech writer for John Howard.

Matt Price is a columnist and parliamentary sketch writer in *The Australian*'s Canberra bureau. He has been with the newspaper almost as long as John Howard has been Prime Minister. Price, who has won awards for his coverage of federal politics, also writes a syndicated column for News Limited's Sunday newspapers.

Stuart Rintoul is a senior writer with *The Australian* and a former Victorian editor of the paper. He has written about indigenous affairs for many years and is the author of *The Wailing: A National Black Oral History* (1993).

Nicolas Rothwell is a Darwin-based writer for *The Australian*. He is a former correspondent for *The Australian* in the Americas, the Pacific, Europe and, most recently, in the Middle East. He is the author of *Heaven and Earth* (1999), *Wings of the Kite-Hawk* (2003) and 'Thirteen Ways Not To Think About Pauline Hanson', published in *Two Nations: The Causes and Effects of the Rise of the One Nation Party in Australia* (1998).

Imre Salusinszky began his career in journalism with *The Age* in 1978. Following a 20-year detour through university teaching, he returned to full-time journalism with *The Australian* at the beginning of 2003. Along with more than 600 columns in newspapers across Australia, he is the author of many articles and books, including, as editor, *The Oxford Book of Australian Essays* (1997).

Dennis Shanahan is *The Australian*'s political editor. In a 35-year career he has worked in Melbourne, New York, Bathurst and Sydney. He has a masters degree in journalism from Columbia University and was briefly an adviser to NSW attorney-general John Dowd. He has been based in Canberra for *The Australian* for the entire Howard prime ministership.

Greg Sheridan is *The Australian*'s foreign editor. He is a veteran of international affairs, including posts as the newspaper's correspondent in Beijing and Washington. He has produced four books on Asia: *Cities of the Hot Zone, A Southeast Asian Adventure* (2003), *Asian Values, Western Dream: Understanding the New Asia* (1999), *Tigers: Leaders of the New Asia Pacific* (1997) and, as editor and co-author, *Living With Dragons: Australia Confronts Its Asian Destiny* (1995).

Mike Steketee is national affairs editor of *The Australian*. He has worked as a political correspondent in Canberra, Washington correspondent and state political correspondent in Sydney. He is co-author, with Milton Cockburn, of *Wran: An Unauthorised Biography* (1986) and has contributed to other books and journals. He won a Walkley Award for journalism leadership in 2000.

Patrick Walters is *The Australian*'s national security editor and the newspaper's senior writer on defence issues. He joined *The Australian* in 1993 as the newspaper's inaugural Jakarta correspondent and covered the fall of President Suharto in 1998. From 1998 to 2003 he was *The Australian*'s Canberra bureau chief.

Alan Wood has been economics editor and an associate editor of *The Australian* since 1990. He entered journalism in the 1960s with *The Australian Financial Review* in Canberra and served as the *AFR*'s European correspondent. He was also economics editor of *The Sydney Morning Herald*, *The National Times* and the Seven Network. He is based in Melbourne.

PREFACE

Anniversaries are the instant noodles of journalism, an unsatisfying meal that the news editor pulls out of the cupboard when there's nothing fresh to serve up at a morning conference.

Occasionally, very occasionally, anniversaries provide copy that screams out to be put on the news pages. A hitherto unknown detail (an eyewitness), who tells more than he or she was previously prepared to or a cogent piece of analysis enriched with hindsight can cast fresh light on a well-known event, helping our understanding of the present and informing our view of the past.

March 2, 2006 marks one such anniversary. A decade after the federal election that made John Howard prime minister of Australia, much has yet to be written about Australia's second-longest serving head of government and the quiet, conservative revolution that has profoundly changed Australia. Apart from a few bilious tracts written by Howard's opponents, there has been only one attempt at a biography and that book, by David Barnett, hardly scratches the surface. By contrast, four books have been published about Mark Latham and one on Kim Beazley, neither of whom has won an election.

In an attempt to redress this imbalance, *The Australian* asked its senior writers and columnists to examine the seismic shift under Howard in the politics, society, workplaces, culture, economy, trade and external relations of the nation. The result is a long-overdue analysis of Howard, his government, its successes and its failures.

This book may well be of service to Howard's opponents, who have failed consistently to get the measure of the man. Ten years ago they portrayed him as an arch conservative in the thrall of Robert Menzies. Christopher Pearson's essay recalls Paul Keating's description of 'yesterday's man, yearning for the era of the Morphy Richards toaster, the Qualcast mowers the Astor TV console, armchair and slippers'.

A decade later Keating's caricature seems as dated as the imagery he evokes. Howard has been a moderniser who has built on and expanded the work of his predecessor to change the nation fundamentally and reframe the national debate. Keating was succumbing to complacency when he boasted that his 1995 budget was 'as good as it gets', while the three Labor leaders who followed him have been the enemies of change. As *The Australian* editorialised last year, the inversion of the old order has been so complete that Bob Dylan's 1964 anthem *The Times They Are A-Changin'* could easily be Howard's rallying call to the upper house: 'Come senators, congressmen, please heed the call, Don't stand in the doorway, Don't block up the hall.'

Under Howard, the conservatives have stolen the mantle of reform and the progressives have become the new conservatives. There are few attacks on Howard's lack of 'political correctness' today because Howard has established a new political orthodoxy, tried and tested at four elections, which has forced his opponents into the role of dissenters.

It is on this turning political wicket that the Prime Minister has proved himself the most skilful political player of his generation, delivering balls that consistently wrong-foot the Opposition. After his first election victory, many in Labor were in denial, holding the deluded belief that Howard was a temporary aberration and that in three years' time voters would come to their senses. With each subsequent election loss it has become increasingly hard for Labor to blame the 'false consciousness' of the workers. Some senior members of the party are now asking the question this book attempts to answer. The issue is not how the voters got things so wrong, but how Howard got it so right.

* * *

In his keynote introduction to this book, Paul Kelly draws on his 2005 Cunningham Lecture to the Academy of the Social Sciences to examine how Howard has reshaped the culture of governance to suit his priorities of economic liberalism and national security. Under Howard's system of prime ministerial government, popular support is invoked to justify the executive's expanding powers while parliamentary supremacy is upheld in the face of emerging demands for a bill of rights.

Cognitive conflict is the subject of Christopher Pearson's essay on the culture war, which describes how Howard's opponents deployed the Zeitgeist of political correctness against him before Howard himself harnessed the Spirit of the Age to his own advantage and, in doing so, changed it. 'The commentators who supposed they were surfing the Zeitgeist like a great triumphal tide found they'd been dumped by it,' writes Pearson.

Dennis Shanahan argues that Howard's pragmatism and ability to change have not only ensured his longevity but also set the limits of his reforms. Howard's starting point is that a party has to be elected to implement its policies and ideas, and his guiding principle is that it is better to get most of a policy implemented than to lose the lot. His uncomplicated rhetoric—'doing the right thing', 'helping our neighbours', 'protecting our borders'—helps him connect with the public. But he is not a simple populist. Howard the conviction politician is a formidable fighter who is prepared to weather bad polling in the cause of the greater good.

Glenn Milne argues that Howard's political dominance comes from the synthesis of two ideas: conservative social values and a pragmatic commitment to the free market. But Howard's supremacy has also been built on darker forces that took hold during his years in the wilderness: fear and failure. He is a politician forged by history and now destined to make it.

Like Menzies, Howard has presided over a period of sustained prosperity. But as Alan Wood shows in his essay on the economy, Howard's golden era is built on very different foundations. The economy has broken away from a past haunted by destructive wage rounds and balance of payments crises. These days the Reserve Bank is more concerned about asset price bubbles than wages or the exchange rates.

In chapter 7, Mike Steketee exposes the paradox of Howard's two-tier welfare state. As a conservative, Howard should be committed to small government, yet welfare spending has increased substantially over the past 10 years, much of it funding un-means-tested middle-class welfare. Meanwhile the doctrine of mutual obligation, first tested with the work-for-the-dole scheme, has spread to include disability pensioners, single mothers and indigenous welfare recipients. But by stopping short of the redesign of the welfare system recommended by the seminal McClure Report, the Government is in danger of creating an intergenerational underclass, permanently marginalising some sections of society.

Howard has also come under sustained pressure to overhaul the tax system but, as George Megalogenis notes, politics have triumphed over policy. Those at the top end of the scale have gained most from what tax cuts there have been, while welfare has been used as a precision weapon to win the hearts and minds of middle Australia.

In chapter 9, Brad Norington goes to the heart of Howard's crusade to reshape workplace relations. Of all the elements of Howard's agenda, this is the most ideologically driven. The 2005 legislation, the biggest change to Australia's industrial relations system since 1907, was the fulfilment of a project Howard had been working towards for much of his political career. 'His philosophy brims with values ingrained from his youth in the 1950s: the Protestant work ethic, individualism, free markets and entrepreneurial opportunity with emphasis on small business,' writes Norington.

Pauline Hanson has left politics and her One Nation party is a splintered and spent force but, as Nicolas Rothwell argues, the battle for the Hansonite vote continues to be one of the most significant dynamics in Australian politics. The rise of Hansonism tested Howard's political mettle but his response ultimately secured his political longevity. By forging his own compact with the voters of middle Australia, Howard harvested the loyalty of the disaffected body of working-class conservatives who constitute the swinging heart of the electorate.

In his second contribution, Megalogenis looks at the politics of race and shows how the colour and culture of Australia have changed during Howard's tenure, a transformation that has at times been obscured by the Prime Minister's tough rhetoric on border control. The country passed a significant milestone on the 40-year retreat from the White Australia Policy under Howard when the European component of our total overseas-born population fell below 50 per cent for the first time.

In chapter 12, Stuart Rintoul chronicles the remarkable turnaround in the indigenous debate under Howard and the emergence of a new paradigm of practical reconciliation. Howard's stubborn rejection of 'black-armband' symbolism was met with bitterness and distrust from some indigenous leaders, particularly during his first two terms. But since then a spirit of dialogue has been gaining momentum, together with a consensus on the mutual obligation principle driven by a common desire to improve the disadvantaged lives of indigenous people.

Samantha Maiden finds the common thread running through 10 years of education and health reforms: the doctrine of choice. Howard plays to the Australian belief in egalitarianism by promoting choice in health and education as a right, not a privilege to be enjoyed by the wealthy few. Choice is the cloak used to disguise his user-pays philosophy as a message of personal empowerment.

In chapter 14, Kate Legge explodes the popular myths about Howard's social conservatism that his critics still delight in perpetuating. Far from corralling mothers behind the white picket fence, Howard has recognised that the age of the single breadwinner is over for most families and is actively encouraging women to return to the workforce.

Howard has also confounded his critics in his handling of foreign relations. Keating warned the nation during the 1996 campaign that Asia would refuse to deal with Howard, yet within 12 days of the election, Keating's nemesis, the then Malaysian prime minister Mahathir Mohamad, announced a highly symbolic visit to Australia. Greg Sheridan points out that, after a stumbling start in international diplomacy, Howard has become a self-taught statesman and has boosted our stocks from Jakarta to London and from Beijing to Washington.

Patrick Walters focuses on national security, showing how Howard instinctively recognised both the threats and the opportunities in the spread of global terrorism. The challenge posed by Islamist terrorism has changed the national security landscape. Howard has been more closely involved in defence and security than any of his recent predecessors, deftly managing the security debate to his political advantage and reinforcing his prime ministerial authority.

September 11, 2001 was a pivotal point for Howard's relationship with the United States, writes Roy Eccleston, who describes how the 50-year-old ANZUS treaty was revived and redefined in the days that followed al-Qa'ida's dreadful attack on American soil.

Steve Lewis looks at another group marginalised by Howard's ascendancy: the Labor Party. Howard's occupation of the middle ground forced Labor to choose between turning left and turning right. The consequence was an unseemly squabble that culminated with the disastrous Latham experiment.

Bill Leak's subversive account of the cartoonist's 10-year struggle to translate Howard's 'ordinariness' into lines on the page offers clues to the qualities that have ensured the Prime Minister's political longevity. Leak, who famously increased the length of Howard's bottom lip by 10 per cent in line with the introduction of the GST, describes how the evolution of the cartooned Howard reflects the changes the man himself has undergone in more than 30 years of public life.

Journalists have often struggled alongside their colleagues in the art department to capture the essence of Howard, a task that has not been helped by Howard's plain-vanilla rhetoric. But, as Imre Salusinszky points out, Howard's choice of words is entirely deliberate. Howard has steered clear of the operatic flourish of Keating and avoided the crude, seething anger of Latham to deliver a message that is perfectly tuned for its audience.

Caroline Overington charts the rise of the 'young fogies' who are responsible for a historic shift in the youth vote from Labor to Liberal over the course of four elections. She draws parallels with the South Park Conservatives of the United States, whose challenge to their boomer parents' political correctness is captured in Matt Stone and Trey Parker's television cartoon series *South Park*.

The final section of the book chronicles the major milestones of the Howard years as a matter of record and as a reminder of the distance the nation has travelled. If *The Australian* has been publishing the first draft of history for the past 10 years, Rebecca Weisser has compiled the second draft, trawling the archives to select the major events as they were reported at the time. With the benefit of hindsight, contemporary comments by the major players, Howard included, range from the prescient to the myopic and are often richly ironic.

One final thought. An anthropological linguist stumbling on these shores in 2006 might well conclude that the collective failure to understand the significance of the Howard decade is reflected by a glaring gap in our lexicography. Britain had Thatcherism and the US had Reaganomics, but there is not yet any noun or adjective to describe Howard's style of government. Perhaps in the process of publishing this book we will start a quest to find one.

Nick Cater
January 2006

I

INTRODUCTION

HOW HOWARD GOVERNS

Paul Kelly

SINCE 1996 John Howard has brought the art of political management to a zenith with his own interpretation of prime ministerial government. This decade under Howard demonstrates the advantage of incumbency with a disciplined and experienced leader. Howard has been an astute chief executive in marshalling the traditional powers of his office, yet he operates as an innovator in his re-interpretation of the role of prime minister. He switches between two models—a leader of intense political partisanship and a leader who symbolises an 'Australian way of life' to the people.[1]

The Howard prime ministership embodies the characteristics of its age—economic prosperity, work and family pressures on households, growing nationalism amid multicultural diversity, a focus on security at home and military ventures abroad, and the rise of the media-driven 24-hour political cycle. The lesson of Howard's uncertain first term (1996–98) was that the priority task of the prime minister was to set the agenda for his government, the media and the Opposition. In the decade since he came to power, Australians have debated Howard's ideas, values and policies. In this process, however, the nation and Howard have moved closer together in a contested embrace.

Howard has introduced a new operating concept—the prime minister in a continuous dialogue with the public. Along the way Howard has moved towards a new synthesis of his office—he is Prime Minister, de facto head of state, a talkback media personality, economic manager, war leader and cultural commentator. He has taken this synthesis into new dimensions of prime ministerial influence. Howard, even more than Bob Hawke, sees the source of his prime ministerial legitimacy originating with the popular will. In his hands the idea of the popular will is a dynamic and radical weapon.

Howard's profile as a conservative is misleading and exaggerated, too reliant on his status as a constitutional monarchist. He believes the political system must adapt to the demands of the people and the challenges that face Australia, from globalisation to national security. I suggest that, on his retirement, Howard's governance record will be more conspicuous for the changes he made than for the changes he refused to make. In my view, he is best understood as a change agent and I believe this is how Howard sees himself. In the context of Australia's debate over republicanism Howard depicted himself as a 'Burkean' conservative, but more recently he quoted Burke approvingly saying that 'a state without the means of some change is without the means of its conservation'.[2]

Howard's record shows him as a pragmatist, uninterested in utopian visions but focused on change that is achievable and utilitarian. His opposition to constitutional change by referendum has disguised the extent to which he supports changes by other means. He brings two distinct views to governance. First, he thinks as a practitioner who judges governance more by its policy and political outcomes than as a system in its own right. He dislikes debate about abstractions or principles of governance, from ministerial responsibility to the separation of powers, and distrusts debate on governmental models. Second, Howard's frame of reference is public sentiment and Australian values—he invokes public approval to legitimate any changes to governance that might diminish accountability or checks and balances. The people become the justification of his prime ministership. This point is widely recognised but its full import is not appreciated.

For example, in relation to federalism, Howard has abandoned the Liberal Party's ritualistic genuflection to state powers. In relation to his industrial reforms he invokes a higher principle, saying that 'the goal is to free the individual, not to trample on the States'.[3] His guiding star, however, is public sentiment. Howard judges that state loyalties are fading and national loyalties are growing. He is fascinated by the rise of national consciousness—what he calls the nationalisation of our society. At rugby league State of Origin games he refuses to barrack for NSW. On talkback radio he finds that the people think national; when he travels into the regions he finds that people are looking to the national government rather than state governments. He seeks to free the Liberal Party from many of its past emotional chains, ranging from state loyalty to the party's orthodox view of institutions such as the Industrial Relations Commission and the Reserve Bank.[4] His military policy is the most adventurous since the Vietnam commitment of the 1960s—and Howard, in effect, has buried the Vietnam legacy.

Over the years, Howard's ministers have criticised the judiciary and Howard himself has embraced a narrow version of ministerial responsibility. He has imposed more restrictions on the public service and he has introduced security laws that alter the balance between security and civil liberty. In each case his justification is the national interest or the will of the people. Howard re-defines existing standards and principles by resort to these arguments. In his approach to governance, therefore, he is a radical populist as well as a Burkean conservative.

It is, however, misleading to exaggerate Howard's break from the past. Howard is no more preoccupied by executive authority than Malcolm Fraser was; no more hostile to the Senate than Paul Keating; no more reliant upon ministerial staff than Hawke. Many of the denunciations of his government are shallow misrepresentations of history—they ignore the fact that Howard's link to the past is more about continuity than discontinuity.

It is important to locate Howard in his office, to perceive him as he is—not as a confected Machiavelli but as a real person working on his prime ministerial project. Such a picture reveals the continuity and the uniqueness in our governance. The Australian system has borrowed from Britain and the US but it is unique. Howard understands this and, in turn, it is a key to understanding Howard. He has no interest in importing external ideas into our system of government—either adaptations from the US presidential model or the universal idea of a bill of rights. The Howard prime ministership is making our governance more nationalistic, more different from (and not more similar to) overseas models. The republic debate obscured this reality. Howard's instinct, so apparent yet so frequently overlooked, is to refine an Australian model.

The heart of prime ministerial government is the House on Capital Hill, opened in 1988 to house the federal parliament.[5] The building is the triumph of executive power, grander than the White House.

Howard arrives and leaves by car from his executive courtyard and has the instruments of his power in proximity—the parliament, his ministers, his staff, the cabinet unit, 300 journalists and, at the foot of the Hill, the main policy departments whose public service chiefs trek up the Hill to advise and to listen.

For the Liberal and Labor parties the prize of executive power has never been so alluring. The major parties are weak, beset by falling membership, decline of voter loyalty and ideological confusions. In Opposition these weaknesses are crippling—witness the demoralisation of the Liberals between 1983 and 1996 and of Labor since 1996. The purpose of these parties now is to provide a structure and a leader to capture executive power. Without executive power, they look non-viable. In government, weakness becomes strength, demoralisation becomes empowerment and a modest leader becomes a giant-killer.

The system of governance is becoming more politicised. Indeed, it can be argued that our very society and culture are becoming more politicised. John Howard is a 24/7 party politician who runs a permanent campaign. He has integrated politics into policy and administration to a degree unachieved by any of his predecessors. Howard is campaigning on behalf of his government each day, almost from the moment he completes his morning walk. Nothing could be more removed from the distant administration of Howard's hero RG Menzies of whom it could be said that the people knew he was there but they rarely saw him.

* * *

The main instrument of John Howard's prime ministerial power is the cabinet—and Australia's cabinet system is unique. There is no functioning cabinet system in Washington, while Tony Blair's Britain has largely abandoned cabinet government. Under Blair most decisions are taken in bilateral or informal networks. In December 2004 Blair's former cabinet secretary, Lord Butler, said: 'The cabinet now—and I don't think there's any secret about this—doesn't make decisions ... the government reaches conclusions in rather small groups of people.'[6]

So Howard's governance is different from that of Bush and Blair. Howard is a cabinet traditionalist, like Fraser and Hawke. An effective cabinet cannot guarantee good government—but there can be no good government without it. Howard's cabinet is tight, secret and collective. Its secrecy is the most abject defeat for the press gallery in 30 years. It is an instrument of collective responsibility and this idea dominates Howard's executive.

In Australia good prime ministers must be good team leaders and 'simply stamping the prime ministerial foot is conductive neither to good government nor to personal survival'.[7] Howard does not stamp his foot, unlike some of his predecessors. On the contrary, Howard is a collectivist. One of his initial objectives was 'to run a proper cabinet system'.[8]

Howard uses the cabinet as an instrument of his authority, of ministerial consultation, obedience and unity. The contentious issues are cleared through cabinet—immigration detention policies, our commitment to the war in Iraq and the goods and services tax (GST). Restrictions on the circulation of cabinet submissions are sometimes so tight that they inhibit debate. Howard's cabinet is the most unified since Menzies and reflects a remarkably shared outlook. The process is formalised and disciplined; meetings are scheduled well ahead. Howard, unlike Keating, is punctual and starts on time. Unlike Fraser, he does not call cabinet at short notice or late at night nor prolong debate to physical exhaustion. Howard is civil; he rarely personalises issues or abuses people. Howard has a businesslike approach. He wants people to have their say, but he does not want ministers imprisoned in the cabinet room.[9]

In 2004–05 there were only 57 cabinet meetings (including cabinet committees but excluding the National Security Committee) and 302 decisions—a modest number.[10] The pace of decision-making is much slower than in the Fraser years and has fallen from 440 decisions in 2002–03.[11]

In 1996 Howard moved the cabinet policy unit from the Prime Minister's Department to his own office. The symbolism was stark—the engine-room of executive government was not to be managed by public servants. It would be supervised by Howard's political staff. The first head of the cabinet office was Michael L'Estrange, a former public servant and Liberal Party staffer, now secretary of Foreign Affairs. The second head was Paul McClintock, from the Sydney business community and a Howard aide from his time as Treasurer. It is the cabinet unit that plans the agenda, lists the items and writes up the cabinet decisions—all from Howard's office under the ultimate authority of his office chief, Arthur Sinodinos.

* * *

John Howard has brought to its zenith a trend that began with Whitlam—the transfer of power from the public service to ministers. This is coupled with a philosophy of administration that also began with Whitlam—public service responsiveness to political will.

In Howard's 1997 Garran Oration, he upheld the idea of impartial advice, saying that no government 'owned' the public service, which he saw as a 'national asset'. But Howard said ministers would take greater control of policy in its 'planning, detail and implementation'—a statement of great import.[12]

His justification for greater ministerial authority was political. For Howard, this was the public's expectation. His judgment is correct and flows from the phenomenon of the 24-hour political cycle whereby the media demands answers from ministers on a daily basis. It is the transformation in politics that has forced a transformation in the conduct of government. The rule defined by Howard is that the task of public servants is to 'recognise the directions in which a government is moving and be capable of playing a major role in developing policy options'.[13]

Howard began by sacking six departmental heads, a third of the secretaries—sackings that were sudden and brutal. One of Australia's public service veterans, Tony Ayers, said later: 'I have no argument if they got the sack for non-performance. My worry at the moment is that people get sacked because someone doesn't like the colour of their hair or whatever.'[14] It was the greatest blood-letting upon any change of government since Federation. Howard's determination to achieve a responsive service informed his choice of Max Moore-Wilton as head of the Prime Minister's Department, a formidable leader with a preference for results over process. In Howard's early years Canberra was a town in a state of high tension. This was accentuated because another of Moore-Wilton's briefs was to reduce public service numbers—the bureaucracy had to do more with less.

Howard's approach was the exaggerated culmination of a 25-year trend. Under Hawke and Keating, power moved decisively in favour of ministers and personal office staff was expanded. In 1987 Hawke created the super-departments, saying his aim was to increase the bureaucracy's responsiveness to the Government's wishes.[15] As prime minister, Keating introduced a contract system for departmental heads that formalised the end-of-employment security for public service chiefs and reflected a new rule of accountability to ministers. Keating had complained earlier about 'the abdication of responsibility by the successive conservative governments in favour of the Commonwealth Club mandarins'.[16]

No prime minister these days—not Keating, Howard or a future Peter Costello—would accept the autonomy exercised by the great public servants of the past such as Roland Wilson, Arthur Tange or Frederick Wheeler. The removal of employment security terminates the age of so-called 'frank and fearless' advice. Despite its mythical afterglow, this was never a golden age and the value of the 'frank and fearless' system remains contested.

The issue now is whether, under Howard, the pendulum has moved too far towards responsiveness. Former public service commissioner Andrew Podger believes that it has. He identifies three concerns—that senior officials may be 'too concerned to please', that the system is too geared to shielding ministers from political embarrassment at the sacrifice of the public interest and that public servants are not sufficiently fulfilling their legal and administrative responsibilities to the public. Such concerns are united in a single theme: the challenge to the public service flowing from Howard's system of political management.

The children overboard incident showed the secretary of the Immigration Department too anxious to pass to Minister Philip Ruddock in an election context advice that proved to be false, notably that children had been thrown overboard by asylum seekers. This was the service being 'responsive', with fatal consequences.[17] The chief of the defence force, Admiral Chris Barrie, later declined to change his advice to his minister or check for himself, the effect being to protect the political position of defence minister Peter Reith and, ultimately, Howard. The issue here is the public service being too willing to shield the government on political issues rather than being party political.

The 2005 Palmer and Comrie reports into the Immigration Department over the Rau and Alvarez cases show the dangers in an over-responsive public service.[18] There are three dominant themes in these damning reports: first, that public servants acted unlawfully and irresponsibly in their dealings with individuals; second, that the department was infected with a cultural mindset that was defensive and dehumanised; and third, that there was a pervasive failure of departmental leadership. The reports, however, missed the over-arching point: these failures are a failure of ministerial leadership. It is extraordinary that mismanagement on such a scale would not be sheeted home to the minister.

However, the widely held view that under Howard the 'correct' relationship between ministers and public servants has been corrupted and that the Howard Government has an unprecedented record of lying are an exercise in political amnesia.

There are many examples that disprove the folklore of a superior past—witness the *Voyager* cover-up, the 1966–67 VIP affair, the Khemlani loan, the bottom-of-the-harbour tax fraud, the unsustainable L-A-W tax cuts, the deception over the 1965 Vietnam commitment, the conceal-ment of the budget position at the 1983 and 1996 elections, and, for sheer political deception, the Kirribilli pact on the prime ministership. We need to see the present in a realistic, not a doom-laden, framework.

The historical debate about relations between ministers and public servants is bedevilled because it overlooks the main point: that the prime responsibility of the public service is to assist ministers to realise their agenda.

* * *

In the Howard Government the primary ideas flow from the top down-wards. As each term advanced Howard grew bolder in the implementa-tion of his own beliefs and policies. The Howard Government has a sharper ideological edge than the former Fraser Government. If Fraser's rule was defined by hard men, Howard's rule is defined by hard ideas.

Howard is a networker who takes ideas from his travels, dialogues and discussions. He is receptive, rarely changes his beliefs and is never an easy touch. The Government's style is anti-elitist, it believes in the opinion of the common man, it is ideological and never values-free, its ministers are down-to-earth and some think there is more wisdom at the local pub than in a university seminar.

Yet the Government remains anchored in a firm political vision that fuses ideology and electoral strategy. Howard's singular achievement has been to win a re-alignment within Australian politics by detaching a sec-tion of the Labor vote and bringing it to the Liberal Party. Menzies was handed this outcome by the emergence of the DLP in the mid-1950s while Howard has achieved this by dint of his insight and appeal. The ideas that shape Howard's governance are economic liberalism, social conservatism, cultural traditionalism, national security, family support and national pride.

It is a complex yet powerful mix—and despite its complexity there is a tenacious grasp of these ideas at the apex of power. Howard, in effect, has created a new Liberal Party ideology, a blend of tradition and innovation that is pitched to the circumstances he faces in office. The defect displayed by his critics lies in their refusal to admit the new challenges that Howard faces, demanding fresh policy responses—from globalisation to Islamist terrorism to the community's quest for order and social stability.

Nevertheless, the intellectual origins of the Howard Government lie in the 1980s and 1990s—the decisive years of Howard's political evolution. Witness his big reforms, the GST and industrial relations deregulation. Amid these epic debates has been the search for a series of sustained and viable policy themes conducted within the centralising concept of whole-of-government administration. Howard is attached to the whole-of-government philosophy to improve service delivery and promote strategic thinking.

This approach was formalised by cabinet policy unit chief Paul McClintock and on 31 July 2002 the cabinet, at an annual 'strategic priorities' meeting, endorsed nine whole-of-government priorities: national security and defence, work and family, demography and an ageing population, science and innovation, higher education, sustainable environment, energy, rural and regional affairs, and transport. Howard took the unusual step of announcing these cabinet priorities, casting his government as 'prepared to carry out vital reforms'.[19]

The results have been mixed. It was tempting, as 2005 drew to a close, to think that the Howard Government might be close to an emerging crisis of ideas. As the Government completes the economic reforms whose intellectual origins lie in the 1980s, there is no apparent source of intellectual renewal. In politics, more of the past is rarely enough. The politicians may not concede the point, but the reality, beyond their media spin, is that they need to discover the new ideas that underpin long-term strategy.

* * *

The people are the centrepiece of John Howard's prime ministership. Howard has no interest in background briefings; he uses the media as an instrument to reach the people. He spends more time on the media than he does in the parliament or in the cabinet. His innovation is the permanent campaign—fighting the 24-hour political cycle for the 1000 days in each three-year term. It is this brand of politics that is transforming governance. Winning each 24-hour political cycle demands a flexible yet focused media message and a 'rapid response'. Howard's office and the apparatus of government are geared to these political demands.

For Howard, an interview before breakfast is not an unusual diet. He has his favourite talkback host in each capital city. Howard markets his ideas, defends his policies and is a commentator on the nation's condition with views from cricket to curriculum. His core tactic is to set the agenda and have his opponents defined according to that agenda. Howard is the omnipresent uncle, transmitting into every household, unless he is switched off.[20] Remember that the main reason given by Labor leader Kim Beazley for establishing a second home base in Sydney was his need to appear on radio.

Howard chooses not to live in Canberra. He lives in Sydney and the symbolism is unmistakable—he leaves Canberra to return to the nation. Howard likes domestic travel and is energised by it—the dinners, speeches and provincial functions. He is the most domestically travelled prime minister in the nation's history—in the regions and in the cities—and is proud of his local knowledge.

Howard's approach to parliament is based on performance, control and negotiation. Prime ministers know that if their government is called to account by parliament then their ministers are being embarrassed, their policies are being modified and their standing is being diminished. The relationship between government and parliament is governed by numbers. When a government is dominated by the parliament its days are limited because its opponents are dominant; witness the Whitlam era.

During the first three terms of Howard's government, the Labor Party and the Senate as an institution were highly effective in holding the Government to account. Any suggestion that the Government was not under intense pressure from the Senate is wrong. Not only were some of its decisive bills rejected or significantly amended but the Senate committee system was used to probe, to disclose and to embarrass. Former Labor Senate leader John Faulkner has argued, persuasively, that the Government was held to account and he has offered a litany of examples.[21]

Howard takes parliament seriously in three respects: first, as the forum in which the Prime Minister and his ministers must perform credibly; second, as the forum in which the governing parties must display their cohesion; third, as the legislature that gives life to Howard's program. He prepares carefully for question time. He expects discipline from his back bench. For his first eight years he chose to negotiate with the Senate and, though tempted, shunned the option of confrontation or a double dissolution in a display of patience that was rewarded with Senate control in 2005.

However, the Howard era that began with high aspirations for ministerial accountability will end with accountability shifting from ministers to public servants. On his first day in parliament as Prime Minister, Howard tabled his ministerial code of conduct. Yet in that first term he lost five ministers and three parliamentary secretaries, the code had to be revised and Howard decided that it was best (politically speaking) to keep ministers, not to lose them.[22]

It seems Howard's working rule of ministerial responsibility is that ministers, in effect, are responsible not to the parliament or the party but to the prime minister. This is the operating reality of the Howard Government. The test Howard applies or rationalises is that of ministerial responsibility to the people, with the prime minister interpreting the public will.

In practice Howard is loath to remove a minister for policy or administrative reasons, a judgment dictated by his political experience. The upshot is that Howard's working rule is for ministers to go only 'if they are directly responsible for significant failings or mistakes or if their continued presence in the Government is damaging'.[23] The result, in the recent scandals documented within the Immigration Department, is that the minister, senator Amanda Vanstone, stays and the department head departs. A literal reading of this example—that ministers cannot be held to account for decisions that are made by their officials—would suggest that Australia has completed a precise reversal of the classical theory that ministers are responsible for their departments. The irony is that, as ministers take more power, the departmental head assumes more responsibility.

One abuse of incumbency under Howard has been government advertising. Australia's guidelines are inadequate, fail to distinguish between government and political advertising and are becoming more influenced by the election cycle. These problems, apparent under Keating, are more intense under Howard; witness the 2005 campaign for the industrial relations reforms. The funds involved overall are substantial—$118 million for the GST campaign and about $50 million on the industrial relations campaign. In 1998 the auditor-general proposed guidelines to ensure that government advertising 'be presented in an objective and fair manner'. The Labor Party has introduced bills to implement these recommendations—and such reforms are essential.[24]

* * *

One of the main themes of Howard's governance—and conceivably *the* main theme—is his effort to entrench the philosophy of economic liberalism. This is best conceptualised as a national project to strengthen Australia as a market economy in the globalised age. It is an extension of the Hawke–Keating agenda.

This project rests upon the view that Australia must succeed as a free-trade nation exposed to global markets without the security of a regional union such as the European Union. It is, instead, a frontline nation close to the economic transformation of Asia now centred on China and India. The pressure to maintain a competitive Australia has marked all federal cabinets since the 1980s. Such pressure drives the quest for a productive, low-inflation, high-growth economy and it will increasingly shape our governing culture. Under Howard, this has happened in respect of monetary, fiscal and industrial policy as well as the drive to privatisation, competition and choice.

The most important institutional economic reform of the past 15 years has been the outsourcing of monetary policy to the Reserve Bank. Howard was elected in 1996 with a pledge to maintain the independence of the central bank—an extension of the more autonomous arrangement set up during the Keating prime ministership. The conclusion was that it was preferable, for both political and economic reasons, to have interest rates determined by the bank and not the politicians.

This view was formalised by the Howard Government in its 14 August 1996 written agreement between Treasurer Peter Costello and the new governor, Ian Macfarlane. The agreement recognised the independence of the Reserve Bank, endorsed an inflation objective of 2 to 3 per cent over the cycle and demanded a series of steps to promote transparency. The agreement formalised a transfer of power. It was successful beyond Howard's wildest hopes, mainly because of Macfarlane's superior judgments. The dramatic evidence was Howard's nomination of interest rates as the main issue of the 2004 election, a decision that some critics depicted as a gimmick. Nothing could be further from the truth. It was a vindication of the Coalition's monetary governance system established in 1996. Howard won an election on interest rates when they are no longer set by his cabinet.

The second most important item of economic governance will be the 2005 industrial reforms whose impact will play out over many years. They are the most far-reaching industrial reform since the doomed effort of Stanley Melbourne Bruce in 1929. The purpose, again, is to gear Australia as a successful economy in the globalised age and, crucially, to apply Liberal Party values to this project. It involves reducing the wage-fixing role of the Australian Industrial Relations Commission, creating a new Fair Pay Commission operating under different rules, the creation of a single industrial jurisdiction and limiting the role of trade unions in the workplace. The 2007 election result will determine whether this new system becomes permanent.

A new framework of fiscal governance was also established in 1996. The main changes were asset sale proceeds mainly being used to reduce public debt; a fiscal policy rule of a budget balance over the cycle; a legislated Charter of Budget Honesty that requires more fiscal transparency and a five-yearly inter-generational report on the long-term sustainability of government policies. These fiscal governance steps are modest. There is no gainsaying that fiscal policy has been dominated by the revenue surge. Yet the new fiscal governance regime has been significant.

This model has delivered low government debt and a surplus position. Howard and Costello have shown the political superiority of this model. Each of Howard's three re-elections (1998, 2001 and 2004) revealed the tactical utility of his surplus and the multiple advantages it gave the incumbents as it was used for targeted spending or tax cuts. Howard and Costello have created a new politics based on the power of the surplus, replacing the Keynesian deficit politics of an earlier age.

* * *

John Howard has introduced a new dimension to his office—the prime minister as national security chief. It is a multiple role—executive, political and presentational. It has been created by Howard during his prime ministership in response to events and crises. The upshot is that Howard has an unmatched grip on the machinery dealing with war, counterterrorism, the military and intelligence agencies. This represents a departure for our governance, driven not by wars that come and go but by the so-called 'war on terrorism' that is assumed to be ongoing. al-Qa'ida and Jemaah Islamiah (JI) are explicit—Australians are priority targets.

The concept of the prime minister as national security chief is buttressed by new institutional arrangements, a new legal regime that alters the balance between security and civil liberty and by a change in community values that underwrites the system of security governance. It gives the intelligence agencies, most notably ASIO, a weight and an influence that exceeds their role during the Cold War—the result of the new home-grown terrorist threat. This will become a permanent feature of the prime ministership and executive governance under a Coalition or Labor. Howard has displayed a restraint in his rejection of proposals for even more ambitious forms of security governance, although his successors are sure to expand upon his security legacy.

The pivotal institutional arrangement is the National Security Committee (NSC) of cabinet. This is the most influential of all cabinet committees. Howard says the NSC 'is the most effective whole-of-government arrangement with which I've been associated as Prime Minister'. He calls it 'one of the very significant successes of this Government in terms of governance arrangements'.[25] Former Howard Government adviser Peter Jennings, a security specialist, says: 'The NSC has been part of the trend of power centralising around the Prime Minister.'[26]

The NSC takes decisions on procurement, security and defence strategy, military deployments from East Timor to Iraq, and all aspects of counterterrorism measures—dealing with intelligence, operations and new laws. Its decisions do not have to be authorised by the full cabinet. It also functions as the crisis management mechanism for the Government. At the height of the East Timor intervention it met twice daily, at early morning and in the evening, to monitor events and take decisions. In the war in Iraq it fulfilled the same function, taking operational decisions such as which targets our fighters would bomb.[27]

Its significance is that the NSC anchors military, intelligence and police chiefs at the heart of government. These collective chiefs, by dint of institutional power and personality, have a position within government that is more influential than before. This represents a shift in bureaucratic and political power whose viability remains to be fully tested but whose results are on display.

Howard had a strong personal link with retired Australian Defence Force chief General Peter Cosgrove and declared, on Cosgrove's retirement, that he was 'the best-known military figure in this country since Field Marshal Blamey', adding that Cosgrove 'popularised the military forces with the mainstream of the Australian community in a way that we have not seen for generations'.[28] It is an insight into the Howard era that it has produced the best-known military chief since World War II.

Under Howard, former ASIO chief Dennis Richardson and Australian Federal Police chief Mick Keelty have become public figures, more prominent than senior departmental heads. Richardson is our new ambassador to the United States. Wired into Howard's Capital Hill system, they have dealt with ministers, politicians and media. Their agencies are being transformed in terms of budgets, responsibilities, closer proximity to the Prime Minister and media relations.

In summary, the office of Prime Minister has assumed a new dimension of authority flowing from the national security role. The influence of military, intelligence and police chiefs is significantly enhanced and this growth in security governance is underwritten by public acceptance. In the hands of an astute leader such as Howard, it represents a fusion of greater political authority and electoral popularity.

* * *

John Howard's prime ministership has opened a new contest within Australian governance: universal human rights versus popular sovereignty. The Howard era bequeaths a sense of human rights injustice highlighted by the post-*Tampa* border protection laws, mandatory detention, abuses of power by the Immigration Department and the new security laws that limit individual freedom.

While much of the Australian debate in 2001 focused, naturally, on the precedent-making border protection regime, there was little debate about the conflict in terms of competing principles of governance. One principle is that in a democracy public consent will sanction, ultimately, the number of people who enter its borders and the manner of their entry. This is the claim of citizens to determine who joins their society and becomes part of their nation. On the other hand, a system of global order means that the claims of refugees must be enshrined in international law and that such provisions should be honoured by nations. If this responsibility of trust is not shared by many nations, then it will be borne by no one.[29] This is a conflict between competing principles with different sources of legitimacy—the first is popular sovereignty and the second is universal human rights.[30]

The momentum for a bill of rights is gathering force—within the Labor Party; within some state and territory jurisdictions; among the Democrats, the Greens, the legal profession, human rights groups and the media. This is the coalition that has lost to Howard on a range of issues for a decade.

Howard has a common-law view of rights. He is opposed to this initiative on the grounds of principle, philosophy and politics. The principle is that he believes it transfers power from the elected parliament to the unelected judiciary; the philosophy is that rights should not be divorced from responsibilities; and the politics are that the practical impact is likely to favour minorities at the expense of majorities. Howard has deemed a bill of rights to be 'totally undesirable'.[31]

The issue here is whether Australia follows Canada, New Zealand and Britain to embrace a bill of rights and accepts the international norms. The alternative is that Australia becomes more nationalistic and distinctive in its own governance arrangements. This might become the real test of the Howard legacy.

2

CULTURE WARS

Christopher Pearson

JOHN Howard's stance on Asian immigration cost him the Liberal leadership in 1988. By the time he won it back, early in 1995, he had developed a far surer grasp of cultural politics.

Howard has never been, by any reasonable definition, a racist. Rather, his mistake was a matter of recognising the threat that the urban proletariat and the rural poor's longstanding anxieties over the rate of Asian immigration posed to social harmony. Worse still, he was prepared to accept that element of public opinion as a legitimate factor in framing public policy.

In democracies, governments generally make some concessions to popular sentiment, if they want to minimise the sort of tensions that led to the recent race riots at Cronulla. But at the time the *bien pensant* orthodoxy was that the Government should defy and override popular sentiment, as a matter of high principle. Anything else was, it seemed self-evidently, despicable redneck populism and pandering not just to xenophobia but to racism itself.

The gap between the elites, including almost the entire political class on the one hand and popular opinion on the other, may never have been greater. Howard positioned himself on the wrong side of the Zeitgeist and was anathematised accordingly. For racism, or anything remotely resembling it, had become the secular equivalent of the sin against the Holy Ghost, for which there can be no forgiveness.

The concept of 'Culture Wars' is a nebulous one. The term has been used to cover a multitude of struggles, from debating the place of metaphysics in the public square to the triumphs of US neo-con domestic and foreign policy. In this chapter, my focus is on the ways Howard's opponents have—with varying degrees of success—deployed the Zeitgeist and its values against him and how he, in turn, has defied, neutralised or harnessed the Spirit of the Age to his own advantage and, in doing so, helped to change it.

These fencing manoeuvres for moral ascendancy increasingly became the stuff of Australian politics in the Keating era, as the major parties came into an embarrassingly close convergence on most policy issues. Afterwards, without the discipline that being a governing party imposes, unresolved tensions between the trade unions and the economic realists, and between the parliamentary Left and Labor's social conservatives, re-emerged with a vengeance. But in 1993, Paul Keating's main weapons were not fundamental matters of policy but a scare campaign on an unpopular new tax (which he himself had previously advocated) and the prospect of a republic.

Keating's republic was an emblematic issue for the bourgeois Left. It seemed to be progress and multicultural modernity incarnate; a visionary change for the nation to enter a new millennium with a new identity, free at last of its anachronistic ties to Britain and the monarchy. To oppose constitutional change was to fly in the face of destiny, to single yourself out as a reactionary, enthralled by the damaged glamour of the House of Windsor and the class system.

Although Howard was the most conspicuous Liberal monarchist, the main target of this onslaught was not Howard but his party, especially its younger and more impressionable members. It was a very successful divide-and-divert exercise, which helped distract public attention from the Government's problems and get it re-elected. The media played their anticipated role magnificently. In retrospect it is plain that the republic was no more than a chimera, a *coup de ballon*, but it certainly served its purpose.

Howard was acutely aware of the extent to which his own views on constitutional matters could be used against him. Well before the lead-up to the 1996 poll, he borrowed a suggestion made by his predecessor, Alexander Downer, and proposed, if elected, to convene a constitutional convention to frame questions for a referendum. In doing so, he effectively neutralised it for electoral purposes, once again leaving the Keating Government, not himself, as the issue. He sensed—rightly, as will be apparent when we return to the topic—that incumbency in office can very rapidly reconfigure the terrain on which the Culture Wars are contested.

By mid-1995, Howard had intuited what party polling would confirm: that Keating had over-reached himself in the public relations equivalent of total war. It may have played well among the commentariat and the cultural elites, but it had thoroughly alienated pivotal constituencies. Howard's task in Opposition was to present a proverbial small target on issues where Labor appeared to occupy the high moral ground, such as multiculturalism and Aboriginal affairs, to offer a plausible alternative account of Australian history and national identity that was less partisan and self-serving than his opponent's and to appeal to the innate social conservatism of what he called 'the mainstream'.

As his speechwriter, I was a minor player in that project. If in retrospect its success seems inevitable, that was not always how it looked at the time. An Opposition leader's most important audience is the press gallery, and many members of that audience, if not most, were Keating loyalists. Even where they had serious reservations about the Labor leader, they tended to share baby-boomer assumptions about modernity and Keating's version of the Zeitgeist's imperatives. When the prime minister caricatured Howard as yesterday's man, 'yearning for the era of the Morphy Richards toaster, the Qualcast mower, the Astor TV console, armchair and slippers', it passed for a serious argument and sometimes he seemed to be winning it.

However, the electorate at large did not find Howard's ordinarinesses anywhere near as threatening as did the Fourth Estate. Many found them rather reassuring, compared with the antics of the self-styled Placido Domingo of Australian politics. Others noted that 'the most conservative Liberal leader in a generation', as he described himself, was also the first to have a female chief of staff, the feisty Nicole Feely, and to employ an openly gay speechwriter.

Howard did not choose his staff in obeisance to a politically correct agenda, although our presences did serve to unsettle the PC brigade. Rather, it was a reminder that he was a pragmatic, modern politician, unfazed by differences of gender, ethnicity and sexuality, and prepared to seek advice from what might once have seemed unexpected quarters.

Prevailing PC pieties on race and gender had driven the Keating Government throughout its years of mismanagement of the Hindmarsh

Island affair, in what was arguably the most important battle in the Culture Wars of the mid-1990s. Robert Tickner, the minister for Aboriginal affairs, was constitutionally incapable of imagining that the Ngarrinjeri people of the Lower Murray might confect a tradition overnight, as the basis of a heritage site claim. When told that it was a case of 'secret sacred women's business', he declined even to view the evidence in a sealed envelope sent to his office.

Federal heritage legislation allowed for the fact that cultural traditions are evolving rather than static phenomena. However, in doing so, it over-compensated by defining tradition very loosely as almost anything Aboriginal people claimed as customary, no matter how recent.

It was obvious to anyone who followed the story that the mythography surrounding Hindmarsh Island was as fresh as paint and had evolved at the urging of NIMBY conservationists when all other pretexts to stop the construction of a bridge to the island had failed. At first it was promulgated by a woman who said that she was the sole custodian of the secret and unable to divulge it to any man. But four other female elders denied its authenticity and testified that the story had originally come from a group of men, some of them white.

It is a measure of Howard's success in the Culture Wars that no one nowadays would try to mount such a reckless claim. But at the time it was taken at face value and passionately defended. The ALP, the ACTU, the Australian Broadcasting Corporation (ABC), the Fairfax press, the Council of Churches, conservationists and even some anthropologists all asserted that it was an ancient, sacred site. The Stevens royal commission weighed the evidence and found that the women's business was a complete fabrication.

Keating was not prepared to sack Tickner, though privately contemptuous of him. Elements of the Prime Minister's own faction, the shop assistants union, abstained from party-room motions of confidence in Tickner and people with experience of indigenous issues such as Gary Johns, the special minister of state, were dismayed by the turn of events.

As with Johns's and Keating's preferred legislative response to the Mabo decision, privately there was little difference at the highest levels of both government and Opposition about the optimal outcome. But Keating was hoist on his own rhetorical petard and appointed a federal inquiry in the vain hope, as it emerged, of overturning Iris Stevens's findings. Meanwhile, public scepticism and disquiet grew and Liberal polling estimated the Hindmarsh factor at more than two percentage points of the swing that was to unseat the Government.

Labor had expected to lose office in 1993 and had begun stacking the higher reaches of the public service, statutory authorities and quangos such as the Human Rights and Equal Opportunity Commission (HREOC) with partisans capable of destabilising a new government. HREOC marked out the ground for the great set-piece battle of the early Howard years, with its Bringing Them Home Report on the so-called 'stolen generation' and its accusations of genocide.

Once again the Aboriginal affairs activists and federal Labor misjudged popular opinion, overplaying their hand because they paid too much attention to the commentariat. Robert Manne and other bourgeois moralisers may have been prepared to toy with the idea of state-sanctioned genocide—or, at the very least, 'cultural genocide'—but most of the public were not prepared to swallow it. People were quite willing to deplore the policy of removing mixed-race children from their Aboriginal mothers regardless of circumstances, while recognising that some forcible removals were likely to have been in the best interests of the children concerned. Genocide was a bridge too far.

Howard's Methodist origins gave him an insight into the political agendas of the social justice activists, especially on racial issues. He rightly understood the movement for reconciliation as a stalking-horse, a means for opponents to anathematise his government and impugn its moral legitimacy. His response has been primarily a matter of steadily increasing the Aboriginal Affairs budget each year, concentrating on long-term improvement in such key indicators as morbidity and mortality rates and recalibrating events in terms of his preferred model of 'practical reconciliation'. It may sound oxymoronic (and no doubt appals rhetorical purists) but the point is not lost on his blue-collar supporters.

Echoing the new government's emphasis on practical matters, after the election Gary Johns advised Noel Pearson, known at the time as something of a firebrand, to come up with a new model of Aboriginal leadership. He told him to avoid the endless circuit of junkets to Geneva and instead lead his people on the ground, by example. Pearson left his Melbourne law firm and went back to Cape York. He also had another conversation, this time with the new minister for Aboriginal affairs, a doctor called John Herron. They discussed dysfunctional communities plagued by alcohol and violence and the syndrome of welfare dependency. Herron urged Pearson, as one of the few with a universally acknowledged right to do so, to speak out about them.

Pearson's analysis, discussed in greater detail elsewhere in this book, has provided a new paradigm for relations between indigenous Australia and government. Others, including the new federal president of the ALP, Warren Mundine, have helped turn the critique of passive welfare and the preferred model of participation in the real economy into something that verges on a bipartisan policy platform. With it has come a fresh approach to what land rights might mean—from an inalienable form of collective title, which left people land-rich but dirt poor, to exploring the commercial possibilities of leasehold and other options, including personal, alienable smallholdings.

It has been, by any reckoning, a remarkable turnaround. The people who attended the sea-of-hands demonstrations and walked for reconciliation across the Sydney Harbour Bridge, so confident of the shibboleths that asserted their moral superiority, have been confounded. Not only has Aboriginal Australia been able to do business in a very pragmatic way with a conservative government; it has adopted conservatism's analysis not just of the so-called 'nanny state' but also, closer to home, of the land councils as the world's last Stalinist bureaucracies.

Howard once told me that 'the thing about Australians is that they're not much given to grand theorising; they're practical people and they like things and systems that work'. I think this helps to explain his successes in Aboriginal affairs and the bipartisan agreement that the dysfunctional Aboriginal and Torres Strait Islander Commission (ATSIC), should be abolished, a proposition that would have been almost unthinkable five years ago. Pragmatism was also the underrated, not-so-secret weapon in the campaign against the proposed republic.

While Howard maintained some distance from the waging of the republic campaign, he lent his support and moral authority to the 'No' case and reiterated its fundamental arguments. He resisted all demands for a plebiscite, which might have approved a republic in principle without also delivering majority support to a particular model, on the grounds that such a result would de-legitimise the existing arrangements and leave the country in constitutional limbo. By holding the constitutional convention and providing government funding for both sides to state their cases, he guaranteed that the issues would be extensively debated.

The media, almost without exception, campaigned and editorialised for change, describing a republic as inevitable. But those of us who led the charge against change knew that the public had grave reservations about a model which, in retrospect, almost everyone admits was flawed. We were almost the only ones to predict the scale of its defeat. Lulled by its own slogans, the commentariat was slow to come to terms with what the public clearly grasped. We already have a subtle system of checks and balances—one that works. The proposed alternative would, in a crisis, have redistributed power towards whoever was prime minister and weakened the constitutional arbiter. In this and various other respects it would have militated against political stability. The only time people vote for constitutional change is when there is broad agreement that the model on offer will work at least as well as the existing version.

The referendum's defeat in all six states stunned most of what passes for Australia's cultural elite. They had imagined they were in a cognitive majority and that 'the force was with them'. The commentators who supposed they were surfing the Zeitgeist like a great triumphal tide found that they had been dumped by it. Republicanism suddenly lost its visionary cachet and began to look like a passing preoccupation of the baby-boomers—just another fad.

Most accounts of Howard's prime ministership seem to me to overstate his active involvement in the Culture Wars. Certainly he understands the symbolic importance of events such as the opening of *Quadrant* magazine's new offices and makes a point of attending them. But when, for example, it comes to board appointments to major cultural institutions, his approach is far less interventionist than Keating's and the decisions are usually left in the first instance to the relevant ministers, rather than his own office. Nor, contrary to journalistic opinion, are appointees expected to liaise with him or his staff: all other considerations aside, they are far too busy and not much interested in cultural politics.

Even in the case of Donald McDonald, a close Howard friend chosen to chair the ABC, we have the chairman's word that they do not discuss the corporation's business in private conversation, and we have no reason to doubt it. Howard is something of a stickler for form in such matters and, besides, McDonald has surprised many at the ABC by the extent to which he very rapidly became a captive of its world view and what might best perhaps be termed its governing assumptions.

A more activist prime minister would have wanted to micro-manage the cultural institutions and appointed conservative commissars. Some critics saw Michael Kroger's presence at the ABC and mine at the

Australia Council in that light, although it was always obvious that Howard is a policy incrementalist who believes in making change as unthreatening as possible and avoids needlessly antagonising people who might vote for him. As Michael Duffy, the so-called right-wing Phillip Adams of ABC Radio National, puts it, 'Howard is quite content to leave the Australia Council and the other institutions to muck around like kids in their own little sandpits, while he gets on with the main game. He doesn't think most people pay them much heed and he's right, of course.'

Duffy's point—that the arts and the cultural and educational elites have become so overtly politicised that they have lost much of their credibility with the electorate at large—is one the elites themselves find hard to comprehend. After all, *they* have always taken themselves immensely seriously. But, from Howard's perspective, why would you bother too much about the ways that artists, the commentariat at large or the academy criticise and even demonise you, when most people discount it in advance on the Mandy Rice-Davies principle 'Well, he would say that, wouldn't he?'

One consequence of non-interventionism—in the federal government's allowing the humanities and social sciences in Australian universities to be all but overrun by its ideological enemies—is, as Keith Windschuttle puts it, 'to end up with a couple of dozen publicly funded, left-wing think tanks'. Some see it as short-sighted and say that, as well, the young deserve access to better universities. Others argue that the tertiary sector will follow the same path as secondary education: that students will vote with their feet by shunning Left-conformist faculties and universities in favour of private universities such as Bond and Notre Dame.

A fuller account of the Culture Wars would dwell on the gradual politicisation of Australian education, since Menzies began the ill-considered implementation of the Vernon report. It would touch on the related battles over literacy, numeracy and critical thinking, and the sound educational reasons why about 40 per cent of senior secondary students in Victoria are now in private schools. It would certainly consider Howard's unexpectedly successful engagement with Asia and the liberation of East Timor, which may well come to be seen as his finest hour. It might also look at recent imbroglios in institutions such as the Special Broadcasting Service (SBS) and the National Museum—although, as a currently serving member of both those bodies' boards, I'm constrained in what I can say about them.

There is another dimension to the Culture Wars that has not been widely noticed, about which I can speak freely and which seems a suitable note on which to end. Late in 2004 the Uhrig report into governance structures was released. It has been broadly accepted by the Government and has gradually begun to be implemented. Some of its recommendations are likely to have considerable impact on commonwealth cultural institutions.

Uhrig urged major governance reforms. He found that government business enterprises with a charter to make money should continue to be governed by boards of directors as arm's-length operations. Those quangos that were not primarily commercial concerns should have their boards scrapped and instead the chief executives should be made to answer directly to the minister, in the interests of greater accountability.

The sceptic in me says that no government, whatever its complexion, would willingly surrender so many opportunities for bestowing patronage. However, this is an increasingly managerialist administration. Then again, it may just decide to defer the implementation of politically difficult changes. The most sensitive would be changes that had an impact on the ABC and SBS.

In the case of the ABC, direct answerability to the minister might be hard to sell to an organisation with a long-term problem of staff capture. On the other hand, it could be argued that the corporation was at least potentially a government business enterprise, by virtue of the immensely valuable broadcast spectrum it has, free of charge. If so, one option would be to give it a further injection of capital and let it run as a commercial enterprise, in which case it is hard not to imagine the ABC becoming what Howard would call 'a far more mainstream sort of organisation'. The other obvious option, which would have much the same effect, would simply be to privatise it.

II

HOWARD'S WAY

3

TWO HOWARDS

Dennis Shanahan

JOHN Howard is Australia's most successful prime minister. He has out-served, and maintained his popularity longer than, Labor's longest serving prime minister, Bob Hawke. He has outperformed the Liberals' longest serving prime minister, Sir Robert Menzies. And for his pains he has had more vitriol directed towards him than any prime minister since Billy Hughes.

There are two John Howards. One, a caricature born of the frustration of his opponents and critics, is both an illusion and a delusion. This Howard is divisive, a master of poll-driven wedge politics, a 1950s conservative, too old, inflexible, out of touch with modern Australia, anti-Asian and anti-immigration. The second John Howard is a far more complex and successful character—someone the Australian people have elected four times. He is the one the people identify with and he is the one they trust (even if they disagree with him) to be steady and to admit mistakes. This is the Howard whose record, complete with back-flips, blemishes and blots, they accept as legitimate. This is the Howard who has established two-way communication with the Australian people and who instinctively understands their concerns, interests and aspirations like few leaders before him.

These contradictory images of Howard coexist because his opponents have never conceded his success. To suggest that Howard could win an election with other than luck would be to acknowledge his legitimacy. According to this narrative, Howard did not win the 1996 election—rather, Paul Keating's tired Labor Government lost it; Howard fluked back in 1998 against Kim Beazley with less then 50 per cent of the two-party-preferred vote; Howard robbed Beazley again in 2001 by playing on prejudice and fear; in 2004 he beat Mark Latham by running an interest-rate scare campaign. These excuses hide the terrible bitterness at being beaten by somebody who, the opponents profoundly believe, should never have won the partyroom ballot for Liberal leader, let alone four federal elections.

It is to Howard's advantage to allow all of this vitriol to continue, to encourage the view of a Neanderthal, frozen in ice, because the longer his opponents wrestle with this delusion the longer it will be before they recognise Howard's strengths and contest him at ground level, which they must if they are to defeat him. Much of what is thrown at Howard is, by extension, thrown at the Australian people: they are too stupid to vote the right way, they are racist, they are boorish, apathetic and conservative. The people take exception to this elitist view, and Howard understands them instinctively. When Howard refuses to accept that Australian society is inherently racist, the vast majority agree with him. They consider themselves to be hard working, tolerant and prepared to give generously to those in need—and Howard agrees with them. Herein lies the true wedge of Howard politics: Howard has used hostile media to cement his relationship with the voting public and reinforce the view that he is one of them.

By portraying Howard as a prisoner of his own conservatism, his opponents profoundly underestimate his capacity to change. Sometimes openly, sometimes with stealth, Howard has ditched the baggage from his doctrinaire days of policy purity, inexperience and ineptitude. When Howard resumed the leadership of the Liberal Party in 1995, after the failed experiment with the young 'dream team' of Alexander Downer and Peter Costello, he had already been in parliament for more than 20 years. He was the wunderkind in Malcolm Fraser's government, joining the ministry after only 18 months on the back bench. In the period to 1995, as a tyro minister, treasurer, Opposition frontbencher, leader of the Opposition and backbencher, Howard set out various policy and personal positions that stuck in the minds of the media and the public. Unlike Beazley's defensive 'small-target' strategy, Howard set out what he stood for in the long years of opposition. Not all of it was good and some of it was downright bad. Yet, early in his tenure as Opposition leader in 1995, there were the first signs that Howard was prepared to adapt.

The clearest examples of Howard's ability to change are Asian immigration and Medicare. These are also perfect illustrations of how, 10 years later, Labor is still fighting a straw man instead of challenging the real Howard for the middle ground.

For Howard, Asian immigration became a totemic issue that haunted him for years and put the fire in the belly of many of those who opposed him. On 1 August 1988, while Opposition leader and after a long debate on the merits of Asian immigration, Howard was asked in an ABC radio interview whether he thought the rate of Asian immigration was too high. He replied:

> I wouldn't like to see it greater. I am not in favour of going back to a White Australia policy. I do believe that if it is, in the eyes of some in the community, ... too great, it would be in our immediate-term interest and supportive of social cohesion if it were slowed down a little.

Those remarks stamped Howard as anti-Asian and, despite expressions of regret in September 1989 for his 'loose language', the image stuck. When he became Opposition leader again, Howard went further. In January 1995 he openly conceded, in an interview with *The Weekend Australian*, that he was 'wrong' to say what he did. 'I don't think I've had a more painful time in politics ... Obviously if I had my time over I would have expressed myself very differently ... I was wrong. The remarks were clumsy ... expressed that way it was clearly an error.'[1] It was a rare public admission but, on such an emotive issue, nobody really seemed to be listening. Keating reminded everyone of Howard's words in the dying days of the 1996 election campaign when he suggested that Asian leaders would not deal with Howard.

The anti-Asian chorus was raised again later that year when Pauline Hanson made her maiden speech in parliament, calling for Australia's immigration policy to be reviewed and multiculturalism abolished. Australia, she claimed, was 'in danger of being swamped by Asians while indigenous Australians were getting preferential treatment'.

'Along with millions of Australians I am fed up to the back teeth with the inequalities that are being promoted by the Government and paid for by the taxpayer under the assumption that Aboriginals are the most disadvantaged people in Australia,' she said.

Howard's immediate reaction to Hanson was cautious. He dismissed her call for immigration to be halted but conceded 'there is a link between the high level of unemployment among certain groups in Australia and some past immigration levels in the composition of our program in the past'. Howard was reflecting his belief that too many unskilled and unemployable people were entering Australia under the family reunion program and he pointed to a reduction in immigration under the Liberals. Polls at the time showed Australians thought the level of immigration was too high, and that was the view among traditional Labor voters.

By failing to denounce Hanson openly, Howard exposed himself to accusations of prejudice, fear mongering and populism. Aboriginal and Torres Strait Islander social justice commissioner Mick Dodson accused the Government of pandering to 'prejudice and bigotry and hatred'. Keating told a gathering at the University of NSW: 'If multicultural Australia, and with it our hard-won good name for tolerance and fair play, falls over ... it will be because the Government has stopped pedalling'. The responsibility would be 'on the Government's head, not the people's or Pauline Hanson's'.[2]

Howard justified his position on the grounds of freedom of speech, a stance complicated by his deep resentment towards the politically correct forces that had prospered under Keating. Howard believes that one of the reasons Keating did not succeed is that he surrounded himself with advisers who were too narrow in their outlook and too sharp in their suits. He also knew that condemning Hansonism could damage the Coalition because much of what Hanson said struck a chord in the electorate. Hanson's one million votes at the 1998 election could easily have turned One Nation into a potent force if the party's leader had been smarter and better organised. Howard's ability to draw back many of those who flirted with One Nation, together with its poor organisation, are viewed by some senior Liberals as the only things that stopped One Nation becoming a new Country Party and swallowing the Nationals.

While immigration minister Philip Ruddock, foreign minister Alexander Downer, and trade minister and deputy prime minister Tim Fischer all campaigned loudly against Hanson, Howard was more circumspect. His view was, and still is to this day, that Hansonism would pass and that the media, once again, had misjudged the mood of the people. 'Can I say, quite frankly, that some of the media obsession with this issue has made her something of a martyr in the eyes of sections of the Australian community,' Howard told the Nine Network's *A Current Affair* program in November 1996. 'That's one of the reasons why I didn't say certain things about her that people were telling me to say, because I've seen this happen before. In a sense, the more an individual is broadly attacked, and comprehensively attacked, the more this sort of underdog thing develops in Australia. You know the Australian psyche.' These words could almost have applied directly to Howard, whose declaration 'I find racism evil' was lost in a mess of mixed messages in the media.

Howard's defence of Australians against accusations of racism, which were to be repeated nine years later, after the Cronulla riots in Sydney, were not lost on the public. In 1996 he expressed these words and sentiments:

> The thing that has angered me most is the extent to which there are still so many people in Australia who want to say to the world: 'Please forgive us because we are a bigoted racist country.' I don't believe we are. We have made mistakes, we badly treated our Aboriginal people, shamefully treated them, and we must remedy that by helping them now to have a brighter future. But in the greater sweep of history, Australia has been a very tolerant, humane society.[3]

Howard was accused of racism again in 2001 when he rigorously enforced the mandatory detention of asylum seekers who, as his critics pointed out, were mostly non-European. The most enduring rhetoric of the election came from the Liberal Party's campaign launch in Sydney in October 2001 when Howard declared: 'We will decide who comes to this country and the circumstances in which they come.' It has been often argued that the arrival of the Norwegian container ship MV *Tampa* with it human cargo of stranded Afghan asylum seekers was the turning point that sealed Howard's election win in November. This analysis misses the point that Howard had already clawed his way back from record low levels of support earlier that year to be on level terms with Labor in a Newspoll survey the weekend before the *Tampa* story broke. The Tampa, however, crystallised the issue of mandatory detention for asylum seekers—a Labor policy introduced in 1993 when faced with far fewer illegal boat arrivals with asylum seekers from Asia—and created a division between immigration and immigration detention.

Again Howard's critics miss the mark. Notwithstanding the disgraceful abuses of power and human tragedies that were allowed to unfold under the detention policy, the attempt by his critics to portray Howard's stance as anti-immigration matches neither the available facts nor the perception of the majority of Australians. Tighter border protection, coupled with a strong economy and confidence about finding a job, has lessened opposition to immigration under Howard and allowed a reversal of the immigration trend under Labor and under the Liberals in their first year. Australia's current annual immigration intake is 130,000 to 140,000, excluding the humanitarian intake—much higher than it has been for decades. While accused of being anti-immigration and anti-Asian, Howard has actually overseen the greatest Asianisation of Australia since the Gold Rush.

Asian immigration, much of it business migration rather than family reunion, has hit record highs and the percentage of Asians in our intake is higher than ever. Australia is taking more black African refugees in its humanitarian intake than ever before and in 2005 the overseas-born population passed 24 per cent for the first time since Federation. Europeans now account for less than half—49 per cent—of those born overseas. Howard has done all of this with the endorsement of the Australian people who, barely a generation ago, supported a formal White Australia policy and only 10 years ago thought the level of immigration was too high. By being tough on illegal immigration Howard and Ruddock reassured Australians that the migration program was under control and that, thanks to an unprecedented period of economic growth under Treasurer Peter Costello, their jobs were not at risk. Fear of losing one's job to an immigrant is actually strongest among the lowest paid workers; it has been a recurring theme in many trade union campaigns and has touched many Labor voters. This is a point recognised by many of the old-style Labor politicians who put workers' interests ahead of rhetoric and can see how Howard has outflanked them on immigration.

As for Howard's inability to deal with Asian leaders, there is ample evidence that Howard has used Australia's influence in the region and our relationship with the United States to enmesh Australia with Asian trade and security ties as never before. This has been achieved despite his awkwardness abroad in his early years as Prime Minister. He has become highly enthusiastic and confident as he has developed relations with the regional leaders, particularly in China. Tragedy accelerated the process—particularly with Indonesia, where a strong and close relationship developed after the two Bali bombings, the attack on the Australian embassy in Jakarta and the 2004 tsunami—but trade and aid have underpinned the relations. Howard has identified the development of a strong relationship with China (and a simultaneous revitalisation of the US alliance) as not only his greatest achievement but also one of the three biggest achievements of Liberal prime ministers. Speaking at the Liberal Party conference gala dinner in the Great Hall of Parliament House in June 2005, Howard said Menzies's decision to provide state funding to Catholic schools and Harold Holt's ending of the White Australia policy were the first two high points of Liberal governments.

> If we can fast-forward to the more modern era and to our external relations, it's been this Liberal Government that has been able to do what the Labor Government manifestly was unable to do, and that is to build an important and strong and maturing relationship with China, without it being at the expense of our relations—our deep, abiding and fundamental relations—with the United States of America. The Whitlam Government embraced a relationship with China, and that was a good thing. But they found it necessary simultaneously to distance themselves from the United States—and I've never forgotten the early days of the Whitlam Government when almost daily attacks were made by Whitlam Government ministers on the policies of the United States, particularly, but not only, in relation to Vietnam. It is possible to keep, and to make even stronger, that relationship we have with the United States, and there is no more important relationship to the future security and strength and stability of this country—that relationship will grow more important as the years go by, not less important; let no Australian be in any doubt about that.[4]

Howard's conclusion—that China is the future for Australia—is a realisation that has come to him during his time as Prime Minister. China was not a top priority when he came to power but it is a relationship he has developed since 1996 during meetings of the Asia Pacific Economic Co-operation forum and bilateral visits. For Howard the acme of the China–Australia–US relationship was reached in October 2003 when US President George W Bush and Chinese President Hu Jintao delivered separate addresses to federal parliament within the space of 24 hours.

On the issue of Aboriginal reconciliation—the other topic on which Howard has often been branded as racist—it is becoming harder for the opponents to make their accusations of prejudice and discrimination stick. Howard's preference has been for concrete results rather than symbolism and, as Stuart Rintoul argues in chapter 12, the debate has shifted his way in the last two terms of government. Certainly Howard's worst public performance was in relation to reconciliation, when he lost his temper with hecklers at the 1997 reconciliation conference, beat the podium with his hand and yelled that he would not be cowed into submission. It was an ugly incident and the only public instance of Howard losing his self-control and discipline so violently. The two symbolic gestures Aboriginal leaders were seeking from Howard—a declaration of Aboriginal reconciliation and a formal apology—have both been rejected. In February 2000, Howard abandoned the formal deadline for a reconciliation document of 31 December 2000, set by the Reconciliation Council in 1991, because 'too much store has been put in the document itself'. Howard wanted to emphasise the improvement and delivery of basic services to Aboriginal communities rather than deal with a document that was originally seen as a treaty. The Coalition put forward 'practical reconciliation' as its priority and some Aboriginal leaders, notably Noel Pearson, have advocated self-reliance for Aboriginal communities and the breaking of a welfare and hand-out mentality. Howard's refusal to offer a formal apology because 'you do not say sorry for something you are not personally responsible for' attracted strident criticism, and still does, but the debate has moved on. Howard has publicly expressed regret for the appalling treatment of Aborigines in the past and recognises they are the most disadvantaged group in Australia but he stops short of an apology. Once again, while many critics cite this as evidence of prejudice and discrimination, he is reflecting the majority view.

The other crucial policy dumping in 1995 was Howard's effort to ditch the Liberals policy on, and his own antipathy towards, Medicare. For years Howard has been described as a destroyer of Medicare, someone who wants to kill it off and someone who wants to introduce a US-style medical system. Howard does not cavil with the quotes thrown back at him; he said them all and cannot complain. But, once again, the criticisms are out of date and the reality of the experience of the public is different from the attitude projected by the old quotes about destroying Medicare.

After John Hewson's defeat in the 'unlosable election' of 1993, Howard, then Opposition industrial relations spokesman, came to the view that the Liberal Party's Medicare policy was as much to blame for the loss as the proposed goods and services tax. Labor's television advertisements on Medicare haunted Howard. After years of opposing

Medicare and promoting private health insurance Howard decided that the universal health insurance scheme was a pillar of Australian society that could not be undermined. By neutralising the Medicare debate, Howard believed he would be able to shift the focus of an election campaign to issues of his own choosing.

The extent of Howard's Damascene conversion to funding Medicare became clear in 2003 when reduced access to bulk billing, perceived as one of the fundamentals of Medicare, began to bite deeply with the public. Regional areas were particularly hard hit as doctors' surgeries demanded up-front payments—in the case of children's visits, in the form of $50 cash from their parents. Howard appointed his political hard man Tony Abbott to the health portfolio with a brief to neutralise Medicare as an issue going into the 2004 election. Abbott succeeded, bulk billing bottomed and then it began to climb before the 2004 election. Abbott had enthusiastically promised open-ended support for the Medicare safety net, giving a rock-solid guarantee that safety-net thresholds would remain at $300 and $700, but faced a rude realisation after the election that Howard's attachment to Medicare went only so far when his guarantee was revoked in the 2005 budget process and the thresholds were raised.

On family policy, the Prime Minister has subtly modified his position, widening the gulf between the real Howard and his critics' concocted stereotype. As Kate Legge agrees in a later chapter of this book, Howard's image as an old-fashioned believer in the single-breadwinner family where the father works and the mother stays at home derives largely from the Liberal document *Future Directions*, released while Howard was Liberal leader in 1988. The policy document showed an idyllic suburban family and house with a white picket fence. Yet one of Howard's proudest boasts is the shift towards family payments and support for single mothers. Howard says that the combination of family payments and child rebates effectively delivers income splitting for working couples and that couples with small children effectively pay no tax until they earn more than $40,000.

Heavily influenced by British social researcher Catherine Hakim, Howard now recognises three types of mothers: the one-third of women who are completely home-centred and wish to stay at home; the one-third of women who wish to work part time or go into the workforce full time when their children are older; and the one-third (approximately) of women who want to work full time all the time, even when their children are small. At the Liberal Party national conference in Adelaide in 2003, Howard introduced the new 'typical' family: a working father, a policeman, who worked full time; a mother, a nurse or sales assistant who worked part time; and children who were cared for primarily by their mother. Howard's reshaped family tax benefits reflect this new model, providing a flexible choice to mothers as well as spreading support across the board, not just to full-time working mothers through childcare subsidies.

Howard's political pragmatism is reflected in his three guiding principles: knowing when to cut and run; 'doing the right thing', regardless of popular support; and 'staying the course' when committed to doing the right thing.

Early in the election year of 2001 was, Howard decided, one of those times when he needed to cut and run: he decided to scrap petrol excise indexation. His government was going through its worst period, small businesses were complaining about the amount of paperwork associated with the GST, petrol prices were rising and the Government had lost the safe Brisbane seat of Ryan at a by-election after the resignation of former minister John Moore with a swing of more than 9 per cent. Newspoll surveys showed the Coalition's primary vote dropped to 35 per cent and satisfaction with Howard to 28 per cent, the lowest it has been while he has been Prime Minister. Howard recognised that his prime ministership, his leadership, and the prospect of winning the election were all in danger. The 'inflexible' Howard backflipped. First the Prime Minister overruled Treasurer Peter Costello to offer small business an annual, simplified statement on GST. While only a tiny percentage of small businesses adopted the new option it created the perception that the Coalition was trying to do all it could to alleviate a burden. Then Howard went further by abolishing the indexation of petrol excise after holding out against pressure to do so for months. He made it law that any government that wished to lift the excise would have to do so with legislation. It is worth noting that when, in 2005, petrol prices rose above those of 2001, there was no similar outcry directed towards Howard. The message of the backdown had been burned into the public mind. By August 2001 the Coalition was level with Labor and the predictions of Howard's political demise suddenly looked premature.

That the abolition of petrol excise indexation may not have been good policy and may have been unnecessarily expensive did not matter to Howard, who was determined to get himself out of trouble. Rather than seeming arrogant and unheeding, he showed that he was prepared to listen to the public's reasonable demands and to act.

In Howard's political repertoire, the backdown is played sparingly. There is a fine line between flexibility and vacillation and he has been careful not to cross it. In contrast to the populist touch he displayed over petrol price indexation, he has confounded those who accuse him of being poll-driven by defying public sentiment on several key issues and yet has still been able to finish with strong personal support. It is here that Howard the conviction politician takes over as he follows the principle of 'doing the right thing', popular or not.

Just eight weeks into his first term Howard suddenly faced a challenge that threatened to divide the Coalition: national gun laws. At 1.30 p.m. on Sunday 28 April 1996 lone gunman Martin Bryant took a semi-automatic rifle from his sports bag at Port Arthur near Hobart and began a shooting spree that killed 35 people and moved Howard to a commitment on limiting gun ownership in Australia. The gun lobby, made up of sporting shooters, hobbyists and farmers, was small, but it was powerful and organised. Howard eventually succeeded in limiting the use of automatic weapons but the opposition engendered in the debate, which was to reappear as One Nation, was born and Howard's gun laws became a potent rallying cry. In other sections of the community, however, particularly among women, the limitations on guns were popular and did not challenge Howard's standing.

Howard's resolve to pursue unpopular policies was tested with the sale of Telstra, the introduction of the GST, the invasion of Iraq and the new industrial relations laws. Public opinion ran strongly against all four, yet Howard persevered. In the case of the GST, persistence came at an enormous cost to many of his colleagues, who lost their seats in the 1998 election. The introduction of the GST was the antithesis of poll-driven politics and a risky policy for Howard to take to the 1998 election, just five years after its earlier incarnation—in John Hewson's 'Fightback!' plan—had been roundly rejected and barely two years after Howard's May 1995 promise that there would 'never, ever' be a GST. Yet Howard constructed an argument that the tax system badly needed reform and his claim that personal tax rates were too high struck a chord. By channelling GST revenue to the states, he avoided criticism that he was lining his own government's pockets. Polling showed that while people thought they may be worse off personally, they accepted the GST because it was good for the economy and they were prepared to 'do the right thing', just as they had accepted the first, and toughest, Costello budget. In fact, Coalition support rose after 1 July 2000, when the consumer phase of the introduction of the GST went smoothly.

Howard's resolve to 'do the right thing' is also reflected in his decision to send thousands of Australian troops overseas on active duty over the past decade, including the largest single contingents of troops since the Vietnam War. Australians have served and suffered casualties in East Timor, Afghanistan, Solomon Islands and Iraq as a direct result of John Howard's policies. Yet Labor, notably under Latham, has failed to convert opposition to the war into votes. In part this is because the level of casualties in proportion to the number of troops, all of whom are volunteers, has been extremely low. But there is also a more subtle factor at play: Howard's high regard for the military and his promotion of the defence forces, past and present, as role models and historical exemplars worthy of respect.

The effective invasion of East Timor by Australian-led troops under United Nations auspices had strong sentimental support in Australia. Howard's decision in 1998 to support a slow process towards autonomy turned, almost by accident, into a rush to independence and the creation of the world's newest nation in 1999. The moves, Howard's first major engagement with foreign policy since becoming Prime Minister, overturned a bi-partisan policy of recognising the Indonesian occupation of East Timor, which had begun in the dying days of Gough Whitlam's administration in 1975. Howard did not expect Indonesia's President BJ Habibie to counter his moves with an offer of an early referendum on independence or incorporation into Indonesia. But, having started the process, Howard saw it through, with strong popular backing in Australia. Also worth noting is the fact that it was the invasion of East Timor that was first cited as a reason for al-Qa'ida's hostility towards Australia.

The terror attacks on New York and Washington on 11 September 2001, while Howard was within sight of the smoke from the Pentagon building after it was hit by one of four hijacked airliners, is a crucial development in the character and success of Howard as Prime Minister. The terror attacks, the first invocation of the ANZUS pact and the so-called 'war on terror' ensured that Howard would not lose the 2001 election and gave him a grip on national security that has been unchallenged since. There was little opposition to Howard's commitment to send troops to Afghanistan to fight the Taliban forces and al-Qa'ida, and the professionalism of Australia's troops—and their successes bolstered public support. The invasion of Iraq, on the other hand, executed without UN approval, was opposed by more than two-thirds of Australians. Yet, convinced of the existence of weapons of mass destruction (WMD) and with ambitions, like British Prime Minister Tony Blair, to be a moderating voice in the US camp, Howard went ahead. Public sentiment shifted once the troops were committed and Australian nationalism, which thrives on a military core, began to cut in. Howard's careful promotion of Australian nationalism—which has as its credo 'the Australian way of doing things' without subservience to British history or US power—played a role in this acceptance.

Even when presented with evidence of the lack of WMD in Iraq, the Australian public, unlike the British and Americans, believed that they had not been deliberately misled, although dwindling numbers believed the unseating of Saddam Hussein was worth the effort. Even though the Senate Intelligence Committee, including former Labor defence minister Robert Ray, found no evidence that the Government 'sexed up' the intelligence reports, Howard's opponents continue to claim that he deliberately misled the public about WMD.

Howard's honesty came under scrutiny during the 2004 election campaign with the revelation that Queensland Liberal senator George Brandis had taken to calling Howard the 'lying rodent'. Brandis never denied using the word *rodent* but has claimed he did not attach the adjective. Brandis' rodent reference, which was substantiated by two senior Queensland Coalition figures, referred to an incident that dominated the last week of the 2001 election campaign—the 'children overboard affair', in which Howard and then immigration minister Philip Ruddock erroneously claimed that a group of asylum seekers had thrown their children overboard to ensure they would be picked up by a shadowing Australian naval vessel. The incident became more celebrated after the election as Labor sought to sheet home directly to Howard the blame for misleading the Australian people. Not long before the 2004 election was called, a former Defence bureaucrat, Mike Scrafton, told *The Australian* that he had spoken to Howard before the 2001 election and told him clearly that he believed the story was incorrect.

Yet the Opposition has found it impossible to gain political traction with the children overboard revelations. It may even be argued that media focus on the subject has served only to cement support for Howard in middle Australia, where it reinforced the impression that the Howard Government was tough on border protection and had 'stopped the boats'.

Howard, more than any other prime minister, understands the dichotomy between public interest and public campaigns, believing that the mainstream media, the broadsheet newspapers, ABC radio and television news, ABC and SBS current affairs, academic journals, collected essays and free-floating columnists and commentators demonstrate an obsession with issues that are either not of interest to the public at large or, like the children overboard affair, are viewed completely differently. After his failure in 1989 Howard wrote a long piece for the *Independent Monthly* detailing the role of the media and press gallery in the Coalition's downfall. Howard believed that the Coalition had not got strong support within the media because part of its agenda, particularly 'radical labour market reform', challenged the ethos of insider deal making between journalists, lobbyists, the public service and politicians. It was a lofty and academic view but Howard had a highly pragmatic and effective antidote when he came to power.

Howard has an intimate knowledge of the workings of the media, he understands the production challenges and difficulties, he can talk with ease to proprietors and editors and he has a forensic knowledge of the working lives of individual journalists. But he has no delusions about how many friends or supporters, even people who would respect or accept his legitimacy as Prime Minister, he has in the media. As a result, Howard did not try to charm or coerce members of the press gallery to his cause, as Keating had done. Instead he adopted a deliberate tactic of bypassing the media gatekeepers in the press gallery and on the opinion pages. Conversely Howard has made himself more accessible than any leader in modern times, giving doorstop interviews at the drop of a hat or holding press conferences in the prime minister's courtyard where he will sometimes take questions until the journalists virtually give up. But Howard's first choice of media interview is to go live, preferably on radio. His appearance on talk-back radio programs is prolific and regular. There is a schedule for the big-rating programs and he tries to make time for the smaller programs and smaller states.

The main advantage for Howard in this approach is that it allows him to talk directly to the people over the heads of the media opinion makers. An appearance early in the morning with Neil Mitchell in Melbourne or Alan Jones in Sydney sets Howard's media agenda for the day. The radio stations get an audio feed of what he has to say on the issues of the day, the television networks get an opportunity to film him and the newspapers are given the transcripts. It's a three-way split and all open to the public without pesky editing. Howard has even developed a technique of facing adversarial television interviewers, such as Kerry O'Brien of the ABC's *7.30 Report*, where the image of him being 'set upon' builds audience sympathy. But it is talk-back radio, with its two-way communication advantage, that attracts Howard most. It reaches remote areas and keeps him in touch with popular concerns. Once again it is a question of a media view of Howard being different from the view of the audience that hears him directly. Howard's critics allow themselves to be blind to his success and his support and to look at issues without real reference to what the electorate is feeling or thinking. As Howard said: 'I think what a lot of my critics have missed, what they overlook, is what the real world is about.'[5] That is the reality, and, like it or not, that's the secret of Howard's success.

Howard has recognised the conservatism of Australians. It's a small-'c' conservatism that supports a welfare safety net and public health systems to protect the vulnerable and paradoxically has a high respect for institutions and a low regard for those who put on airs in office. There is also a pragmatism that rates results ahead of symbols and for 10 years Howard has rejected symbols and concentrated on results.

4

PURPOSE DRIVEN

Glenn Milne

OCTOBER 28, 2001. The City Recital Hall, Sydney. John Howard is at the podium launching his bid for a third term as Prime Minister. Defending his government's decision to turn back the ship the *Tampa*, with its human cargo of 433 'illegal' asylum seekers, Howard declares, right hand pumping in the air: 'We will decide who comes to this country and the circumstances in which they come'.

His staff were stunned. The line had come from nowhere. It had not been prepared. No one had written it for him. It was Howard as conviction politician, out ahead, and alone. But so potent was the message that it became the centrepiece of the Coalition's advertising for the remainder of the campaign.

That potency derived from the political genius that has sustained John Howard in office for the past decade: an instinctive synthesis between two divergent forces—pragmatic but reformist market economics on the one hand and conservative social values on the other. The *Tampa* represented the latter, the rest of Howard's 2001 policy speech the former. While these forces have strained against each other at times during Howard's prime ministership, he has managed to keep them broadly coupled and in so doing has re-made Australia in his own image.

But more than that Howard has used the same political fusion to prise enough of Labor's base away from the Opposition to keep it in the political wilderness for the past 10 years. Howard's supremacy is a demonstration that he understands that Labor's blue-collar base has always been socially conservative but economically aspirational. His pact with this critical grouping has been constituted thus: provided you deliver on economic policy—growth, jobs, low inflation and low interest rates—and you remain in step with our social conservatism, we will continue to vote for you.

This, in turn, has created a so-far-insoluble dilemma for the ALP. Every time Labor produces a policy, it must have a dual appeal—not only to the group that has come to be known as 'Howard's battlers' but also to the party's educated middle-class constituency (the 'chattering classes' to their critics). More often than not, this dual appeal is impossible. The 'chattering classes' are socially progressive, the 'battlers' socially conservative. So Labor finds itself on an irreconcilable internal collision course that has seen the party implode at four consecutive elections. The quintessential example of this was what became known as the '*Tampa* election'. Howard hung absolutely tough on the issue of border protection and therefore on the side of the 'battlers' who might otherwise have voted for Labor. 'We will decide who comes to this country and the circumstances in which they come' was the message to which they responded.

On the other side Kim Beazley floundered, trying to thread his way between what should have been Labor's blue-collar supporters, who backed Howard's strong stand, and an educated middle class demanding a more compassionate position on refugees. The resulting confusion proved disastrous. Once again Howard stood between Labor and its natural base. And for the term of his office he has used successful economic management in the same way, in the process re-casting the Australian political landscape.

But it was not always so.

One of Howard's strengths is that his political skills have been developed and tested over time. The two themes that emerge over these years are failure and fear. Like all master politicians, he has learnt from his own mistakes. And according to those closest to him, Howard, having known failure, lives in constant fear of it—the key to his remarkable energy levels and iron discipline. He always feels he may be five minutes from calamity and works like a man possessed to outdistance potential disaster. The prime ministerial morning power walk is the metaphor here: arms pumping, wired to the morning news, purposeful and charged.

That was not the image in May 1989 when Howard lost the Liberal Party leadership to Andrew Peacock in a coup organised by the so-called 'Gang of Five'—John Moore, Wilson Tuckey, David Jull, Chris Puplick and Peter Shack. It was to be the last of the leadership struggles between Howard and Peacock, a contest of personalities and ideas that helped paralyse the Coalition for the 13 years of the Hawke–Keating governments.

Howard in defeat was left looking vaguely pathetic: a small and awkward man with outsize spectacles, teeth that resembled flying bowling pins and eyebrows that looked like they belonged in a garden. His *Future Directions* mission statement, which set out his party's family policy, had been torn to shreds by a commentariat conditioned by the charisma of Bob Hawke and the startling economic reforms of the Zegna-clad Paul Keating. The document featured on its cover the perfect Anglo-Saxon family—a wife and two children (one boy, one girl)—standing at their white picket fence in front of a suburban house with lawns that could have been manicured with nail scissors. The late Robert Haupt, writing for *The Sydney Morning Herald*, depicted the cover as akin to looking at life through a rear-view mirror. The smear stuck and Howard tumbled.

Howard's vision, particularly on the role of women in the workforce, had simply been too conservative. It was a mistake he would not make again. In government his policies would have conservative social objectives but Howard learned that it was always best to include in any program an element of choice—a strategy that fitted perfectly with Liberal Party ideology. He would never again try to prescribe overtly his own social vision for the country.

Economically, though, Howard's ideas were broadly set. By 1983, at the end of his stint as Treasurer in the Fraser Government, he had completed his transition into a full-blown but practical free marketeer. The industrial unrest that dogged Malcolm Fraser had led him to conclude that reform in this area was necessary to unleash the full potential of the economy. On this Howard's compass never wavered—all the way to a narrow Senate majority in late 2005 that finally delivered on his industrial dreams.

What also led to Howard's downfall in 1989 was his mismanagement of people. He was secretive to the point of paranoia, a loner who, as leader, ruthlessly rewarded his own 'dry' supporters at the expense of the 'wets' (now known as moderates). In the process he fuelled the barely suppressed factional warfare in the party and contributed to his own demise. When he finally returned to the leadership in January 1995 that too was another lesson learned. Howard proved inclusive and consultative, more embracing of his former internal ideological rivals, a gesture symbolised by his appointment of leading moderate Robert Hill to the Senate leadership. John Moore and David Jull, two of the assassins in 1988, were given ministries. Says one adviser who observed the transition: 'During his period as Opposition leader in the 1980s he was too ideologically strident. That created a clearly unhappy minority. By 1995 he understood that you have to carry people with you.'

It is an approach that Howard was to apply to the electorate at large. He became an expert in getting 90 per cent of what he wanted, provided his core objectives were met. It was a model he was to apply later to get the GST through a hostile Senate.

As he again took the reins of the Opposition, Howard demonstrated another lesson learned. His teeth had been capped, his eyebrows had been pruned and gone were the nerd glasses, replaced by television-friendly lenses. It signalled Howard's realisation that while ideas are important, so too is image.

Those who had worked in the frenetic and often chaotic orbit of Howard's predecessors, John Hewson and Alexander Downer, breathed a sigh of relief on his return. He was calm and directed. 'It was the hand of experience,' said one. 'Suddenly things worked.'

> You'd prepare Hewson for a media interview and he'd get on,
> and there'd be the curly one and he'd fall straight into it. We'd
> be mopping up the mess for three days. With Howard, he'd just
> go around the tricky left field question he hadn't prepared for
> and no one would even notice. That's the difference.

In March 1996, Howard swept into office, confirming the famous prediction by the defeated Queensland Labor premier Wayne Goss that Queenslanders were waiting on their verandas for Keating with baseball bats. The size of the election victory proved that it was not just Queenslanders who were loitering with intent.

Howard's critical judgment call during the 1996 campaign and the period immediately beforehand was to recognise that Goss was right. The electorate had wanted to vote Keating out of office in 1993. But the manic John Hewson and his 'triple whammy' platform of a GST, radical industrial relations reform and the virtual dismantling of Medicare frightened the life out of voters. At the 1993 election Hewson prevented them from punishing Keating for the 1991–92 recession.

In 1996 Howard made certain he did not get between voters and Keating. He adopted a 'small target' strategy of modest policy proposals. The fact that he was an experienced leader and that voters had become familiar with his central values of small government, family and—at that stage—some limited industrial relations reforms was of comfort to the electorate. He presented himself as a safe pair of hands and in doing so gave licence to voters to dispense with Keating.

Despite that experience, those close to Howard at the beginning of his prime ministership say he was tentative and uncertain of himself. Then, in April 1996, came the Port Arthur massacre, one month into Howard's first term. Former British Conservative leader Harold Macmillan was asked by a journalist during the 1956 Suez crisis what was the most difficult thing about being prime minister. Macmillan is said to have replied, 'Events dear boy, events'. The point being that it is often circumstances—or more accurately a leader's response to circumstances—that shapes a prime minister.

The horror of Port Arthur gripped the country. As much as the awfulness of the 35 dead it was the situation in which the slaughter occurred: a historic site where families went to connect to the nation's past. Howard's response to the event was the first indication that he was an emerging leader instinctively in tune with the national mood. After the initial grief the question that emerged from the tragedy was this: how was Martin Bryant able legally to arm himself with automatic weapons that gave him the capacity for such butchery?

Howard immediately sensed that Port Arthur demanded national laws for limits on the use of such guns and set about framing them. Again it was conviction politics in action. Howard had longed believed that one of Australia's strengths was its positioning half way between the US and European models of democracy and society. Howard knew that, as a result of Port Arthur and existing gun laws, the country was at a tipping point, in danger of going down the road of the United States. He was intent on restoring the balance. To achieve that he was forced to take on his Coalition partner, the National Party, and the Government's natural constituency in regional and rural Australia. He did so at some political and personal cost: remember the pro-gun rally where Howard was forced to wear a bullet-proof vest?

But overall the political outcome was a plus. The process proved a number of things. First, Howard had read the national psyche perfectly.

Second, it became clear to him that being involved in a fight with your own base over issues of principle is not necessarily a bad thing. It would be a pattern he would repeat on issues such as the sale of Telstra. The guns debate demonstrated to him that while people may oppose you they respect the fact that you stand your ground.

Howard won overall support from the electorate at large and grudging admiration from part of his own constituency for his tenacity. Others, however, galvanised into One Nation—a problem he would have to confront at a later date.

Port Arthur and what flowed from it proved to be defining events for Howard. He emerged in voters' minds as more than a cardboard cut-out. He showed strength in achieving his goals. And for the first time in his career he showed public compassion. His gesture in putting his arm around one of the grieving relatives at Port Arthur was the first step on a path that led all the way to the Bali bombings and his claim on the status of being 'father of the nation' at times of national calamity.

Then came Howard's nadir as Prime Minister: 1997.

The events that conspired to wear him down were many. The euthanasia debate flared nationally. After the Northern Territory legalised assisted death the federal parliament became consumed by demands to override the Territory's law. It eventually did. But in the long process of debating the conscience issue, government MPs and cabinet ministers were pitted against each other. The impression was of a government at war with itself and lacking internal discipline. A few months earlier, in December 1996, the High Court had handed down its decision in the Wik case. The court found that pastoral leases did not give exclusive possession to pastoralists and therefore did not automatically extinguish native title—thereby destroying a central tenet of the existing Native Title Act. The result through the early part of 1997 was uproar throughout rural and regional Australia and within the National Party. Unfounded scare campaigns were run about the legal security of the Australian quarter-acre block. The family Hills hoist was alleged to be under threat. It was a complex issue. And the political damage came to Howard, delivered by time; the debate dragged on for months. Little else was on the national political agenda.

The seeds of further destruction had also been sown late in 1996 when two junior ministers, Jim Short and Brian Gibson, resigned after allegations of conflict of interest over shareholdings. About the same time industry minister John Moore survived an attack over his $100,000 shareholding in venture capital company Bligh Ventures Ltd.

In February 1997 the parliamentary secretary to the minister for health, Liberal senator Bob Woods, announced his retirement as federal police investigated allegations against him of misuse of parliamentary entitlements.

Meanwhile in the Senate, the Government had enlisted the support of former Labor senator Mal Colston, who had quit the ALP in August of 1996 after Labor refused to back his candidacy for deputy Senate president. Colston's crucial vote ensured the passage of a Bill authorising the sale of 49 per cent of Telstra. The party went after him with a fury only a Labor 'rat' can provoke. The result: accusations against Colston of rorting government travel allowances, most of which were subsequently proved.

That produced a cascade effect in which all MPs' travel entitlements were trawled by their opponents on both sides. By the end of September 1997 Howard had lost seven ministers and parliamentary secretaries to scandals of one sort or another, as well as his chief of staff and confidant, Grahame Morris, and his office manager, Fiona McKenna.

The Government was in disarray and directionless—victim of Howard's high-minded code of ministerial conduct, which had been one of his election commitments to raise executive standards. On top of that Howard caught the flu, which developed into a chest infection. He was forced to take time off. The Government, from the top down, was sick. Some MPs privately questioned whether Howard was up to the job. 'He worried then that he was going to be this generation's Billy McMahon,' says one Liberal insider at the time. 'A oncer.'

But again Howard's political instincts and determination prevailed. He had already realised by early 1997 that he was going to have to claw his way out of the hole into which he had fallen. And based on his experience of the gun debate he also realised that the best way of doing this was to fight for an idea, even though it might be unpopular. In May 1998 he put the GST on the agenda.

The big idea prevailed over the scandal of the day and the 1998 election was dominated by the tax debate, followed by the emergence of One Nation. Howard largely neutralised One Nation by denying that the party's supporters were racist and acknowledging, correctly, that Pauline Hanson was simply the lightning rod for the victims of globalisation. He was accused of political 'dog whistling'—condoning racism by not condemning it. But it worked. Just. Howard took a pounding (Beazley actually won more of the primary vote than the Government) but he survived. One of his advisers at the time summed up the equation: 'He knew it [the election] was going to be a close- run thing. But eventually the punters concluded: I'm not sure about the GST but Howard obviously believes in it and he's not doing it for political advantage. He must be doing it for Australia.'

It was the 1998 election, the closest he has faced, that tempered the Howard steel. All the political skills he has since demonstrated were fully formed as a result of that contest. It became clear to Howard that he had to avoid becoming consumed by issues peripheral to the concerns of the electorate. When these issues surfaced, he had to act decisively to change course. He also recognised the political value of fighting for an idea, even though the electorate initially might be spooked by it. Starting with the GST these two conclusions have helped drive nearly every major policy offensive mounted by Howard since: the full sale of Telstra, the war in Iraq and radical industrial relations reform.

He understood that governments are elected to get things done in areas that are important to voters; this was the primary lesson of 1997, with the malaise over Wik, euthanasia and government scandal. He also now understood the need to bring the electorate and the party with him on the substance of these ideas. If this involved some compromise to achieve core objectives, so be it. Hence the May 1999 deal on the GST with then Democrats leader Meg Lees. And so it was also in 2001 when the Government had its back to the wall, reeling under the impact of high petrol prices, allied with the introduction of the GST. That low point culminated in the shock loss of the Ryan by-election.

Howard again immediately fought his way out, cutting fuel excise by 1.5 cents a litre and abolishing automatic indexation at a cost to revenue of $555 million a year. But it was a small price to pay for the very public message it sent to voters: that Howard shared and identified with their pain, a technique he would return to often during periods of pressure. In July 2001 the Aston by-election proved Howard had re-asserted his leadership credentials and was on track to win the subsequent full election. The *Tampa* was simply the icing on the campaign cake.

The 2004 election again showed Howard's capacity to compromise strategically—rather than on points of principle—where he sensed vulnerability. So when then Labor leader Mark Latham wrong-footed him, proposing a winding back of the generous superannuation entitlements enjoyed by federal MPs, Howard matched him.

But the formidable tactical mix that now defined John Howard— flexibility at the margin and firmness on central principles—was again on show over Iraq. With the polls demonstrating increasing concern about Australia's involvement in the war, Latham went down the cheap route, pledging to 'bring the troops home by Christmas'. Once more, on the big idea, Howard held firm, despite voter disquiet, declaring that Australia would not 'cut and run' from Iraq. It was another example of the precedents set by the GST, the sale of Telstra and industrial relations reform. And once again in 2004 voters rewarded Howard for sticking to his core principles, even though they might not have liked them.

Since 1988 Howard has applied the same skills to his internal management of the Liberal Party. Abandoning the 'winner takes all' principle, he is prepared to negotiate within the party if that is what is needed to achieve his main goals. Witness the late 2004 compromise with internal party rebels, led by Petro Georgiou, over changes to refugee policy. Howard divined an electoral mood greatly changed since the 2001 *Tampa* election and worked through the concessions needed to reflect the altered climate.

John Howard is of the Liberal Party and for the Liberal Party—a 25-year activist who implicitly understands the organic nature of the organisation. He knows that he and his prime ministership are creatures of it. Hence the commitment he has made over and over again: to remain as leader only for as long as the party wants him to.

Now, though, Howard faces a test of a type not seen before: the question of a leadership succession to Treasurer Peter Costello. Externally the test is to judge whether, after 10 years as Prime Minister, his popularity is durable enough to take the party to the next election and win. Internally the test is to weigh whether the best interests of the party he professes to love so much are best served by a smooth transition or a bloody and divisive brawl. This could yet prove to be the toughest challenge faced by the political master. And there are no templates.

5

GETTING PERSONAL

Matt Price

IT'S FASTER than a trot yet not quite a jog. Much closer to a clip than a walk, which denotes a faint disposition towards leisure and languor. And as anyone who has wheezingly struggled to tag along knows, there's nothing remotely languid about the Prime Minister's exercise regime. Indeed, practically everything you need to know about John Howard can be garnered by observing his vigorous dawn constitutional. Iron discipline. Ferocity. Concentration. Energy. Doggedness. Power. And, yes, a touch of unselfconscious nerdishness that has characterised Howard's political ascent.

Howard was an irregular exerciser before winning the 1996 election. On assuming high office he determined to start every day with a 30- to 40-minute burst around Kirribilli or, whenever parliament sits, the banks of Lake Burley Griffin. Now, wherever Howard is, no matter how jetlagged, jaded or busy, he'll hit the streets around sunrise. At the beginning of Howard's prime ministership there was a comic 'Where's Wally?' dimension to the morning routine, especially when Howard ventured overseas. Look, there's the PM—knobbly of knee, floppy of hat—in front of the Eiffel Tower. Or the Lincoln Memorial. Or Piccadilly Circus.

Typically, Howard was entirely unfussed by this sort of ridicule and simply continued to rise early, leap into his runners and take off. Exactly when the PM's walk morphed from national embarrassment into badge of success isn't clear, but after 10 years the exercise regime is widely acclaimed and admired. Older Australians are impressed by Howard's mental and physical tenacity and even those not especially enamoured of the Prime Minister attest to astonishment at his capacity to soak up the near-endless demands of the job.

Jeff Kennett, the former Liberal premier of Victoria and now chair of Beyondblue, the national anti-depression initiative, believes the example set by Howard's daily exercise ritual may yet prove one of the Prime Minister's most enduring legacies. 'If ever there was an important message being sent out by our most senior leader, it is John Howard walking every morning,' Kennett told ABC TV. 'If I want to help a lot of our aged from becoming depressed as they become aged—and more and more are, particularly as they're taken out of their own environment—I would say that they should follow John Howard's lead.'[1]

This, incidentally, is the same Jeff Kennett who delivered arguably the most spectacular insult of the thousands directed at Howard during his lifetime in politics. Captured, infamously, in mid-mobile-phone conversation in 1987 with Howard's long-time adversary Andrew Peacock, Kennett was regaling his close friend with a fruity opinion of the then Opposition leader:

Kennett: And I said to [Howard], 'Tomorrow, I'm going to bucket the whole lot of you.'

Peacock: 'No! Don't do that, Jeffrey.'

Kennett: Hold your flow. I said 'Tomorrow John' and he said 'I know where your sympathies lie' and I said: 'I don't give a fuck. I have no sympathies any more. You're all a pack of shits and tomorrow I'm going berserk.' Well he went off his brain and in the end I said to him, I said: 'Howard. You're a cunt. You haven't got my support, you never will have and I'm not going to rubbish you or the party tomorrow but I feel a lot better having told you you're a cunt.'[2]

They're all friends now—Peacock would later be appointed ambassador to the United States after Howard won office—but the excruciatingly frank exchange, intercepted by a goggle-eared punter with a domestic scanner, bespeaks another of the Prime Minister's key traits, perhaps the most useful of all: his thick hide.

Public office is a very harsh school in knockabout Australia; nobody reaches the giddy heights of party leadership without suffering free, frequent and frequently unkind character assessments. Yet the PM has endured more barbs, slings, arrows and rockets than seems humanly feasible. At every juncture of his political career—minister, treasurer, Opposition leader and even prime minister—Howard has been abused, lambasted and written off. He has weathered gibes about his teeth, his eyebrows, his bottom lip, his height (in truth, the PM's stature is nowhere near as diminutive as the 'Little Johnny' stereotype would have you think), his wife, his lack of sporting prowess, his voice and the afore-mentioned morning walk. If any of this overly upsets Howard, he does an excellent job of keeping the umbrage to himself.

Even Howard's initial brush with political power produced a wonder-fully unflattering anecdote. According to his biographer, David Barnett, Howard took six weeks' holiday from his legal practice to assist belea-guered Liberal Prime Minister William McMahon during the 1972 elec-tion year. Howard hadn't yet met McMahon, so a meeting was arranged in the Prime Minister's office in the Old Parliament House. According to Barnett, 'Howard was ushered in and Bill McMahon jumped to his feet. "No," he said. "I don't want to see him." Then McMahon, who also had an appointment with a Japanese delegation, stopped himself. "I thought you were the Japanese," he explained [to Howard].'[3]

* * *

By any measure, Howard enjoyed extraordinarily rapid success in the early stages of his political career. He entered parliament in 1974, was a minister the following year and by the age of 40 had risen to treasurer in the Fraser Government, a position he held for five years. Yet through all these years Howard was roundly derided as the 'boy' treasurer and Fraser's lapdog. During his subsequent stint as Opposition leader, Howard was frequently dismissed as hopelessly unelectable—the Kennett–Peacock conversation being just an explosively impolite ver-sion of the conventional wisdom surrounding the member for Bennelong during the 1980s.

Even Howard's ultimately triumphant return to the leadership in 1995 was driven much less by enthusiasm for the veteran than by a desperate lack of acceptable alternatives. And as the Prime Minister seemed to falter during his initial years in the job, the critics were relentless. Here, spectacularly, is Labor MP Anthony Albanese's breathless and savage appraisal of the Prime Minister as delivered to parliament in April 1998:

> Today my grievance is against the Prime Minister for his failure to provide leadership. You can trim the eyebrows; you can cap the teeth; you can cut the hair; you can put on different glasses; you can give him a ewe's milk facial, for all I care; but, to paraphrase a gritty Australian saying, 'Same stuff, different bucket.' In the pantheon of chinless blue bloods and suburban accountants that makes up the Australian Liberal party, this bloke is truly out of the box ... In John Howard, here is also a man, small in every sense. Some have said he is the worst prime minister since Billy McMahon. That is unfair to Billy McMahon ... The gulf, Mr Deputy Speaker, between the man in his mind—the phlegmatic, proud old English bulldog—the Winston of John Winston Howard—and the nervous, jerky, whiny apparition that we all see on the box every night. When he looks on the box he gets to see what we see—not the masterful orator of his mind but the whingey kid in his sandpit. Spare a thought for us, Mr Deputy Speaker, because we have to watch this performance every day—the chin and top lip jutting out in full duck mode ... Here is a man who lived at home until he was 32. You can imagine what he was like. Here were young Australians demonstrating against the Vietnam War, listening to The Doors, driving their tie-dyed kombi vans, and what was John Howard doing? He was at home with mum, wearing his shorts and long white socks, listening to Pat Boone albums and waiting for the Saturday night church dance.[4]

This catalogue of insults and abuse running through 30 years of political life helped forge the characteristics that have driven the Prime Minister's improbable long-term success. It's true Howard cut a nerdish figure in his youth; concrete proof of this is preserved in the National Screen and Sound Archive, which unearthed a 1955 radio quiz featuring 15-year-old John Winston pitting his wits against popular disc jockey Jack Davey in front of a live studio audience. In a cheeky, squeaky voice, Howard oozes geeky self-confidence:

Davey: What is a mezzanine floor?

JH: A what?

Davey: Well, where do you find a mezzanine floor?

JH: Oh, on the floor of a house in an eastern country?

Davey: You mean, a harem?

JH: How do you know?

Davey: How many people does it take to make a tete-a-tete?

JH: A tete-a-tete?

Davey: Yes. Have you ever been out with anybody?

JH: Two.

Davey: You've been out with two people?

JH: Two's the answer.

Davey: Yes ... What is the unusual characteristic of a kiwi?

JH: It's got a ...

Davey: No, it hasn't.

JH: It's on the face of a tin of boot polish.

Davey: Anything else?

JH: Well, it comes from New Zealand.

Davey: So do I, but I'm not on a can of boot polish. You're a nice boy. And remember, plenty of work and not too much tete-a-tete and everything will be fine.

Eventually, of course, everything *was* fine, but over the next 40 years John Howard weathered the kind of pasting that would deter ordinary mortals from pursuing a career in politics. As Daryl Melham, a veteran Sydney Labor MP, conceded on Howard's 64th birthday:

> If you were watching the races, if you went to the saddling enclosure in the races to pick out a horse for a winner, you know, what you're going to back in a race, you'd never pick John Howard to be Prime Minister. Because he would be probably the worst looking horse in the saddling enclosure, and yet this bloke's become Prime Minister over all the odds and, you know, I've got to say, I admire that.

That Howard has been constantly underestimated—not least by his Labor adversaries—has both contributed to his success and enhanced his unbridled enjoyment of the top job. Living well, they say, is the best revenge.

In *Recollections of a Bleeding Heart*, Paul Keating's speechwriter, Don Watson, writes eloquently of Keating's 'tiredness, languor, withdrawal, sadness and melancholy' on reaching the apex of political life. In contrast, Howard attacks the prime ministership like a fellow still mildly astonished that he's managed to pull it all off. Consequently, while Keating appeared forlorn, aloof and detached, Howard bristles with energy and never allows himself the luxury of feeling overly comfortable in the top job. This constant political paranoia—a sense of always expecting the unexpected—is born of bitter experience and has served Howard well. 'That's right, I've always been like that,' he told me in 2003. 'Somebody said to me this morning something complimentary, and I just looked around and said, there's always an Exocet coming over the horizon ... you can never tell in politics.'

* * *

There has been no shortage of Exocets during Howard's 10 years in office. He was almost a one-term wonder, a quivering nervous wreck, on election night in 1998 when the massive majority he had won two years before began to vanish. Through most of the Coalition's second term Labor seemed poised for victory, only to falter in the months before the 2001 poll. Mark Latham, the crude, unpredictable, volatile Exocet from western Sydney, had Howard in his sights during 2004 before spectacularly backfiring on the Labor Party. Through victory and turmoil Howard has remained grounded, adhering to Kipling's famous advice about regarding triumph and adversity as similar impostors. For all the cruel, amusing and inventive insults that have been hurled his way, nobody has ever accused the Prime Minister of being up himself.

That such a remarkably successful politician comes across as such an unremarkable character infuriates his critics. 'John Howard, as I say, is the most deeply ordinary person that I've ever confronted in Australian politics,' former premier and federal health minister Carmen Lawrence once huffed, 'And, for God's sake, he's leading the Liberal Party and everyone thinks he's a political genius.'[5]

To a point, Howard is astonishingly ordinary and, for a senior politician, admirably unpretentious. 'He is in tune with a big majority of the mob,' wrote former Labor minister and powerbroker Graham Richardson. 'The over-55s love him because he talks like them. He has the same values. He harbours the same suspicions they harbour about newcomers and bludgers ... he knows instinctively what really matters to those who decide his fate.'[6]

A mildly eccentric friend of mine from Canberra still dines out on her story of attending a leadership and ethics conference near the Prime Minister's Kirribilli residence. While exercising early one morning she stumbled upon the power-walking Prime Minister and conspired to front him the following day with an offer to address the conference. The next morning she hooked up with Howard—he was happy to have a chat—and on the homeward stretch summoned the nerve to invite the Prime Minister across the road to speak to her colleagues. 'I'll be there in 20 minutes,' Howard said, forcing my friend to race back and wake still-sleeping confreres. True to his word, Howard turned up and stayed for half an hour.

On the day Sydney was to win the 2005 AFL grand final, I found myself seated at a pre-game breakfast with Howard's youngest son, Tim. We were talking sport and I wondered aloud whether his father, an avid St George fan, would manage to return to Sydney in time to catch the Dragons play in an NRL knockout final that evening. Musing about the logistics of leaving the MCG after 5 p.m. to reach Sydney by kick-off, we agreed it would be difficult. But the Prime Minister, I suggested, could easily arrange for a helicopter to ferry him to Melbourne airport after the grand final. Tim just burst out laughing: 'C'mon, Dad would never be that flash.'

It's true, Howard is conspicuously unflash; none of the senior staff in his office has a government credit card or expense account. Still, this image of Howard as über-ordinary is illusory. There's nothing remotely normal about Howard's fervid dedication to his profession. The Prime Minister is an avid, nigh-obsessional consumer of news, starting his walk plugged into morning radio bulletins and retiring after the closing credits of ABC television's *Lateline* program. Every government decision or appointment requires Howard's imprimatur. During holidays—rare and rarely devoid of duty—Howard reads about politics and politicians. Once the latest developments in world cricket have been dealt with, small talk with the Prime Minister is inevitably steered towards his favourite subject. Even those who have known Howard for decades remain in awe of his recall of seemingly arcane political details. Almost everything Howard says and does is calibrated for maximum political effect.

* * *

In any consideration of the Prime Minister's success, the role of Janette Howard cannot be overstated. They are truly soul partners, bonded by clear-eyed ambition, a boundless fascination with politics and deep love of family. Young Janette Parker took a liking to Howard when he was a journeyman solicitor, stuck with him through the nerdish and wilderness years and has plainly relished her husband's success. They met at a Liberal Party do, hooked up immediately and have sailed the stormy seas of Howard's career together. 'I think he's gorgeous' was what Mrs Howard said to *Woman's Day* about her husband when he became treasurer. Mainly, though, she has eschewed publicity, creating an air of mystique that adds to the popular image of Mrs Howard as influential gatekeeper to her husband. If this is exaggerated, Howard makes no attempt to hide the importance of his beloved 'one-person focus group'.

'Janette has been the greatest source of support and companionship that anybody in public or private life could possibly have, and I am very lucky to have met her some 35 years ago,' the Prime Minister told parliament as it adjourned for summer in 2005. 'I am very fortunate indeed, and I thank her for the three wonderful children that she has given me and for the joy we have had with our kids. My greatest achievement, if I have had any, is to have a wonderfully close relationship with my three adult children. It is the greatest joy you can have in life.'[7]

This wasn't merely Yuletide-inspired hyperbole; Howard frequently expresses thanks and no small wonder that children Richard, Melanie and Tim have survived his tumultuous political journey intact. For this he attributes most credit to Janette.

'As somebody sagely said,' he told the house, 'what you can hope for is that when you depart this life you have your family around holding your hand. That is a reminder to all of us that having our children with us and having the support of our family is the most important thing.'[8]

For so long a stiff, awkward social figure—Howard's deafness in one ear hasn't helped—in latter years Howard has palpably softened. The first Bali bombing in 2002 had a profound effect on the Prime Minister, who took it on himself to be counsellor-in-chief to the families and friends of 88 Australians who died in the blasts. When Howard told the parliamentary commemoration service that 'this terrible tragedy has perhaps revealed another side of our nature—the uninhibited out-pouring of compassion towards those who have lost so much', he might have been speaking of himself. Afterwards, in a powerful and indelible moment on the parliamentary forecourt, a hefty mourner wearing Doc Martens, tattoos, reflector sunglasses and a ponytail all but lifted Howard out of his shoes while applying a despairing bear hug to the Prime Minister. Both men were weeping openly.

Despite his reputation for stubbornness and resilience, it has been Howard's ability to shift deftly with the times that has most confounded his critics. He has become more tolerant to internal dissent and increasingly willing to admit mistakes and move on. The disparagement continues apace but, like Popeye and his spinach, ridicule and denigration seem only to strengthen the Prime Minister's resolve to prove his naysayers fools. How John and Janette must privately marvel at the way events have turned out.

III

PROSPERITY AND REFORM

THE GOLDEN YEARS

Alan Wood

'Firstly, let me deal with the economic challenge. If we do not succeed there
every other ideal we share will be unachievable.'
—John Howard, Opposition leader, first Headland speech,
6 June 1995

JOHN Howard's 10 years at the pinnacle of Australian political power
have been remarkable ones for the nation's economy. International
observers such as the Organisation for Economic Co-operation and
Development have called it an economic miracle. Although by no
means free of economic shocks, viewed through the haze of history the
decade will be seen as another golden age, similar to the 1960s. Musing
on this three years ago, the Prime Minister thought that there was
something insubstantial about those earlier years.[1] There was. The
economy then was far more protected, far more inward-looking and
insular, with a controlled exchange rate and high tariff walls. Exports in
the 1960s comprised only 8 per cent of the Australian economy. It is a
very different economy now. The tariff walls have largely gone and the
Australian dollar is a floating currency, free of exchange controls and
government manipulation. Exports and imports each account for about
20 per cent of this much more open economy, and foreign investment

by Australian companies now exceeds direct foreign investment flows into this country.

The periodic wage explosions, exchange rate and balance of payments crises that typically ended economic expansions in earlier decades no longer dominate economic policy. The last time monetary policy had to respond to the threat of an inflationary wage breakout was in 1994–95. The Reserve Bank put up interest rates by 2.75 percentage points between August and December 1994. According to then governor Bernie Fraser, this was necessary to counter overheating in the economy and rising wage pressures. It was the last gasp of the old wages system. The RBA will still respond if wage pressures threaten inflation, but in contrast to earlier episodes, in 2005 strong wage pressures in some areas of skills shortage, such as mining, did not spread rapidly through the economy via national wage increases and the pernicious doctrine of comparative wage 'justice'.[2] This reflects a more flexible labour market, partly the outcome of labour market reforms but largely the result of the opening up of the economy to global competition.

Fears about the possible impact on interest rates, the exchange rate and economic growth of big current account deficits and rapidly rising foreign debt lingered well into the 1990s—the political and policy aftermath of the mid-1980s Banana Republic episode. Playing on fears about the high level of foreign debt was a prominent feature of John Howard's successful 1995–96 election campaign, with a 'Debt Truck' touring electorates displaying the latest debt figures. But attempts by Labor leader Kim Beazley to revive these fears on the back of a current account deficit that exceeded 7 per cent of GDP in the March quarter 2005 (compared with about 6.5 per cent in the Banana Republic years), and foreign debt much higher than it was in the mid-1980s, have so far had little impact on the political debate, in the electorate and in financial markets, or on economic policy. Now our foreign debt belongs to the private sector, the Howard Government having eliminated net public sector debt, and is overwhelmingly denominated in Australian dollars not, as before, in US dollars. This makes us much less vulnerable to a run on the currency and distinguishes us from the Latin American countries with chronic balance of payments problems[3]—one of the most important economic developments of the past decade.

Through the Howard years economic growth has averaged 3.75 per cent, compared with 5.25 per cent in the 1960s, 3.25 per cent in the 1970s and 3 per cent in the 1980s. While the 1960s performance stands out, Howard was right when he said it had shaky foundations and could not be sustained. Each of these earlier decades experienced at least one recession, but over the past decade growth has been much less volatile and there has been no recession.

This experience is not unique to Australia. In what have been called the Anglosphere countries—the United States, Australia, Britain, Canada and New Zealand—the 10 years from the mid-90s to the mid-'noughties' have been years of prosperity and relative economic stability. Even in the United States the recession that followed the bursting of the stock market bubble in 2000 was the mildest in the post-war period. However, Australia's performance has been a global standout. In the four decades after 1950, Australia's GDP per capita growth rate rarely exceeded the OECD average, but there has been a dramatic improvement since the early 1990s and we have regularly outperformed the OECD. It has been a decade of rising living standards and falling unemployment, of low inflation and cheap money, and of new financial opportunities (and risks) for households, which have geared up their balance sheets and fed an extraordinary boom in housing prices, now cooling off. These days the Reserve Bank worries more about asset price bubbles than wages or the exchange rate.

Just how extraordinary the economic transformation has been was strikingly captured in a speech by Treasury secretary Ken Henry in March 2005:

> If, at the start of the 1990s, we had predicted that our largest trading partner [Japan] would experience average growth of just one per cent and suffer four recessions over the coming decade, that a large part of emerging East Asia would experience a financial crisis and severe recession (1997 and 1998), that US bond markets would effectively grind to a halt for a period (late 1998), that US equity markets would experience the emergence and bursting of a major bubble (2000), that the US economy would experience a not insubstantial recession (2001), that significant acts of terror would occur in New York and elsewhere, that Asia would experience health scares like SARS and avian flu, and that oil prices would rise sharply to levels not seen since 1985, most of us would have thought that the next 15 years would be pretty miserable ones for Australia. Yet this has been a period of historic economic prosperity for us.[4]

How did this historic change in our economic performance come about? How much was luck and how much good political and economic management? How much can John Howard and his Treasurer, Peter Costello, claim credit for?

In attempting to answer these questions it is important to recognise that while 10 years as Prime Minister is a notable achievement, it is a completely arbitrary period over which to assess a country's economic performance. Australia's run of growth is now heading into its 16th year and its foundations were laid in the preceding decade and even earlier. To recognise this is not to belittle Howard's contribution, which also reaches back beyond his term as Prime Minister. In a speech to the Business Council of Australia in 2003,[5] reflecting on the previous 20 years, he spoke of the 'five great economic reforms that have transformed the Australian economy', and went on to list six: financial deregulation, the floating of the Australian dollar, tariff reform, industrial relations, tax reform and fiscal consolidation.[6]

The first three of these, Howard acknowledged, were under the previous Labor government and the other three under his government, although he noted that financial deregulation and tariff reform were implemented with strong support from the then federal Opposition, which from September 1985 to May 1989 was under Howard's leadership.[7] His role is acknowledged by John Quiggin, a leading left-wing academic economist who is no fan of Howard:

> Although he had not taken a particularly ideological stance during his period as treasurer in the Fraser government, John Howard emerged in the 1980s as the strongest and most consistent advocate of free-market reform in Australian public life. As treasurer, shadow treasurer and then leader of the Opposition during the 1980s, Howard played a crucial role in pushing Australia towards microeconomic reform.
>
> In Opposition, Howard could have taken an opportunistic line, attacking the Labor government whenever its reform measures proved politically unpalatable. Instead, he adopted a position of bi-partisan support for reform, attacking Labor only on the grounds that it was not going far enough, particularly where proposals for reform were opposed by the union movement.[8]

By the time he won the 1996 election, Howard still had this reputation, earned in the 1980s, as a champion of economic reform. However, he was a much more cautious one, having been through the loss of Opposition leadership in 1989, having seen Opposition leader John Hewson's radical Fightback! policy (including the Jobsback labour market reform policy that was Howard's responsibility as shadow minister) defeated at the 'unloseable' election of 1993, and having seen the public mood turn against the reforms of the Hawke and Keating Labor governments that he had supported. Equally importantly, as Prime Minister, Howard lacked the support of a reform-oriented Opposition, instead facing a Senate controlled by a Labor Party and minor parties with little interest in, or open hostility to, economic change and the longer-term national interest.

This caution has not been without its economic and political costs. Such was Howard's new modesty as a reformer that he had been Prime Minister barely a year when it began to look ominously like his might be a one-term government. Influential business groups began to talk of a do-nothing government, and Howard's approach was often characterised as vacillating. A prime example was his labour market reforms. Although he and his industrial relations minister, Peter Reith, had got the *Workplace Relations Act 1996* through parliament, this was widely regarded as a seriously compromised piece of legislation—because of Howard's unwillingness to confront the Senate, which would have required at least the credible threat of a double-dissolution election, and his pre-election promise that nobody would be worse off under the changes. As a result Reith had to negotiate with Australian Democrats leader Cheryl Kernot to get the legislation through the Senate, significantly weakening it. Now Howard has used an unexpected, if fractious, Senate majority from the October 2004 election to step up labour market reform. This is less radical than the unions (who made similar wild claims about the 1996 Reith legislation) would have us believe: more of the unemployed will get jobs, productivity will increase over time and average incomes will rise. The role of the Australian Industrial Relations Commission and wage awards will be reduced significantly. However, the labour market will still be highly regulated, although the nature of the regulation has changed.

With his government at risk in 1997, Howard decided to embark on a major structural reform of the Australian tax system, with the introduction of a goods and services tax, compensated for by substantial changes to income tax. This, too, was compromised in negotiations with the Democrats, weakening the economic benefits from its introduction. Since this politically bold move there have been further cuts in income tax to compensate for bracket creep, but no further attempt at fundamental tax reform, despite burgeoning budget surpluses and strong pressure from business, some academic economists and others, including *The Australian*.

Two very important reforms introduced under Howard, both in his first term, involve the conduct of fiscal and monetary policy. On both fronts Australia now has an enviable international reputation, which has stood it in good stead through shocks such as the 1997 Asian exchange rate and banking crisis.

In May 1995 the Opposition's treasury spokesman, Peter Costello, used an address to the National Press Club in Canberra to lambaste what he called Paul Keating's budget deceit.[9] 'Too much government effort goes into pulling slick tricks to hide the real outcome of the budget,' he said, going on to declare that Australia needed an honest budget. While there had been a clear improvement in the budget papers under Keating, there was certainly room for more, and Costello committed the Coalition to introduce a charter of budget honesty if elected. The charter did not make it into legislation until 1998, but the principles underlying it were reflected in Howard government budgets from the first one in 1996–97. In his budget speech of 20 August 1996, the novice treasurer reaffirmed his commitment to a charter intended to make fiscal policy much more disciplined and transparent.

> Before its defeat on 2 March, the previous [Keating Labor] government maintained that the budget would now be in underlying balance. The truth was nearly $10 billion to the contrary. Financial dishonesty of that magnitude undermines public confidence in our political system. We will never let it happen again. Our Government will enact a charter of budget honesty ...

The *Charter of Budget Honesty Act 1998* sets out, among other matters, the principles for sound fiscal policy. There are five. They cover: the prudent management of financial risk faced by the commonwealth, such as excessive net debt; ensuring fiscal policy achieves adequate national saving and moderates cyclical fluctuations in economic activity; tax and spending policies consistent with reasonable stability and predictability in the level of the tax burden; maintaining the integrity of the tax system; and requiring government to have regard to the financial effects of its policy decisions on future generations—that is, generational equity. The charter also covers other matters such as mid-year budget updates, pre-election fiscal reports, five-yearly inter-generational reports and annual statements of fiscal strategy. It has improved the fiscal policy framework but not the transparency of the budget papers, which changes introduced along with accrual accounting have made harder, not easier, to read.

Ironically, while the charter was motivated by the desire to prevent governments from concealing budget deficits, the problem for the Howard Government has been a string of budget surpluses much larger than forecast by Treasury. More accurate forecasts might have encouraged the Government to tackle fundamental reform of the income tax system, instead of tax cuts being periodic hand-backs of what is left over after the budget spending has been done, or when there is a political need to stop middle income earners from slipping into the top tax bracket. Then again, perhaps not. The Labor Party is right when it claims that the Howard Government has been a high-taxing, big-spending government.

Although Costello—who has to fight off big-spending ministers in every budget round, year after year—would vigorously deny it, the Howard Government has only had one really tough budget: it is first. Since then it has progressively enjoyed the revenue riches flowing into its coffers. However, it has stuck with the basic operating principle of its budget strategy—a balanced budget over the economic cycle—which means budget surpluses in the good years and deficits in the bad. So far it has been fortunate enough not to have had any bad years. It has also eliminated net federal government debt. Its surpluses and debt elimination have made it a stellar fiscal performer in a world dominated by the massive US budget deficit.

There has been another important effect of setting fiscal policy in a long-term framework: it has removed the pressure that bad fiscal policy puts on monetary policy. This is a virtue that has been emphasised by former Treasury secretary Ted Evans and his successor Ken Henry. In a 2003 speech on fiscal policy,[10] Henry said there were two ways in which ill-disciplined fiscal policy could create problems for monetary policy. First, it can put pressure on inflation, forcing a monetary policy response. Second, it can generate instability in the economy, interfering with the operation of monetary policy. On the other hand, a credible medium-term fiscal strategy provides room for an effective monetary policy. The Prime Minister has been highly, indeed excessively, sensitive to the connection between interest rates and fiscal policy.

In the same Press Club address in which he announced the charter, Costello said that monetary policy would be the responsibility of the Reserve Bank and 'there won't be any sort of midnight calls or pressure or boasting, as you've got from Mr Keating on how he pulls the levers'.[11] He gave effect to this undertaking with the release on 14 August 1996 of a *Statement on the Conduct of Monetary Policy*, agreed between the Treasurer and the incoming governor of the bank, Ian Macfarlane. This was a watershed in the conduct of monetary policy in Australia. It formally gave the RBA policy independence and ended the practice of consulting the government of the day before making interest rate changes, which were then announced jointly by the governor and the Treasurer. The Government reserved the right to comment publicly on monetary policy from time to time, which the Prime Minister has exercised frequently—more often than not to make clear that he did not agree with rate rises. But it is the RBA board, not government, that now makes the decision.

This independence has been particularly important because of a fundamental difference in the way Ian Macfarlane and John Howard view interest rates. For the central banker, interest rates are the policy instrument the RBA uses to achieve its inflation target of 2 to 3 per cent, on average, over the economic cycle. For the politician (low) interest rates are themselves the target, which is precisely why central banks need policy independence. Howard was Treasurer in an era when governments ran monetary policy, and his comments on interest rates sometimes leave the strong impression that he wishes he still did. All the Government's research shows that the high interest rates of the late 1980s permanently scarred a generation of voters, particularly in small business—research it used to effect in the 2004 election campaign.

However, there is no evidence of any attempt by the Howard Government to privately influence the RBA's interest rate decisions, perhaps because the conduct of monetary policy has changed in ways congenial to it (or any government). First, the central bank is much more relaxed about the inflationary dangers from a falling exchange rate. This means it is less likely to respond to a fall in the Australian dollar with higher interest rates. Second, despite some disagreement with Treasury and the Government in the late 1990s and more recently on the issue, the Reserve Bank believes its anti-inflation credentials are strong enough, and the Australian economy is flexible enough, to be able to grow more rapidly without generating the inflationary pressures of the past. The disagreement has been over how rapidly it can grow before rates rise, with the RBA more conservative but not dramatically so.

These and the other policy changes outlined earlier have been a central feature of the story of Australia's decade of prosperity and its ability to break away from a past haunted by destructive wage rounds and balance of payments terrors. But luck has also played its part, inevitably. John Howard was lucky enough to be elected early in the long run of prosperity across the Anglosphere economies, which has generally been kind to incumbent governments. Even Bill Clinton would probably still be president of the United States if presidents were allowed more than two terms of office.

Another piece of luck, although not for Paul Keating, the man who coined the phrase, was the 'recession we had to have'. Keating was right, but Howard enjoyed the benefits. Ian Macfarlane put the early 1990s recession into long-overdue perspective last December. 'I mean the episode in Australia which returned us to a low-inflation, sustainable-growth economy is regarded as a policy error, whereas in America it is regarded as a policy triumph.'[12] The low-inflation economy, with its reserve of spare productive capacity, has been an important part of Australia's 15 years of growth. So, of course, has the emergence of China, which has been important to Australia in many ways, from helping to sustain low inflation to the huge boost to our terms of trade and domestic incomes.

John Howard and Peter Costello have been lucky, but they have also followed macroeconomic policies that have been important in getting Australia through some potential rough patches, such as the Asian crisis of 1997 and the US recession of 2001. However, anyone remembering the Howard ('the strongest and most consistent advocate of free-market reform'[13]) of the 1980s would have been expecting more in March 1996 than he has achieved over the past decade.

7

THE CARROT AND THE STICK

Mike Steketee

'The role of government has grown too much. It ought to be reduced.'
—John Howard, 1986

WHEN Robert Menzies retired as the Liberals' longest serving prime minister in 1966, the federal government took 22.1 per cent of Australia's income in taxes. Twenty years later the figure had risen to 26.1 per cent of a much larger national economy and John Howard as Opposition leader criticised Bob Hawke's big government in the Alfred Deakin lecture.

These days the Prime Minister rarely invokes the conservative touchstone of small government. In 2006 government tax, including the GST, accounts for 25.6 per cent of income, which is hardly a basis to argue for smaller government. In fact, during Howard's 10 years in office, revenue as a proportion of national income has risen, not fallen: the Keating Government in its last year raised 24.2 per cent of income in taxes.[1]

The figures on the size of government say a great deal about the Howard approach. His career has displayed a constancy of belief in many areas. Free enterprise, individual initiative and self-help, combined with active support for the traditional family as the bedrock of society, have been major themes through three decades of public life.

Smaller government is the corollary of the first three of these themes but it has been overwhelmed by two forces: dramatic economic change, which Howard supported in Opposition and carried forward in government; and equally drastic social change, which he has mostly opposed but which governments have limited power to influence. There is a third factor. Above all else, Howard is a political pragmatist, as any prime minister has to be to stay in power for a long period, and he has learned the art of spending his way out of political trouble, most notably in the 2001 and 2004 elections. The interaction of these three elements means that the role of government has not been reduced under a prime minister who once described himself as the most conservative person ever to lead the Liberals.

Not only that but the welfare state—that part of government to which conservatives supposedly have the strongest ideological objection—has grown significantly. In 1995–96, the last year of the Keating Government, spending on social security and welfare made up 35.4 per cent of the federal budget. Ten years later unemployment has almost halved, to about 5 per cent, but the figure has risen to 42.5 per cent.[2]

Opening up the Australian economy to the rest of the world, particularly through tariff cuts, has seen industries grow and shrink at a rapid rate, along with the number of employees in them. Many workers made the transition successfully, often parlaying their skills into higher paid jobs. Others moved down into rapidly growing areas such as the service industries, with lower rates of pay and a higher proportion of casual and part-time work. This meant that more working Australians qualified for welfare benefits to top up their incomes. Those most vulnerable to structural change were older and blue-collar workers and many of them ended up on the Disability Support Pension (DSP) after being assessed as unlikely to work again. In 2004, more than 40 per cent of DSP recipients were 55 or over, and just over 20 per cent 60 or older. While those receiving unemployment benefits have been falling with strong economic growth, the numbers on the DSP have been rising steadily, with the two figures intersecting towards the end of the 1990s. There has been a similar increase in single parents receiving the parenting payment. The result of this economic and social upheaval is that over the past 30 years, the proportion of working-age Australians receiving an income support payment has quadrupled to 20 per cent, representing 2.6 million people.[3]

Arguably, much of this increase could not be influenced by Howard in the short term, at least if he were to survive politically. But the biggest growth area in the welfare budget in the past decade has been in an area that he has made a priority: assistance to families with children. Whereas overall spending on social security and welfare rose by 87.5 per cent over the decade, that on families with children increased by 134 per cent. At a cost of almost $27 billion in 2005–06, it represents the second-largest item in the welfare budget after assistance to the aged.[4] The Government has fashioned family tax benefits to be the equivalent of a large tax cut, but one targeted to families with children. In terms of directing resources to the area of greatest need, this is an effective strategy, given that large families in particular are over-represented among the poor. Research by Canberra University's National Centre for Social and Economic Modelling (NATSEM) found that the disposable income of the lowest 20 per cent of families rose by 18 per cent in real terms between 1997 and 2004, thanks mainly to increases in family payments in 2000 and 2004.[5]

But family tax benefits are more than a welfare measure: they represent a conscious shift towards providing greater government support for families. The scale of the measures is not always appreciated, at least not by Australians without children. After taking family tax benefits into account, families with two young children in 2005 effectively did not start paying tax until their incomes reached between $44,951 and $47,891, depending on their circumstances. The maximum rate of family tax benefit A is $5157 a year and it is not phased out completely until family incomes pass $101,495 for families with young children and an even higher figure for larger families and those with older children. On top of this, assistance of up to $3066 is available under family tax benefit B, which goes to single parents and non-working spouses and is not means-tested at all on the main earner's income. In addition, from 2004 the Government provided a maternity payment of $3000 for each new child, with the rate rising to $4000 in 2006 and $5000 in 2008.

As the name suggests, the Government does not want family tax benefits to be regarded as welfare, even though that is the only sensible description for them, as acknowledged by their inclusion in the social security and welfare category of the budget papers. Their generosity stems from their ability to meet two government goals: support for families and providing the equivalent of a targeted tax cut. Family tax benefits constitute both traditional welfare and middle-class welfare that reaches well into swinging-voter households.

There is another group on which the Government has lavished largesse. Particularly in the 2001 and 2004 elections, it granted a raft of concessions and payments to the aged, including extending access to the Seniors health card; a utilities allowance; an income tax offset that lifts to more than $33,000 a year the threshold before retired couples start paying tax; and removing the superannuation surcharge introduced in the Howard Government's first budget. Many of the concessions will impose an increasing burden on future budgets as rising numbers of Australians retire, running counter to other measures the Government has taken to encourage people to stay in the workforce, such as a tax offset for mature-age workers, a pensions bonus scheme and allowing people to draw on superannuation while they are still working.

By contrast the Government has been tough, even punitive, in traditional areas of welfare. Unemployment and youth allowances are indexed to prices, whereas pensions for the aged, disabled and single parents increase faster in line with wages, meaning there has been a growing gap between the two types of payments. This has created a perverse incentive to establish eligibility for a pension rather than stay on allowances and meet the much more rigorous requirements of looking for work. Means tests also are much stricter for allowances than for pensions and family payments, creating another barrier to work. Even relatively minor breaches of the conditions for receiving allowances, such as missing interviews, attract tough penalties, including up to two months' suspension of benefits for multiple offences.

All this is part of the Government's aim to change the culture of social security from an entitlement to a last resort. It exploits public perceptions of welfare bludgers and of people ripping off taxpayers, though the truth is that this is relevant only to a small minority and a shrinking one as the conditions for receiving payments become increasingly onerous. The Government has made much of its crackdown on social security fraud, such as the advertisements it ran in the 1998 election campaign boasting it was saving $46 million a week. The figure looked impressive but it represented just 4.5 per cent of federal spending on social security at the time. Most of the money came from overpayments, due in part to the complexity of the welfare system and was offset to some extent by underpayments. In the first two years of the Howard Government, just 4471 of the 7.8 million receiving a welfare benefit were convicted of fraud. The Government reinforced such measures with rhetoric, such as former social security minister Jocelyn Newman's description of welfare as a safety net rather than a hammock and Tony Abbott as employment minister referring to 'job snobs' and arguing that many Australians were too fussy about the kind of jobs they were prepared to take. The Government introduced a program with the populist and pejorative title of Work for the Dole to emphasise the principle of mutual obligation, under which the unemployed are required to give something in return for receiving a payment from the Government. Starting with young people, the program has been expanded and extended to include long-term unemployed. In the words of Workforce Participation Minister Peter Dutton, 'it is a compliance mechanism, highlighting the Government's strong commitment to mutual obligation, and it is an important tool in developing a work ethic, the value of teamwork, investment in our local communities and valuable work experience'.

But its goal, even though an indirect one, of putting the unemployed into work, has had at best modest success. The Government has been sceptical of labour market programs, breaking its 1996 election commitment to retain the Keating Government's Working Nation programs and instead cutting them drastically in its first budget. It argues that this form of active labour market intervention is too expensive. But in Britain, where the Blair Government adopted many of the ideas of Working Nation, long-term unemployment has fallen faster than unemployment overall, whereas in Australia the opposite is the case. Working Nation was framed on the same principles of mutual obligation emphasised by the Howard Government: it imposed a 'reciprocal obligation' to participate in training, work experience or wage subsidy programs or otherwise face the reduction and ultimately the loss of benefits. But apart from paying the benefit, this government has been less willing to fund its side of the obligation.

There is however a continuity in government policies often overlooked in the adversarial rhetoric of politics. While the bureaucracy increasingly tailors its advice to the political preferences of the government, it also is a repository of experience that sees similar solutions advocated for continuing problems. The Howard Government gradually brought back elements of labour market programs, such as access to training, wage subsidies and more individualised assistance, though it has funded them at only modest levels. It took a large step towards privatising the welfare system through Job Network, contracting out the job placement work of the Commonwealth Employment Service to non-profit and commercial organisations. A similar step was being considered within the Keating Government and it might well have been implemented if Labor had not lost office. Arguably the largest step towards privatising welfare was taken by the Keating Government with the introduction of a national superannuation scheme operated by private funds and with the ultimate, though very long-term, goal of replacing the aged pension for many Australians.

The clearest expression of the Howard Government's philosophy came with its implementation of 'welfare to work' reforms previously blocked by the Senate. From 1 July 2006, only people assessed as unable to work at least 15 hours or more a week will qualify for the Disability Support Pension (DSP), compared with the previous threshold of 30 hours. This means that many people who previously would have qualified for the DSP will be moved to the Newstart allowance, worth $46 a week less. From July 2006 those receiving parenting payments, mostly single parents, must seek work voluntarily within a year or when their youngest child turns six. After that, they, together with new applicants, will have to work or go on Newstart if assessed as able to work 15 hours a week, reducing their allowance by $29 a week. The carrot to go with the stick is some easing of the means test for Newstart but it still is less generous than the pension. As well, vocational education and training, literacy and numeracy and childcare programs are being expanded. These measures represent the biggest assault on welfare dependency in the 10 years of the Howard Government.

But the investment in moving people from welfare to work is still small in relation to the large numbers of recipients. Over three years, the Government is funding 20,600 more places in open employment services and 41,600 in rehabilitation to help people with disabilities find and retain jobs. This compares with the 700,000 people now receiving the DSP. A total of 52,000 families will receive help to meet the gap in childcare fees and 84,300 extra places for outside-school-hours care will be created but there are more than 600,000 people receiving the parenting payment. Added to the guarantee that existing DSP recipients will not have to meet the new requirements, this suggests that the changes will have a significant effect only in the long run and will need the assistance of demographic change, which will see the competition for labour increasing as the numbers entering the work force decline.

Former employment and workplace relations minister Peter Reith identified the problem of long-term welfare dependence as long ago as 1998 in a letter to Prime Minister Howard that was later leaked. 'There is plenty of evidence that permanent marginalisation of particular groups will generate high social costs down the track and can have intergenerational consequences as well,' he wrote. The 2000 report that the Government commissioned from a committee headed by Mission

Australia head Patrick McClure recommended reducing the high effective marginal tax rates for families caused by the compounding effect of income tax, the withdrawal rate of family tax benefits and the income test on youth allowances. It suggested simplifying and rationalising benefit payments, particularly through introducing an integrated income support system. A common base payment across pensions and allowances would be supplemented by additional needs-based payments according to family and other circumstances. As well, participation supplements would help the transition to employment.[6] While there has been some movement in these directions, the Government has stopped well short of a redesign of the welfare system, including a rationalisation of the 15 different income support payments for people of working age. One reason is that striking a common payment would involve raising the level of unemployment benefits, with the only other option for a common payment the politically unpalatable one of cutting pensions. The withdrawal rate over most of the range of family payments has been reduced from 50 cents to 20 cents in the dollar and a working credit introduced for people on benefits who take up jobs. But the withdrawal rate for unemployment benefits has fallen only to 60 per cent, typifying the distinction the Government draws between deserving and less deserving recipients of government benefits.

The goals that the McClure report set for measuring the success of welfare reform were a significant reduction in both the number of jobless families and the proportion of the working-age population relying heavily on income support, together with stronger communities that generated more opportunities for social and economic participation. Data from the national census shows a rise from 12.1 per cent to 18.2 per cent in the 15 years to 2001 in the proportion of families with dependent children under 15 that are jobless, bringing the rate to one of the highest in the OECD.[7] Two-thirds of jobless households in 2001 were headed by single parents, a category with an unemployment rate of 53 per cent. Eight per cent of two-parent families had no one in work. Together, there were 670,000 children in these households, representing the nation's biggest social challenge, given the potential for inter-generational unemployment to develop into an Australian underclass. A different measure suggests that rates of child poverty have fallen slightly from 16.7 per cent in 2001 to 14.5 per cent in 2003. This is based on a calculation by the Brotherhood of St Laurence from Household Income and Labour Dynamics (HILDA) surveys of a poverty line drawn at half median household income, with adjustments for the size of households. The HILDA data also gives an insight into the persistence of child poverty and jobless households. Over the three years from 2001, 24.6 per cent of children were in a jobless household for at least one year, 15.3 per cent for at least two years and 8.9 per cent in all three years.[8] Future surveys will give a better indication of the extent to which such families regularly move in and out of unemployment and poverty.

McClure's second objective of a significant reduction in the proportion of the working-age population relying heavily on income support has yet to be achieved. The 'welfare to work' measures may have an impact in the long run, as may the falling rate of growth of the workforce as the population ages. But labour market reform and the likelihood of a widening gap in earned incomes that it produces may have the opposite effect, with more people in low-paying and part-time jobs relying in part on government benefits. As well, the incentive for those on government payments to take up work will be reduced if wages at the bottom sink closer to the level of benefits.

In terms of welfare the Howard years have been marked by a shift to a two-tier system. There has been a concerted effort to change the culture of welfare for the unemployed, disabled and single parents from one of entitlement to imposing new obligations to look for work or engage in programs such as Work for the Dole. But the Government has been unwilling to embrace wholesale reform and rationalisation of the welfare system along the lines suggested by McClure, including through the scale of investment in transition to work that experience in countries such as Britain suggests is needed to make a significant dent in unemployment among the disadvantaged. This risks leaving a pool of permanently unemployed spilling over into second and subsequent generations, constituting the makings of an Australian underclass. The Government has taken a quite different approach to families with children and the aged, significantly increasing support and extending the reach of the welfare state.

8

TAXING TIMES

George Megalogenis

POLITICIANS reveal their true selves when they hand out money, because the transaction compels them to choose between voters. As a tax cutter, John Howard has wound up preferring higher-income males over the blue-collar battlers, and working mothers over the stay-at-homes. Neither fact fits the political cliché, because supporters and opponents alike view the Prime Minister as being both the battler's mate and ambivalent towards working mothers. He may, in his gut, be that person, but his record in office says otherwise.

The moment of clarity came in the run-up to the 2004 election, at the eight-year mark of Howard's cross-century decade in power. The budget surplus had been restored to rude health by a booming economy, which tallied in raw politics to a tax cuts kitty of almost $34 billion for the next four years. There was more than enough here to make every man, woman and child feel loved. But Howard was in no mood to waste resources on those people he didn't need to impress. One in three of the nation's 9.5 million households would receive absolutely nothing from that budget, because their vote was judged as holding no value. They were younger singles on lower and middle incomes (usually renters) and older couples without dependent children (who were more likely to own their own home outright).

The personal tax cuts were restricted to upper-income earners on more than $52,000 a year, which is the elite male rung on the income ladder. The tax rates were left untouched. All that changed were the thresholds at which the top two tax rates of 42 cents and 47 cents applied. At first blush, it seemed as if the Government had missed its mark, because the Liberal Party's polling suggested that women, not men, would decide the coming election. The pivotal voter was the second earner in the typical two-income household, the mum, who worked part time on $12,000 to $15,000 a year.

But Howard knew what he was doing. The tax cuts were not the main game of the May 2004 budget; they compromised less than half the total giveaway—$14.7 billion out of $33.9 billion. The larger amount was a $19.2 billion increase in family payments. The cash was skewed, deliberately, to working mothers in middle- and lower-income households, where many of the dads were denied tax cuts and where both parents were feeling squeezed by their mortgage.

Howard passed up the opportunity to reduce personal tax rates across the board—even though he had the means to do so—because family payments delivered a bigger political bang for the buck per target voter. When families entered the ballot box five months later, they did so with their wallets full but fearful of higher interest rates under Labor's Mark Latham. The Government picked up eight Labor seats in the mortgage belt, which more than offset the loss of five Coalition seats where there was a below-average number of home borrowers.

Did this vindicate Howard's pragmatism, or did he waste money from the welfare side of the budget on voters who were always going to stick with him because of interest rates? Once the election was over, it took a measured but biting comment from Max Moore-Wilton, a former head of the Prime Minister's Department and a Howard ally, to suggest that the latter was the case. 'Both sides of politics have been favouring to some extent an increase in middle-class welfare,' he said on the Nine Network's *Sunday* program on 9 October 2004.

Now some elements of the community believe that that's a retrograde step. I might even think that myself. But the Howard Government has expanded government benefits to very wide-ranging elements in the community, and I'm not altogether sure that that's been totally necessary, but it's part of the reality. It's an entitlement mentality. I think we will see in the future, with an ageing population, that that will be very costly to the economy and there will probably be some winding back.

No doubt the Government that will have to remove the taxpayer props for the prosperous will be blaming the Howard years for the black hole in the budget. But the truth is that middle-class welfare is usually the last to go when the axe of fiscal responsibility is wielded. One of the little understood features of the tax system is that more than one in three households ends up paying no tax once their family payments and tax breaks are counted. The proportion of voters in this pampered position has not shifted in Howard's time. It was 38 per cent of all households at the end of Paul Keating's Labor government in 1996, when the budget was in deficit; it is 38 per cent 10 years later, when the budget is in surplus. One thing Howard's tax system *has not* done is encourage an increased rate of self-sufficiency in the electorate. What *has* altered is the mix of households in the tax-free club. There are fewer couples with dependent children—26 per cent, compared with 31 per cent under Keating. But Howard has more sole parents on the drip—91 per cent, versus 82 per cent.

* * *

The end of a soap opera episode is sometimes the best time to turn on the television, because it reminds the viewer they didn't really miss anything. For all the energy and political capital that Howard expended on matters tax, his tenth year, 2006, began as his first did: with business groups calling for tax reform. Chief among the demands are a reduction of the top personal rate of 47 cents in the dollar, to be paid for by the winding back of tax concessions.

Part of the pressure for a new round of tax reform is the operation of hindsight. The 2004 budget was the first pain-free document of the Howard era, when the 'quid' came without a 'pro quo'. What the Government did not know then was that it had an even fatter surplus to play with. It spent some of it at the election later that year. Then another $21.7 billion in personal tax cuts was announced in the 2005 budget. Like its immediate predecessor, this tax cut was delivered mainly to elite males via the back door, by fiddling with the thresholds for the 47 cent and 42 cent rates. But a tax rate was also reduced; 17 cents paid on lower incomes became 15 cents. It was only the second time in 10 years that the Government had cut a marginal tax rate.

But the clamour for tax reform had a less flattering undertone. It showed that Howard never did achieve the modern personal tax scales that he promised in return for the GST, which was the most significant achievement of his early years. When he unveiled his GST reform package in August 1998, Howard claimed that the income tax cuts would inoculate low- and middle-income earners from the evils of bracket creep. 'I am immensely proud of the fact that under this plan the top marginal rate paid by 81 per cent of Australian taxpayers will be 30 cents in the dollar or less,' he said at the 1998 launch.

> In other words, you can pass from $20,000 of annual income to $50,000 of annual income without going into a higher tax bracket. You can almost call it the 'bracket creep abolition provision' of the tax plan.

For Howard's formula to hold, no more than 19 per cent of taxpayers should have crossed over the $50,000 mark in the short term. But the promise was broken on the day the new tax system began: 1 July 2000. By 2002–03, the last year for which official data exists, 26.1 per cent of taxpayers were facing the top two rates. At that point, the budget cupboard was bare, because Howard had sacrificed the surplus to buy off the voting blocs that had been alienated by the implementation of the GST in 2000–01.

Estimates prepared for *The Australian* by the Melbourne Institute show that Howard will not have achieved his goal of 81 per cent of taxpayers on 30 cents or less until 1 July 2006, six years late, when the last round of the 2005 budget tax cuts is paid. Moving from the 30 cent to the 42 cent and 47 cent thresholds is only one part of the bracket creep equation. The other, which Howard also urged voters to test him on, was the total tax paid by a worker on average earnings.

'The average tax rate—the amount of income tax that people pay as a percentage of their income—has also been increasing for middle-income earners during the past 40 years,' the tax package said by way of explaining what was wrong with the old tax system. Guess what? The new tax system reduced the real tax burden on average earners just once, in 2000–01, after which it began rising again. It will return to 23.4 per cent in 2007, which is where it was at the 1998 election, unless another tax cut is announced beforehand.

In a perfect world, a government should return bracket creep to where it came from, so that no voter is worse off. But Howard, like

Keating before him, had no interest in indexing the tax scales for inflation. He preferred to pick the winners himself.

This is where the detail of Howard's tax record may bamboozle his supporters. About 4 million lower- and middle-income earners happen to have gone backwards in real terms under the new tax system, despite three rounds of tax cuts in between—in 2003, 2004 and 2005. Because they are childless, they have not been able to make up the difference with family payments. Their loss may seem trivial—a mere $2 a week for those earning between $23,000 and $59,000 a year. But this gold-coin donation adds up to more than $2.5 billion over the past six years, and it has been redistributed into some unexpected pockets.

Part of the tax redistribution has been in favour of working mothers, which fits with the pattern of the 2004 budget. About 1.3 million part-time earners on between $15,000 and $22,000 a year boast a real tax cut of about $1 a week after inflation, before family payments are added to the picture.

The shock is that the biggest winners are at the top of the income ladder. About 1.3 million upper-middle and high-income earners are much better off in real terms. Their gains are instructive and belie Howard's reputation as the battler's friend. A top earner on $125,000 a year will be paying $3991 (or almost $77 a week) less in personal tax from 1 July 2006 than they would have if the personal tax scales had been adjusted to remove inflation since 2000.

It begs the question: why the clamour to lower the 47 cent rate, when only 3 per cent of taxpayers will be facing it and when higher earners are already better off after inflation? For the tax reform cheer squad, it is all about efficiency.

Howard's tax system operates on a twin delusion that the very rich face the top rate—they do not—and that ordinary workers do not have the smarts to play the avoidance game—they do. The nation's wealthiest people are not the same group as the nation's highest income earners and they pay less tax because there are enough shelters in the system for them to hide their money. The taxpayers on the top band are not, generally speaking, that much different from the wage slaves further down the income ladder, according to the Melbourne Institute's survey, 'Household, Income and Labour Dynamics in Australia'. The main source of cash is their wage; and they do not have substantially greater levels of private assets than the battlers. They are affluent, sure, but not the super-rich that the tax system assumes them to be.

The super-rich are another group altogether, with enough wealth to reduce their tax bill to the levels of the battlers. This is one angle of the dilemma. The other is the very strong smell that tax avoidance has become a mainstream hobby. The deductions that lower-income wage slaves are claiming, from cars to negatively geared property, are growing at double the rate of the income they declare to the Australian Taxation Office. Wages and salaries happen to be the slowest revenue stream of all under the Howard Government. Over the seven years between 1995–96 and 2002–03, they have risen, in dollar terms, by just 39.1 per cent. Blame the disappearing bloke.

The number of male taxpayers has flat-lined over the period, increasing by just 0.9 per cent in seven years. This is simply not believable. It is a clue that the cash economy is alive and well, despite the GST. By contrast, the ranks of female taxpayers have expanded by 9.1 per cent over the same period.

To track where the revenue has gone, follow the loopholes. Capital gains used to be taxed at a person's top marginal tax rate minus inflation. In September 1999, Howard reduced by half the amount of capital gains that were subject to the tax. In a nutshell, someone who faced a marginal tax rate of 47 cents on their wages could choose to take their income as a capital gain—say, through shares—and pay a tax rate of 24.5 cents in the dollar. Not surprisingly, the amount of capital gains being declared has boomed by almost five times the growth in wages and salaries under the Coalition—190.8 per cent compared with 39.1 per cent, with most of the action coming since 1999. Dividends have been almost three times stronger, at 104.5 per cent.

The capital gains tax concession was sold as a pro-investment measure, to help Australian business compete for funds in the tech age. What it became, instead, was the trigger for an investment boom in property. In the final year of the old rules, 1999–2000, the tax office was $698 million in the black in its dealings with property investors, because rental income exceeded interest and other deductions. Each year of the new capital gains tax regime has reversed the flow, with deductions swamping incomes. At first it was a trickle—property investors declared a loss of $696 million in 2000–01 and $622 million the following year. Then it exploded into a flood: $1.2 billion in 2002–03, and $2.6 billion in 2003–04. Either Australians are the dumbest property investors in the world, or they think the tax system will pick up the tab for their mortgages.

Now look at the other deductions people claim. Work-related car expenses are running twice as fast as wages and salaries—88 per cent versus 39.1 per cent. Greed alone is not driving the trend because gifts and donations are also up 77.9 per cent. It is all perfectly legal, and it is the means by which wage and salary earners, the well-paid and the battlers, have been helping themselves to the tax cuts that Howard, for whatever reason, did not give them directly.

To paraphrase the 1960s folk rock group The Byrds, the motto for Howard's tax system is 'churn, churn, churn'. It is a world away from his GST mantra in 1998 for a 'broader tax base and lower tax rates'. The problem is that once people get on the tax drip, they can never be satisfied. The calls for tax reform now, as the economy enters its sixteenth year of uninterrupted growth, are the sound of both frustration and avarice. It is the demand for more reform, but also more cash. The electorate demands a tax cut from the Government. The Government delivers, but receives no credit because the electorate is already anticipating the next tax cut.

'The tax politics of prosperity have been interesting,' Howard said in an interview for this chapter. 'The revenues have come in stronger on just about every occasion over the last five years that we had predicted. That's difficult, but I'd rather it that way than the other way around. It's a credit to the Treasury Department for having conservative revenue estimates.'[1]

One of Howard's formative political memories was his first budget as Treasurer in Malcolm Fraser's government in 1978. It fell to Howard to announce the cancellation of the 'fistful of dollars' tax cuts that Fraser had promised in the 1977 election campaign. 'Terrible that 1978 budget, shocking, because the 1977 tax cuts were clearly too optimistic. I'm never going to get into that situation. That was awful.'[2]

Yet for all the money that has been pouring into federal coffers in recent years, the Government has not been able to guarantee that there will be no losers after allowing for the effects of inflation. There are three strikes against the tax system. First, the proportion of sole parents who pay no tax has risen from 82 per cent to 91 per cent because many cannot afford to take a job. Any private income they do earn sees between 60 cents and 80 cents in the dollar confiscated in taxes and reduced family payments. Second, the four million singles and childless couples in the middle, who have gone backwards because of inflation, are being tempted to rort because they see people below them not working and people above them getting the lion's share of the tax cuts and tax breaks. Third, the nation's wealthiest people are paying only 25 per cent of their income in tax, which is similar to the rate they helped themselves to a decade earlier.

In the end, Howard has played the politics of tax reform better than the policy. The GST was not popular when he presented it to voters in 1998. Labor won the two-party-preferred vote 51 per cent to 49 per cent, but the Coalition held on to its most marginal seats, which spared Howard the indignity of being a one-term prime minister. He had said before the 1996 election that a GST or anything resembling it would 'never ever' be Coalition policy again. He meant it at the time, but his first term in office lacked policy definition. Business said he was a do-nothing leader. The GST became Howard's way of answering that criticism. But the job of selling and implementing reform of the indirect tax system gobbled up four years of public debate. Half of Howard's first term, from May 1997 to August 1998, was spent building the case for a GST. Almost all of the second term, until August 2001, was needed to get it through the Senate, albeit in a compromised form, without food in the tax base, and to ensure that every last lobby group had its gripes attended to. The experience seemed to return Howard to his former cautious self. The third term contained no big-ticket reform to speak of, only bribes.

When the Senate fell into his lap unexpectedly at the 2004 election, Howard took the opportunity to revive his reform brand with a revolution in industrial relations, a welfare crackdown on single parents and disability pensioners to lure both back to work, and legislation to sell the rest of Telstra. But there was no temptation to revisit the GST. Food would stay out of the tax base, and the automatic indexation of petrol excise, which was abolished in February 2001 at the height of the community revolt against the GST, will not be restored. But personal tax reform is on the agenda, he says.

'The personal tax thing clearly didn't end with the GST, for the most obvious of reasons. Until we got control of the Senate [on 1 July 2005], the idea of doing anything expansive in the middle and upper brackets was not on our agenda, because we never had any hope of getting it through the Senate. That was the political reality of it.'

The final judgment of Howard's tax record will have to wait until the 2006 budget, when many of his supporters will be hoping the Government makes up for lost time.

9

UNFINISHED BUSINESS

Brad Norington

JOHN Howard is often branded an ideologue, a label he disputes. But there is no better example of his dogged commitment to a political philosophy than his passion for reform of Australia's industrial relations system.

As he approached his tenth year as Prime Minister, Howard's opportunity to implement far-reaching changes to laws governing the nation's workplaces arrived. The surprise bonus in winning the October 2004 election—control of the Senate—meant he could pass all his legislative agenda on industrial relations without Labor and the minor parties obstructing his government. Finally he could realise his goals of weakening trade union power and creating a modern workplace based on market conditions.

In December 2005 Howard pushed his historic 'Work Choices' legislation through parliament, brushing aside calls from trade unions and the Labor Party to moderate his plans on the grounds that they represented a threat to living standards.[1]

Howard argued the opposite. For him, workplace reform was essential to guaranteeing the nation's future prosperity by putting the economy on a more competitive footing internationally. Higher productivity and employment would yield higher wages. Howard promoted a workplace culture based on individual initiative and entrepreneurship. He wanted to shift responsibility back to individual workplaces to sort out their own arrangements without interfering 'third parties'.

Howard rarely indulges in grand rhetorical flourishes or the 'big picture' sentiments of his predecessor Paul Keating. He captured the significance of the moment, though, as he revealed to parliament a detailed outline of his government's proposed workplace changes in May 2005. 'This package embodies one of the great pieces of unfinished business in the structural transformation of the Australian economy,' he declared.[2] In a personal interview for this chapter,[3] Howard said 'unfinished business' referred to his frustration at failing to implement, in 1996, his first batch of IR changes in their entirety. He rated his industrial relations changes as more important than the other big-ticket domestic items of his prime ministership: the GST, gun control and the sale of Telstra. There is, however, a much deeper level at which Howard's achievement represents unfinished business. It is best understood by appreciating that Work Choices is the fulfilment of a 20-year quest to revolutionise the Australian workplace. As commentator Gerard Henderson told Paul Kelly for his book *The End of Certainty*, Howard was 'very much traumatised' by the early 1980s recession when he was Treasurer in the Fraser Government.[4] He was determined to make amends, believing the answer lay in a total overhaul of the IR system.

The other key to Howard's motivation is his little-explored psyche. Much of the inspiration for Howard's laws can be traced to his personal background. His philosophy brims with values ingrained from his youth in the 1950s—the Protestant work ethic, individualism, free markets and entrepreneurial opportunity, with emphasis on small business. His parents were also 'very anti-Labor'.[5]

Howard's father, Lyall, a World War I veteran, was a tradesman laid off from his job at the CSR factory in Sydney during the Great Depression. Lyall took a risk, buying a petrol station with his father at Dulwich Hill in Sydney's inner west. Howard accepts that his focus on industrial relations was linked to his upbringing as the son of a small-business operator.

> I didn't grow up in a home where unions were, sort of, routinely denigrated. I mean, they didn't entertain the idea that unions are bad, but they didn't talk about unions.
>
> The whole idea of doing something with your life was about personal achievement, and starting a business. That has

influenced my attitude, because my father had a garage open. I remember as a child, the first unpaid job I had was serving petrol on Saturday and Sunday mornings. So this idea that life is not quite a five-days-a-week existence was with me at a very early stage. I guess working for yourself, working for private enterprise, and not working for the government, was something I was brought up to believe in.[6]

Howard was just 16 when his father died and his deeply conservative mother, Mona, became the dominating influence in his life. He later admitted to having inherited her values based on the Protestant work ethic.[7]

The Howard family home in Earlwood was comfortable but clearly modest. One of Howard's three older brothers, Bob, recalled how Mona talked about buying a new lounge suite and new carpet. She never got around to it because 'she had no great ambition to create an atmosphere of luxury'.[8] A dislike for pretension and overt displays of wealth stayed with Howard. It helps explain why he has never been completely at ease mingling with the big end of town. At the same time—and also like his mother, according to journalist Milton Cockburn—the young Howard appeared 'never to have questioned why social divisions exist and why some people in an affluent society are forced to scrounge for a living'.[9]

By studying straight law and no outside subjects at university, Howard was not exposed to political theory.[10] On one level, it meant he lacked an early structured intellectual framework for his political leaning (he had joined the Liberal Party at 15). It also meant he did not deviate from the conservative mould, unlike his brother Bob, an academic who walked away from the Liberals over the Vietnam War and became an active member of Labor's left wing.

Howard's growing distaste for unions reflected his loyalty to the Liberal Party and abhorrence of socialism. His hero was Bob Menzies and he was keenly aware of union links to the ALP and the Communist Party. His antipathy grew in an era of frequent strikes.

Howard lived with his mother until he married in 1971, aged 32. He entered federal parliament in 1974 after stints as a city solicitor and NSW Liberal machine man. His career advancement was rapid, thanks to Malcolm Fraser promoting him to treasurer in just three years. Howard agrees that industrial relations were not on his mind during this period, apart from introducing 'secondary boycott' provisions 45D and E of the Trade Practices Act.

'It is fair to say that I began to develop a big interest in this issue after I went into Opposition,' he recalls. 'It was a very difficult time for the Liberal Party, but it was productive in one sense—that we actually had some significant internal debates about issues and directions. Industrial relations was one, and I got very interested in the issue then.'[11]

Howard was very critical of Fraser after the Coalition's 1983 election defeat, which ushered in 13 years of Labor rule under Bob Hawke and Keating. For all Fraser's tough talk about taking on the unions, it was not matched by action. Howard concluded that the way unions operated, on the basis of 'comparative wage justice', was fundamentally flawed and needed overhauling.[12]

Australia had a unique system of industrial relations before John Howard turned it upside down. Under the Constitution's original provisions, the settlement of industrial disputes was hived off to a separate court—later known as the Australian Industrial Relations Commission. The system evolved from the famous 1907 Harvester decision in which judge Henry Bournes Higgins ruled that the free market should bow to a system of 'fair and reasonable' wages determined by compulsory arbitration.

Over time, to regulate working conditions, the Australian Industrial Relations Commission (AIRC) developed highly prescriptive documents called awards. These became the ideal vehicle for unions to amass better pay and conditions. Using collective bargaining, they would increase pay rates across whole industries where they had muscle and then resort to centralised arbitration, getting the AIRC to pass on negotiated rates as an award standard without regard to higher productivity.

The union-backed wages explosion of 1981 triggered a recession, throwing many thousands out of work. Howard believed the ravages of the recession could have been avoided if businesses had been able to set their own pay rates based on market conditions. And so he became the champion of the individual enterprise. He drew his earliest support from small business leaders while employer groups representing large firms played safe by seeking the protection of wage restraint under the Hawke Government's accord with the unions in which the AIRC had a special place.

Howard made plain his intentions as early as August 1983, six months after the Fraser Government was tossed out of office, when he declared in an address to the National Press Club: 'The time has come when we have to turn Mr Justice Higgins on his head.'[13]

The epiphany for Howard came undoubtedly with the publication of an article, 'The Industrial Relations Club', by former bureaucrat Gerard Henderson. Henderson wrote about rituals of a self-serving IR club involving government, unions, employers, academics and compliant journalists. The club, he said, exuded an ethos of complacency and self-congratulation as 'they alone understand industrial realities; know how the system works. And it is they who can do deals and fix agreements'. So successful was the club, wrote Henderson, that its members controlled a key sector of the Australian economy. After almost 80 years, the club used its longevity as a rationalisation for its continued existence.[14]

Howard was inspired after reading a piece by columnist Des Keegan in *The Australian* that praised Henderson. So much so that he added the inflammatory line about Higgins that very day to his Press Club speech.[15] He also employed Henderson as his senior adviser.

The Liberal Party's dries and wets quickly polarised over IR. Howard, then deputy leader and Opposition treasurer, was on the side of the free market lobby seeking to dismantle the arbitration model. Ian Macphee, industrial relations spokesman, wanted to retain the centralised system. The seeds of Howard's modern-day system are to be found in a compromise he forced on Macphee during the drafting of the Coalition's 1984 industrial relations policy. While Macphee reinforced the power of the commission to make and enforce awards, Howard scored an 'opt out' clause for employers that allowed 'voluntary agreements'. The groundwork was laid for a system based on enterprise bargaining that would eventually bypass the AIRC.

The National Farmers Federation was already pushing hard for reform, along with the New Right and its labour market reform lobby, the HR Nicholls Society. Eventually the Business Council of Australia, representing the nation's 80 top companies, jumped on board. Howard's cause was helped further in the mid-1980s by a series of emblematic industrial disputes involving unions that made serious misjudgments in breaking away from the ACTU's solidaristic wages policy under leaders Bill Kelty and Simon Crean.[16] These disputes proved that employers could step outside the Higgins arbitration model and use legal remedies to tame unions.[17]

By mid-1986, Howard as Opposition leader won his fight with Macphee. He was now upfront about creating a system of 'voluntary contracts' for businesses with fewer than 50 employees. The relevant award would be the minimum hourly pay rate and the commission would have no involvement. 'We really nailed our colours to the mast,' Howard recalled of the policy, 'because the whole culture and attitude [were] so different.'[18]

Hawke's corporatist style, in which the ACTU and some on-side employers were included in decision-making to the exclusion of others, was especially galling for Howard. It made him more fiercely determined to impose an alternative system if and when the Coalition won office.

Though he makes light of it now, there is a sense of lingering resentment as Howard recalls how the union leadership treated him— the alternative prime minister—with short-sighted disdain.

> I remember having a meeting with Simon Crean. He was then president of the ACTU, and he rather reluctantly, I think, agreed to see me. I was Opposition leader and he didn't want to come to my office. He wanted to meet me in a coffee lounge, or something or other. Maybe I didn't want to go to his office. Anyway, there was no … he spoke as a person who was riding high (laughs) but it was sort of, 'well, what's this?' Every time you'd make a suggestion, 'Why would you want to change that? Why don't you leave this to the commission, the unions and the employers?' Tripartite was king in the 1980s.

'You mean corporatism,' I said. 'It was,' he replied. 'It was very powerful, as powerful as some of the large companies and business organisations.'[19]

By 1990 Howard was no longer leader and the Coalition was still languishing in Opposition. But he returned to his industrial relations portfolio and lost none of his drive. Interviewed by Henderson shortly before being deposed by Andrew Peacock, Howard made a rare boast. 'The debate now is not as hard because, in a sense, I've won,' he said of his contribution to IR and privatisation.

'One of the frustrations for me in having led the debate in these areas is that I find I've won but we're still in Opposition'. Howard was blunt about how he would alter the law to put unions on a 'level playing field' with everyone else. 'Implement our policy root and branch,' he said. 'If we do that we'll effect a revolution.'[20]

Howard insists that his 2005 reforms are not radical. They are, he agrees, significant and underpin a historic change in the industrial relations culture. Yet without the changes that occurred in the interim, his 'revolution' *would* have appeared radical. What made the difference was a decision by Hawke and Keating in league with ACTU secretary Kelty to embrace a limited form of decentralised enterprise bargaining in the early 1990s. Their objective was to appease union frustration with wage restraint after years of the accord. It was also a way to answer criticism that Labor was not tackling labour market reform. Howard's response—this time as industrial relations spokesman under Opposition leader John Hewson—was to draft an even tougher reformist industrial relations manifesto called Jobsback in 1992.[21]

Billed as the economics policy centrepiece of Hewson's Fightback! blueprint released the year before, Howard proposed that all awards be terminated from a certain date and that companies could stay with the award system only if they opted back in. Compulsory arbitration would end. Workers would be encouraged to sign individual contracts. The adult minimum wage would be linked to award rates but the youth wage would be cut to between $3 and $3.50 an hour. There would be five minimum conditions under a new statutory safety net. A new authority, the Office of Employment Advocate, would hear worker grievances. Compulsory union membership would be banned and unions would be required to hold secret ballots before all strikes. Howard's Jobsback policy is remarkably similar to the legislative package eventually passed in 2005. All the central elements of WorkChoices were there, although Howard later dropped the mandatory cut-off date for awards.

Keating tried to regain control of the agenda after his surprise 1993 election victory by legislating his own form of enterprise bargaining. He shocked unions by suggesting that enterprise bargains should be not mere add-ons to awards but 'full substitutes'.[22] Keating's legislation, however, reflected more modest goals. While the powers of the AIRC were reduced and enterprise bargains became the preferred form of employment agreement, awards remained the benchmark. The only real irritation for unions was allowing registered collective agreements in the (majority) non-union sector.

A significant task with Howard back as Opposition leader for the 1996 election campaign was to ward off Labor–union scaremongering about the impact of his industrial relations policy.[23] Hence Howard's guarantee, when announcing the policy in January that year, that no worker would be worse off. 'Under a Howard government you cannot be worse off, but you can be better off,' he said. 'I give you this rock-solid guarantee. Our policy will not cut your take-home pay.'[24]

After every election since the 1996 victory that heralded the Howard decade, the man who has made it his mission to transform

Australia's labour-market regulation has nominated yet more industrial relations reform as his priority. The Workplace Relations Act that he introduced in his first year as Prime Minister was significant in establishing the alternative agreement system he wanted and in further weakening the arbitral powers of the AIRC. In Peter Reith, Howard had the ideal minister to implement the agenda because of his command of the portfolio and relentless approach. However, Howard and Reith were limited in what they could achieve because of the brake applied by the Senate.

The compromise deal negotiated with then Democrats leader Cheryl Kernot in late 1996 introduced Australian Workplace Agreements (AWAs) as a legislated form of non-union individual employment contract overseen by the Employment Advocate. These contracts were an important cultural break with the past, as Howard wanted, because they denied collective bargaining and were outside the AIRC's union-friendly reach.

But the AWA take-up rate was slow among employers, apart from some key sectors such as mining. Before the 2005 election only 2.5 per cent of the workforce had signed up, hardly a ringing endorsement.

Howard achieved a partial breakthrough on hundreds of highly prescriptive awards accumulated over 80 years by compelling the AIRC—with Democrats support—to cull them to a universal list of just 20 conditions. Awards, though, remained pivotal to the system because all agreements, collective or individual, had to be compared with them under a new 'no disadvantage test'. Workers could not be worse off than under the award 'in overall terms'.

One big win for Howard was banning compulsory unionism, thus officially ending the old 'closed shop'. But the Democrats rejected his plans for secret ballots and other measures to clamp down on union activity. Howard, again via Reith, made one further attempt to push his full agenda through the Senate with his ambitious Workplace Relations Amendment (More Jobs, Higher Pay) Bill in 1999. But it was a futile exercise. The legislation was ultimately withdrawn when the Democrats made it plain they would reject it.

The only course for Howard to further change the industrial landscape was to press for reform from within. That meant encouraging, even cajoling, business into using the law to the fullest extent and selling the case for more reform to the public. Australia's waterfront was an obvious target. It was a perfect example of an industry that continued to ignore the realities of global competition. Reith spread the public message about rorts and thieving on the docks, making wharfies a soft target. Backed by government money for redundancy payouts, Howard and Reith found in Chris Corrigan, head of Patrick, one of the nation's two big stevedoring companies, an entrepreneur willing to risk entrenched warfare with the Maritime Union of Australia. While Howard failed to bust the MUA in the 1998 waterfront dispute, settlement of the dispute did force labour flexibility and higher productivity on the docks that put Australia on par with world's best practice. Ever since, Howard has tried, through Reith and his ministerial successors Tony Abbott and Kevin Andrews, to spread his reformist zeal. In almost all cases he failed because of reluctance among employers to co-operate.

Howard's tactic for his next big target, the union-dominated big city construction industry, was a royal commission to investigate the extent of industrial lawlessness and thuggery on building sites. He hoped its predictable findings would morally browbeat the Senate into passing legislation to crack down on the militant Construction Forestry Mining and Energy Union. The Democrats refused. So again Howard was forced to wait until laws passed with the Coalition's Senate majority.

When Howard outlined the detail of his workplace changes to parliament in May 2005, he said the Government trusted employers and employees to make the right decisions in the workplace. 'The era of the select few making decisions for the many in Australian industrial relations is over,' he said.[25]

Howard's new order, grand in its scale, went far beyond his election policy. For the first time Australia would get a national industrial relations system, covering up to 85 per cent of the workforce, using the corporations power of the Constitution in a forced takeover of remaining regimes in Labor states.

Howard's chief method of achieving workplace flexibility was a much-reduced set of five legislated minimum working conditions for people on enterprise agreements—a minimum wage, four weeks' annual leave, 10 days' sick leave, 12 months' unpaid parental leave and a flexible 38-hour week.

The standard for agreements applying to the majority of the workforce became much simpler. Previously, award conditions—including overtime, penalty rates, shift penalties, public holidays, allowances and annual leave loadings—had to be taken into account in enterprise negotiations under the 'no disadvantage test'. Howard's abolition of this test meant that everything except for the five conditions was up for negotiation and could be traded away—with or without financial compensation. Awards continued with a larger set of 16 minimum conditions for about a fifth of the workforce still employed on them. But once people switched to an employment agreement, they could not return to the award. Howard also made the agreement-making process much simpler. All agreements came into force at the time of lodgement with the employment advocate. There was no requirement to check that minimum conditions were met. It is obvious that Howard's eventual goal was to make awards obsolete as all workers gradually shifted to agreements, and to make the AIRC so irrelevant that it might as well be abolished, although he would not admit to it.

The powers of the AIRC were significantly reduced. Its job of setting minimum wages was handed to a new five-person tribunal called the Fair Pay Commission, with a special brief to put the interests of the unemployed and the economy first. The AIRC also lost the right to alter awards or approve collective agreements, which had so infused it with union culture. That left a weak tribunal with the role of helping to settle disputes (but with no ability to arbitrate). It also handled unfair dismissal claims in big firms. Howard's downgrading of unions was obvious too. While still entitled to represent workers, their access to worksites and right to strike were severely restricted. Unionists faced heavy penalties for legal breaches, including fines and deregistration.

Preference under Howard's system was given to AWAs. Unlike in the US or Britain, unions had no collective bargaining rights. An employer could refuse to negotiate a collective agreement even if all employees wanted one. An employer could legally persuade workers at any time to opt out of a collective agreement and sign an AWA. And as before, signing an AWA could be a condition of employment for new staff.

Howard's new order was buttressed by his overhaul of unfair dismissal laws, which were introduced by the Keating Government in 1993. It had been Howard's policy until the 2004 election to abolish unfair dismissal claims for employers with fewer than 20 staff, following protests from small business that these laws were a disincentive to hire people if they could not be sacked. After the election—with his Senate majority in hand—Howard decided on a much more ambitious exemption threshold of 100. This was a politically deft move that gave the whipping hand to employers. It meant that not only small businesses but medium to large firms were much freer to hire and fire. Most workers were theoretically on notice all the time. As well, employers could dismiss workers at any time for broadly defined 'operational reasons'.[26]

In framing his 2005 reforms, Howard dispensed with his old guarantee that no worker would be worse off. It was not a pledge he could realistically sustain because removing the award 'no disadvantage test' and replacing it with five minimum conditions meant that some, perhaps many, workers who lacked muscle might forfeit income as they lost penalty rates or were bargained down on pay. Those reliant on minimum pay rates could also expect a fall in real wages because of smaller increases granted by the Fair Pay Commission.[27]

Howard's revised pledge was a more general one—that his guarantee is his record after average wage increases of 14 per cent over his term in office. He also identified what he called a new breed of 'enterprise worker'—people whose 'attitude of mind' accepted that their future was tied to the performance of their business and the economy generally.[28]

Despite promises to the contrary, nothing in WorkChoices was geared to help employees 'better balance work and family responsibilities'. The flexibility of Howard's changes all ran in the employer's favour at a time when Australians were working longer, not shorter, hours. Essentially, Howard placed faith in the benevolence of employers.

Conservative economist Mark Wooden, from the Melbourne Institute of Applied Economic and Social Research, is among those who regard the changes as one-sided. He also questions why Howard has gone to so much trouble in giving preference to individual employment contracts when there is no evidence they are more advantageous than collective agreements.[29]

One of the significant criticisms of Howard from other supporters of reform is that he has not gone far enough. Unlike New Zealand, where the award system was junked in favour of individual contracts in 1991, Howard's laws do not so much deregulate the Australian labour market as dismantle some of its machinery and add a complex new layer on top.[30]

Howard disagrees. He argues that the system is much simpler because agreements are much easier. Most of the new regulations, he says, are transitional arrangements made necessary because the states refused a voluntarily handover. Howard also rejects that he should have abolished awards and the AIRC and set a single minimum wage, as the United States did.

How low is the [minimum wage] in America? I mean, I have never supported their approach to welfare or IR. In fact, I have regularly said that the Americans' approach to these things is too harsh. I think you can have an enterprise culture, an entrepreneurial approach without the harshness of the American system.[31]

Much public debate about the workplace changes has focused on issues such as pay rates, working hours and the future of public holidays. But much of the law is devoted to restricting union activity, perhaps odd considering that union membership has slumped to 17 per cent in the private sector where most people work and that strikes are at a record low. Howard's concept of the future of work is based on the independent individual with little role for unions. 'I regard them, the culture of unionism, as being something that is increasingly out of touch, out of date,' he said. Collectivism? 'Yes, of course, of course, it's part of my own belief system.'[32]

One obvious effect of further weakening unions is that it will also hurt the organisational base of Howard's political enemy, the Labor Party. Howard is emphatic.

Look, it could have that effect, although one of the problems the Labor Party has had in recent years is that it has been dominated by the inner-metropolitan elites and they are not necessarily the same as the blue-collar trade unionists. In fact, I think we probably have got a fair share of trade union votes at the last election. That's not the goal. If it has that effect, well, so be it, but that's not the goal.[33]

John Howard's industrial relations reforms are a personal triumph, given his quest to overthrow the orthodoxy. Their impact, however, will not be known for some years. Much depends on the willingness of employers to use the laws. Those with skills in high-demand occupations will continue to do well, but unskilled workers at the bottom who are easily replaced could find life harder. Smaller wage rises for the low paid are likely to mean some boost in employment. The effect on productivity remains unclear. Howard believes that less union interference and greater flexibility derived from shedding restrictive work practices will deliver lasting economic benefits.

IV

THE HOME FRONT

10

PLEASE EXPLAIN

Nicolas Rothwell

OFTEN, the pattern of a political era becomes plain only in time's unfolding perspective; often a leader's character emerges only once his moments of greatest ordeal and struggle have come and gone—and so it is with today's Prime Minister, a decade into his reign at the nation's helm. Australians from all walks of life are waking to the astonishing fact that John Howard—who seemed, on his rise to power in March 1996, a stop-gap, intermediate figure—is still there, still reshaping and reinterpreting the nation to itself, still forging and strengthening his intimate tie with the electorate. Only now, in the concluding phase of Howard's ascendancy, with Australian troops deployed in Iraq and the 'war on terror' casting its shadow across the world, has the Prime Minister's brand of conviction politics flowered. It is a patriotic populism, it marks a drastic break from the prime ministerial styles of the past generation, and it has a startling point of origin. For John Howard's brilliant latter-day career and persuasive approach to national leadership owes a great deal to the cardinal challenge of his first term—the rise of Pauline Hanson and One Nation—to Howard's response to that challenge and his decision to forge his own compact with the disaffected voters of middle Australia.

How easily we rewrite the record of the recent past! Who now remembers the uncertain tone of Howard's early months, the missteps and policy fumbles, the low-level ministerial scandals, the long quest for core themes and a personal style?

Even though Howard had swept to power with a vast swing and a 44-seat majority, that win was widely seen as a vote against Paul Keating, the man who seemed still to overshadow Australian politics. Howard had been chosen by his party as the ultimate safe pair of hands. His persona was still that of an establishment politician, a Sydney solicitor, a conventional liberal, if one with a nostalgic sympathy for the ways of the old Australia.

In the same election, in the once-safe Labor seat of Oxley, an obscure, disendorsed Liberal candidate secured a striking victory. But Pauline Hanson, a former fish-and-chip shop proprietor from Ipswich, only came to national prominence with her maiden speech in federal parliament that September. This was the vehicle she used to set out her policy preferences and prejudices; this was the device that pulverised the codes of political correctness governing discussion of race and multiculturalism in 1990s Australia. Howard's response is well known, and was fiercely condemned at the time: he did next to nothing, allowed Hansonism a degree of oxygen, and opted to let the phenomenon run its course.

Like all crazes and cults, Pauline Hanson's One Nation Party surfed the rise and fall of potent waves, with Hanson herself doubling as heroine to the masses and laughing-stock of the intelligentsia, fanned to prominence in both roles by obsessive media coverage. During much of Howard's first term as Prime Minister, Hanson was the most famous—in the sense of most recognisable—individual in Australian public life: a permanent walking scandal, flame-haired, bold, outspoken, always on the verge of controversy, temper or tears. For a leader such as Howard in those days, a leader lacking in immediate lustre, she was a fascinating phenomenon. She had a public: that disaffected body of working-class and lower middle-class conservative voters who then constituted the swinging heart of the political map. These were men and women who thrilled to Hanson's symbol-laden message: who wanted to be told that mainstream Australia counted, that the core of the nation had value, that the elites were not the only virtuous class. Howard's strategists had already identified these voters: they were already becoming known as 'Howard's battlers'—natural Labor supporters who had been alienated by the drastic cultural shifts of the Keating years. But Hanson brought them into focus as a distinct group, and threatened to steal them away from their fragile new allegiance to the Coalition parties. They were men and women who lived in the fringing suburbs, edge cities and rural towns; they were people who felt betrayed by the political class. Howard, as he heard the distant clamour of their grievances, could feel the rules of Australian politics cracking apart. In July 1997, midway through his first term in office, during the period when these trends were becoming prominent, he spent a week in hospital for pneumonia … and went through something of a dark night of the soul.

In that period of reassessment, Howard seems to have reached certain sharp conclusions after deep thought. He emerged from this time of ill-health with fresh resolve and an interlocking set of priorities. First, he had decided to fight the next election on a high-stakes gamble. He would push through reform of the tax system and bring in the GST—a move that swiftly revolutionised public finances and made possible the vast pork-barrelling populism of his later years. Second, he would fight the 'culture wars' with new strength and position himself as an unapologetic national enthusiast; and, last, he would learn from Hanson's style of intimate appeal and deepen his direct relationship with the electorate. Already known for his willingness to appear on talk-back radio, Howard now became an almost constant presence on the airwaves: avuncular, available, a man of the people.

Set this against the Hanson saga, and the interplay of influences becomes clear. It is not that Howard hit the same accents as Hanson, but he was certainly pitching for her public. It is not that Howard wanted a Hansonite Australia, but he realised his preferred future might be built with the backing of her supporters. It dawned on the Prime Minister that One Nation's voters, who felt excluded and abandoned, could themselves form the basis for a new, expanded conservative majority—and he spent much of the following decade, unnoticed, recasting the levers of economic and social policy to ensure their support.

Hanson's political romance reached its soap-opera climax within a couple of years. Even as the strains within her party were becoming apparent, One Nation attracted 22 per cent of the vote in the June 1998 Queensland state election, and its candidates won 11 seats in parliament. At a stroke, the political space for conservative nationalism had been dramatically widened. Howard staged his first bid for re-election later that year, taking care to place One Nation last on Coalition ballots. Hanson's party was still able to win almost one million votes across the country, securing 8.4 per cent of the primary vote, and 14 per cent in

Queensland. But, thanks in great part to the Coalition's decision not to give its preferences to One Nation, Hanson lost the contest for the newly redistributed seat of Blair.

Returned to power by the narrowest of margins, Howard was transformed by his second victory. Now he was a leader with his own mandate and with the financial resources to re-craft the relationship between government and the people; he was presiding over a protracted economic expansion; and he had found room to develop his political persona. Hanson's destruction, and Labor's leadership void, had left him the space to redefine the prime ministerial role in the age of the permanent news cycle.

His next term as Prime Minister was an intriguing transitional phase: Howard's popularity was still low but his character was gaining definition. Two events helped fix him in the minds of his public. In late 1999, when the referendum on an Australian republic was held, Howard played the most cunning of guiding hands. He was a supporter of the existing constitutional monarchy, so he ensured that the referendum would ask voters whether they favoured a specific model: the choice of a president elected by two-thirds of the federal parliament. But polls suggested that most Australians were in favour of direct popular election of their head of state. The republican model on offer went down to heavy defeat. It was Howard's definitive blow to the dreams of the 'new class' Australians. He had managed, in the space of a few months' manoeuvring, to kill off the first of the two great symbolic issues dear to this social group. The campaign for Aboriginal reconciliation would be dispatched soon afterwards, in May 2000, when the Council for Reconciliation's recommendations were rejected in a brisk government press release.

Howard had also handled with consummate skill the first high-level foreign policy challenge of his prime ministership—the East Timor emergency and Australia's successful peace-keeping intervention, which began in September 1999 and had the effect of raising in dramatic fashion the prestige of the armed forces. One could sense, as a result of these events, a new kind of self-image for the nation beginning to take form: one marked by a distinct sense of patriotic pride, a rejection of the 'elite' agenda for Australia, and a rather striking demotic tone. It was the kind of Australia where Hanson's voters felt gathered in and listened to, not scorned and rejected.

Howard's courtship of this constituency stemmed from an unusually clear-eyed analysis of Australian politics. His instincts had long told him that the old, class-based political brands attaching to the major parties were becoming obsolete. He believed he could create a new consensus, embracing both traditional liberals and the men and women who felt that Labor had left them behind. He also had a new generation to convince: these were the 'aspirationals', for whom frankly populist Howard policies such as the first-home owner grant and the baby bonus proved vital incentives. The Howard decade has been a time of startling increases in property values, rising wealth and rising employment levels: it has proved to be a good time for social engineering on a grand scale. Yet at the halfway point of this decade Howard, even as a successful Prime Minister, still lacked some crucial connection to 'his' voters. He was tolerated, rather than admired; seen as capable, rather than heroic. He had begun edging his way towards the recipe of a conservative populism but had not yet found a direct avenue of appeal.

This was no surprise. Populism, for all its heady immediacy, has been a road rarely travelled by modern Australian prime ministers. Gough Whitlam's message was crafted to a fresh generation of idealists. Malcolm Fraser's electoral successes rested upon a managerial reputation. Bob Hawke's overwhelming charm allowed him to pursue ambitious economic reforms, while Keating offered to his true believers a wild personal immediacy and to the nation at large a series of drastic cultural revisions. But the eager adoption of crowd-pleasing political initiatives has generally been avoided by Australian leaders, who have tended to focus their energies on the arduous tasks of nation-building.

This recipe was stale when Howard first became Prime Minister. There was a jaded feel to national politics, a disconnect between rulers and ruled. Hanson and One Nation exploited the gap. It is worth recalling just how persistent One Nation proved. Despite a fierce series of internal feuds, and its federal eclipse, the party was still able to perform well at the regional level and to function as a kind of conductor of discontent. In the West Australian state election of February 2001, the conservative parties lost power—One Nation secured almost 10 per cent of the vote. A week later, in the Queensland state election, One Nation candidates attracted 20 per cent support in the seats they contested. But the contours of Australian politics were on the verge of being redrawn, in the most rapid and unpredictable fashion.

Late in August 2001, the Norwegian vessel MV *Tampa* appeared, with its cargo of rescued asylum seekers, close to the territorial boundary of Australian waters. The Government set in motion its elaborate 'Pacific solution'. The following month, Howard was in Washington when the

9/11 attacks unfolded. That November, after a campaign dominated by these transformative events, Howard led the Coalition to a strong election victory. Pauline Hanson was heard to lament that the Prime Minister had stolen One Nation's policies. In fact, something much more significant had occurred. Howard had at last found the symbolic key to middle Australia's heart. His popularity, and that of his government, surged—for reasons that had more to do with emotion than policy. At the time of the *Tampa* crisis, there was a pervasive sense that the asylum seekers reaching Australia were acting 'unfairly', queue jumping, exploiting legal loopholes. A perception was spreading that Australia's identity stood on the verge of being swamped by an unchecked human flood. The sheer drama of the Prime Minister's decision to take a stand on the *Tampa* and to defy the vociferous protests of the intelligentsia—these were the things that resonated with much of the public. One Nation's vote migrated to the Coalition camp. A new tone shrouded national politics. Australian troops were sent to Afghanistan, and eventually to Iraq. The following year, the Bali bombings, which claimed 88 Australian lives, brought home the meaning of the 'war on terror'.

In all this, the *Tampa* moment was central, as both Howard haters and enthusiasts agree. It was the great lightning strike that redefined Howard's time as leader. What happened? In practical terms, Howard launched a draconian policy to defend territorial integrity, and crowned this stand with the sound bite that will define him in history: 'We will decide who comes to this country and the circumstances in which they come.' On the symbolic level, he had affirmed not just Australian sovereignty but Australian values of 'fairness' against an unruly, threatening outside world. But far more than this, he had found a way to reach out to the inchoate nationalist feelings lurking in a broad segment of the public. *Tampa* was the volcanic shaft that allowed Howard to stretch down into this emotional magma: it promptly flowed back up to him in responsive support.

Since then, the Prime Minister has converted himself into a kind of patriotic father figure, and barely placed a foot wrong on the critical issues of cultural symbolism. Grieving chief mourner at Bali, patron of the troops on their departures for Afghanistan and Iraq, chief celebrant at Gallipoli, Australian member of the international 'coalition of the willing', he has made the Australian flag his natural prop. Given this abrupt breakthrough to a successful populism, it was inevitable that the Labor Party would turn to a maverick 'man of the people' as the only feasible choice in its unsuccessful bid to stop Howard at the last federal election. There has also been a certain inevitability to Hanson's demise, even as the Prime Minister's star shines with ever greater strength: jailed briefly for financial irregularities but later cleared on appeal, the former One Nation leader is now engaged in a bizarre afterlife as a minor star in the galaxy of popular TV.

This leaves Howard standing unchallenged at the focal point of the national stage. It also raises questions about Australia's centre of gravity. Has the country, at the Prime Minister's promptings, shifted towards a more relaxed understanding of itself? Has it become, as Howard's critics contend, a darker, less tolerant kind of place? The Cronulla riot of December 2005 and the anguished reactions to this episode throw matters into distinct relief. The beachfront clash, with its overtones of tribal warfare, gang rivalry and racial confrontation, served as meat for some of Howard's most committed ideological opponents, who claim that his removal of the checks of political correctness has created an open season for voices of intolerance in Australia. The opposite point of view argues that the violence stemmed from the incapacity of today's social institutions, afflicted by the doctrines of multiculturalism, to gather in the different ethnic and religious identities of a polymorphous society and create something whole and new.

Howard's response was measured, slow and detailed, and laid out a middle ground between these extremes. It bears close examination—for the Prime Minister, although constantly condemned for speaking in code, tends to be exceptionally clear on his core beliefs about Australia. He waited a day before offering his commentary. When it came, it was a profession of the principles that have shaped his approach to matters of race, class and values, through the Hanson years and through the more recent passages of his time in office.

'I do not accept that there is underlying racism in this country,' he said when interviewed by the electronic media. 'I have always taken a more optimistic view about the character of the Australian people. This nation of ours has been able to absorb millions of people from different parts of the world and we have done so with remarkable success. I think it would be an enormous mistake if we began to wallow in generalised self-criticism, because the overwhelming majority of Australians have the proper instincts and decent attitudes and decent values.'

Howard was careful to affirm the non-discriminatory nature of Australia's immigration policy and to defend freedom of religion but he also called for a greater emphasis on 'integration' into the broader community. 'I don't think Australians want tribalism. They want us all to be Australians.'

Howard would have been able to lay out this credo at any time over the past 10 years—but he has felt free to speak out plain only in these days of his ascendancy. It is a credo that marks his deliberate pact with a softened, watered-down form of multiculturalism. It also marks the end destination of his populism. He has successfully redefined and defended Australian identity, recasting it around notions of fairness, equality and a patriotic heritage, with Anzac strong in the mix. This is far from being a closet form of Hansonism: there is no fearful exaltation of the old Australia at the expense of the new nation still being born. In truth, Howard is trying to shape a much more radical future. It is his ambitious, extraordinary hope that race will be drowned in national identity, that Australian values will completely trump ethnicity. The strange twist in this political journey remains, for only the outspoken, untutored political virago from Ipswich was able to clear the way for Howard to break the chains of conventional, class-based politics and build his paradise of mateship.

11

MIXED RACE, MIXED MESSAGES

George Megalogenis

AUSTRALIA changed colour and culture under John Howard, who reduced the European component of our total overseas-born ranks below 50 per cent for the first time in history. Part of this was the inevitability of demographics, as Europe dried up as a source for new Australians and as the men and women of the first post-war migration wave began to pass away. But part of it was a deliberate decision to restock the workforce with skilled immigrants from Asia, in particular China. Ironic, because Howard had made his name in the 1980s as a critic of Asian immigration.

Here is another statistic that may surprise. Our overseas-born crossed 24 per cent of the total population in 2004. The proportion had been higher in the past, but that was in the pre-Federation 1890s, when the intake was overwhelmingly white. Australia had never been more foreign, and never less white, and the prime minister who pulled off this switch was Howard.

When told of his record in an interview for this book, Howard beams like a child who had just topped his class. 'Really?' Then he adds: 'I think it demonstrates that we have run a truly non-discriminatory immigration policy.'

Three of the most divisive images of Howard's career involve the politics of race. In August 1988, he attacked Asian immigration and was punished for his misjudgment with the loss of the Liberal leadership to Andrew Peacock the following May. When he prepared to return to the Liberal leadership in January 1995, he gave an interview to *The Australian*'s Greg Sheridan to clean the slate. The page one headline read: 'I was wrong on Asians, says Howard'. In his first term as Prime Minister, 1996–98, Howard found himself sharing the limelight with Pauline Hanson, a politician whom he would describe much later as Australia's version of France's far-right Jean-Marie Le Pen. And at the 2001 election Howard shook his fist at the boat people who were then testing Australia's borders. Future generations will agonise over each episode. Was he, and are most Australians, xenophobes? That is the inevitable, if unfair, question. But it is only in posing the riddle so harshly that the real Howard, and the real nation, can be gleaned.

The difference, if there is any, between Howard and the electorate on race is that the community was quicker to accept the Asian wave of immigration in the 1980s and 1990s than he was. They also got over Hanson, as he had predicted, but not because he had handled her well. To the contrary, most of his supporters think he was wrong to allow Hansonism to flourish without challenge for two critical years between September 1996 and the October 1998 election. Howard underestimated Hanson. He was surprised she had won the previously safe Labor seat of Oxley, south of Brisbane, at the March 1996 election. He did not give her much thought until her maiden speech to parliament six months later. Howard did not agree with her claim that Australia was 'in danger of being swamped by Asians'. His electorate of Bennelong, in Sydney's affluent inner north, offered the best rebuttal. The Asian-born were 13.7 per cent of the voters in 1996 and would rise to 18.4 per cent five years later. Hanson said that Asians 'form ghettoes and do not assimilate'. By making it to Bennelong, they had proved the opposite, that they were as upwardly mobile as the southern Europeans of the first immigration wave. Years later, when Hanson has disappeared from view, Howard paid Chinese and Vietnamese Australians the ultimate compliment by saying they were 'the new Greeks and Italians'.

Howard could have said this in 1996, but he chose not to. His office had expected Labor to ask a question about Hanson's maiden speech and an answer was prepared to reaffirm Australia's colour-blind immigration program. But Labor did not challenge Howard immediately, because it had also underestimated her. When it became clear in 1997 that Hanson was speaking for a sizeable chunk of the Coalition's base, Howard was reluctant to take her on, for fear of elevating her further and sending more voters her way. His fumbling was symptomatic of a wider malaise, not some deliberate race ploy. His government's first term was hesitant, contradictory and prone to mind-boggling bouts of incompetence. Seven frontbenchers would lose their posts in the first 18 months for breaching the ministerial code of conduct. In the end, Hanson flourished for the most mundane of reasons: Howard had yet to find his own voice as Prime Minister. Almost one million people voted for Hanson's One Nation Party at the 1998 federal election, with the majority of her support concentrated outside the capital cities in her home state of Queensland and Howard's NSW. It could have been the start of a third force in politics, but Hanson had lost her seat in the House of Representatives and with it her soap box. Howard assumed Hanson was finished, but he didn't count on her supporters returning to haunt him early in 2001, as another election loomed. Only it was not race they were worried about, but rising petrol prices.

Labor believes that Howard stole the 2001 election when he turned back the MV *Tampa* in late August. The Norwegian freighter had rescued a stricken boatload of mainly Afghani asylum seekers en route to Christmas Island. Howard wanted the *Tampa* to return her human cargo to Indonesia, but the asylum seekers forced the captain, Arne Rinnan, to change course and resume the journey to Christmas Island. Howard stood his ground and the navy was used to intercept the boat. The asylum seekers were taken at gunpoint to Nauru to have their claims processed under international law, where the Government assumed fewer of them would be accepted than if they had been allowed to use the Australian legal system.

The confrontation switched Howard's poll numbers. Immediately beforehand, 50 per cent of voters were dissatisfied with the job he was doing as Prime Minister, while only 40 per cent were satisfied. The *Tampa* made it 50:40 his way, and a fortnight later, after the September 11 terror attacks on the United States, Howard's numbers jumped again to 61 per cent in favour and only 31 per cent against. He couldn't lose from here, and didn't.

* * *

It is important to draw breath at this point and recall what went wrong for Howard in the first half of 2001, because it will help explain how much of his election triumph was due to the refugee issue and whether the public response to the *Tampa* was an expression of xenophobia. The Government had finished 2000 in front of Labor. 'We weren't a long way in front, but we were comfortable,' Howard says.[1]

He had assumed the implementation of the GST would be more difficult in the short run. But the first inflation number had come in lower than forecast and there were no obvious signs of a consumer backlash. But it was the balmy calm before a cyclone. The revolt was brewing in three areas that the Government had not anticipated to be that much trouble: the housing market, the red tape associated with the new tax system and petrol prices. Yet border protection decided the election in Howard's favour, because it brought back the Hansonites in the cut-throat electorates in Queensland and NSW that had threatened to turn against the Government earlier in the year. In each seat, the One Nation vote fell by about half, and the Coalition primary vote increased by the same amount. But did this confirm that the nation's heart had darkened? Not quite. Only 10 per cent of the electorate changed its vote because of border protection. For the remaining 90 per cent, the economy, leadership and existing party loyalties were pivotal.

Here's the rub. Howard would have won without the *Tampa*, because September 11 was driving voters all over the Western world into the laps of the incumbents, at the national and at the state levels. But what if there had been no *Tampa* and no September 11? It is hard to imagine the Hansonite vote coming over to the Coalition to the same extent. The best scenario would have been a narrow win for Howard; the worst would have been a narrow loss.

Where border protection mattered most to Howard was in the fact that it allowed him to sharpen the contest with Kim Beazley. Before the *Tampa*, the public mood towards the two leaders could best be described as one of boredom. Sure, Howard had appeased the electorate on the GST, but that did not make him popular—only less *un*popular. Importantly, the exercise had left him without any funds to run a positive election campaign. The budget had, in fact, slipped into deficit, although voters were not to learn this until after the election. The *Tampa* allowed the Government to run a bribe-lite campaign, by presenting Howard as a patriot, and Beazley as a flip-flopper.

It was after the event that the detail of the border protection regime began to bedevil the Government. Between late August and December 2001 the navy intercepted a total of 14 boats carrying more than two thousand people. Ten boats were taken to Nauru and Manus Island for processing, while the other four were turned back to Indonesia. Of the 1547 people who passed through Nauru and Manus Island, 985 were found to be genuine refugees and a further 77 were accepted on humanitarian grounds. Most of them wound up in Australia. Add the 131 Afghanis who were taken straight off the *Tampa* and accepted by New Zealand, and the success rate for claims is above 70 per cent. In September 2003 Howard said, incorrectly, that 'the great bulk of them were not found to be legitimate refugees'.

The defining image, though, was a government in the midst of an election campaign telling a lie about the occupants of the fourth boat to be intercepted, carrying 219 mainly Iraqi asylum seekers. The boat was sabotaged, according to the navy, and it eventually sank. Somehow, the Government convinced itself that the asylum seekers had thrown their children into the water in an attempt to intimidate the crew of the HMAS *Adelaide*. Photos from the rescue at sea were presented by the then defence minister, Peter Reith, as evidence that children had been thrown into the water.

It didn't happen, of course, and to this day Howard insists that he learned that the allegation was wrong only after the election. His colleagues are inclined to agree with him. One cabinet minister close to Howard has told me he was sure that Reith knew the truth during the campaign, and can only assume that he tried to shield the Prime Minister from any embarrassment. Yet Mike Scrafton says he told Howard three days before polling day that no one in the department believed the story any more.

The best reply came from the asylum seekers themselves. The people on the so-called 'children overboard' boat happened to have the highest success rate for claims under the 'Pacific solution'. The final tally showed that 96.5 per cent were accepted as genuine refugees. They were, after all, fleeing Saddam Hussein, a despot against whom Australia would go to war in March 2003.

Howard has no regrets about the incident. 'They don't carry any visible signs of being demonised, to the extent that they have been accepted,' he says.

[This issue] figured far less prominently in the public's mind before the election than it did afterwards, because it became the great excuse why Labor lost the election. But if it had never arisen, I don't think there would have been any difference in the result, I don't think a vote would have shifted. People voted for our tough border protection policy. They didn't vote for us because of children overboard.[2]

Asked whether the incident gives his critics an easy line of attack against him, Howard is unapologetic, saying:

> The most powerful reply to that is that they irresponsibly sank the damn boat, which put their children in the water. I'm sorry, if I had have been told definitively, if I had been told that that story was completely wrong, I would have said so, but I wasn't and my last act before the election was to put that video in the public domain so that I wasn't accused of concealing it, because it was ambiguous. Watching that video, you couldn't tell whether people were being thrown in the water or not. It was just impossible. But after all, they did sink the boat.[3]

It is a fascinating window into the Howard psyche. He offers no apology for the tone of the border protection policy. What he has changed at the margin is his attitude to the Immigration Department. He became increasingly uncomfortable with the detention of children and the long delays in settling the onshore case load. From 2003, Howard began writing to the then minister Philip Ruddock to suggest the process be improved. But the message did not seem to be getting through, and Howard became frustrated. Part of him would have welcomed the mini backbench revolt, led by Liberal MP Petro Georgiou in 2005, that forced the Government to adjust the detention regime. The mood in the electorate had shifted by this point, as evidence of systemic bungling by the department was revealed. It had detained one mentally ill Australian citizen and deported another to The Philippines.

Yet the border protection policy remains popular. Howard's critics struggle to understand the distinction between the principle of keeping out the boats and any blunders made in the application of the regime. The 'children overboard' fiasco did not swing votes to Labor at the 2004 election; nor did the examples of Cornelia Rau and Vivian Alvarez in 2005. What motivates voters has always been much simpler than race. It's the economy, stupid, as Bill Clinton one said.

That said, it is important to note that Howard today is probably ahead of public opinion on Muslim immigration. A joint university study in 2002 found that 53 per cent of voters in NSW and Queensland would be concerned if a relative married a Muslim. By contrast, 72 per cent said they would not mind an Asian in-law.

Asked whether he thinks the Muslims will follow the same track as the Asians, Howard says he is confident 'most of them' will.

> But I do think there is this particular complication because there is a fragment which is utterly antagonistic to our kind of society, and that is a difficulty. You can't find any equivalent in Italian, or Greek, or Lebanese, or Chinese or Baltic immigration to Australia. There is no equivalent of raving on about jihad, but that is the major problem, and I think some of the associated attitudes towards women [are] a problem. For all the conservatism towards women and so forth within some of the Mediterranean cultures, with which you would be familiar, it's as nothing compared with some of the more extreme attitudes. The second one of those things is a broader problem, but to be fair to them, it's an attitude that is changing with the younger ones.[4]

The interview was held on Friday 9 December 2005.[5] By the end of that weekend, Australia had witnessed its most violent race confrontation of the television age. The setting could not have been more incongruous: North Cronulla beach, in Sydney's south. Until then it was one of the postcards of Australian settlement, a suburb overlooking the Pacific Ocean. Now it risks becoming an enduring symbol of Howard's Australia, the seeming paradox of prosperity and prejudice.

Previous immigration waves could count on the economy as their saviour. Xenophobia would abate as gross domestic product accelerated and as the Australian-born children of non–English-speaking immigrants made the trip from outcast to middle class. What Cronulla demonstrated at the end of 2005, the sixteenth year of an uninterrupted boom, was, in a way, the very thing that Hansonism had proved seven years earlier, at the 1998 federal election. Support for Hanson's One Nation Party was concentrated outside the cities in Queensland and NSW where the overseas-born population was substantially less than the national average. The towns they lived in were also on the bottom of the income ladder.

North Cronulla had only one part of the Hansonite equation: a higher than average Australian-born population. Howard had once described the area as a 'bit of an Anglo–Celtic enclave'. But it was a high-income postcode, so the backlash against the Lebanese Australians who that afternoon had taken the car or the train from Sydney's west to use the beach was an expression of tribalism at its most ugly. As was the retaliation over the next two nights from the young Lebanese Australian gangs who smashed parked cars and yelled abuse at the locals. These two groups did not know each other, and did not want to know each other. Yet Howard's Australia had never been more accepting of the regular immigration program, according to the private research of the Liberal and Labor parties. Howard has enjoyed the best of both worlds since he turned back the *Tampa*. The voters who worry most about immigration in the former Hansonite belt of Queensland and NSW think Howard is keeping out all foreigners, when he is bringing them here at a rate Paul Keating never contemplated during his term and a half as Prime Minister between December 1991 and March 1996.

Howard has overseen the transformation of the content and the tone of the immigration debate with barely a whisper of dissent from the conservative side of politics. Imagine what people would have thought at the 1996 election if Howard had promised to beat the standard the Hawke Government set in the 1980s, when the net immigration intake was above 100,000 for five years in a row. Howard's record is six, with a seventh on the way in 2006–07. Amazing, when you consider that he began his first term in office as an immigration cutter.

12

BEYOND SORRY

Stuart Rintoul

WARREN Mundine found himself in strange territory. He was president-elect of the Australian Labor Party but one of the pin-up boys of the Howard Government in Aboriginal Affairs, where he spoke in terms the Government found appealing. He was a member of the government-appointed National Indigenous Council until he resigned in January 2006. He was also awarded a 'Bennelong medal' by the archly conservative Bennelong Society, which was founded on the principle that Aboriginal people should integrate into the broader Australian community. He was a lightning rod in a volatile area. 'And I've got the scars to prove it,' he says, laughing.[1]

Pat Dodson was in strange territory too. Regarded by some as 'the father of reconciliation' and by any measure one of Australia's greatest indigenous leaders, Dodson now found himself airily dismissed as 'old guard'. In August 2003, he had described the new direction of Aboriginal policy as a 'virulent form of assimilation' and a throwback to the debates and philosophies of the 1950s. Dodson, a key player in black politics for the past 30 years, said that graphic accounts of violence and dysfunction in remote communities made it clear that something had failed dismally, 'but that doesn't mean you ... rearrange the direction of Aboriginal society'.[2]

But changing direction was precisely John Howard's intention. Over 10 years, Howard had stopped what he called the pendulum swing to Aboriginal rights and sent it arcing back towards integration into the broader Australian dream. 'Thirty years of failure' became the catchcry, as the era of self-determination introduced by the Whitlam Government and championed by economist H C 'Nugget' Coombs[3] gave way to new policies aimed at ending the misery of welfare dependency. Aboriginal collectivism was packed off and replaced by calls for individual and family responsibility. Reconciliation—a concept introduced by the Hawke Government—fell from discussion as the focus sharpened on life and death in Aboriginal communities. Separateness, in the form of ATSIC, was ended. The days of 'conspicuous compassion'[4], declared Indigenous Affairs Minister Amanda Vanstone, were over.

It was December 2005. The speech in front of Vanstone was titled 'Beyond Conspicuous Compassion'.[5] She began, in a style that had become pro-forma:

> I acknowledge the traditional owners of the land on which we're meeting today. I acknowledge the richness of the culture that prospered here in the past and also the strength of the culture that continues to enrich Australians in the 21st century. However, I must also acknowledge the frustration of looking at the last 30 years of Indigenous policy in this country and not seeing anywhere near good enough to show for it. Life for too many of our first Australians continues to be unhealthy, unhappy, violent and short ...

Vanstone spoke of 'an extraordinary opportunity for change' but she warned:

> The environment will be challenging for those who are comfortable indulging in what has been called 'conspicuous compassion'—a culture of ostentatious caring which is about feeling good, not doing good. Caring but not making change condemns Aboriginal people to some sort of cultural museum where they should expect less than others ... For too long we have accepted a different standard for Indigenous people. The understandable abhorrence of the injustices of the past has led in some ways to a reluctance to be critical and to respond

firmly when we should have. A fear of doing more harm led us to doing very little.

Throughout the Howard years, there has been increasing pressure to address the question of perpetually uneconomic remote Aboriginal communities that have become breeding grounds for violence and ignorance. A former Aboriginal affairs minister, Peter Howson, led the conservative chorus, writing frequently of the 'awful horror of social disintegration' in these communities, which were former ration depots and the remnants of a failed socialist fantasy, places where, to borrow from Thomas Hobbes' *Leviathan*, there was 'no Knowledge of the face of the Earth; no account of Time; no Arts; no Letters; no Society; and which is worst of all, continuall feare, and danger of violent death; And the life of man, solitary, poore, nasty, brutish, and short'.[6] Now Vanstone questioned the viability of a thousand remote Aboriginal communities with less than a hundred people living in each. 'No more cultural museums that might make some people feel good and leave Indigenous Australians without a viable future,' she said. 'Continuing cultural identity does not require poverty or isolation from mainstream Australian society.'

What was the response to Vanstone's comments? Virtual silence. In Melbourne, Howson, who advocated a return to the policy of assimilation,[7] which he said had been changed from a word of hope in the future to a synonym for genocide, was staggered—and delighted. He regarded Vanstone's speech as a watershed. He believed the argument for radical conservative change had been won. It was inconceivable that such a speech could have been made at the beginning of the Howard years. But so much had happened in between times and so many of the images of black Australia were images of despair. Dreams had turned sour.

In 1992, at Redfern Park, in a speech despised by conservatives for its dark interpretation of history, Howard's Labor predecessor, Paul Keating, spoke of the ignorant and prejudiced dealings with Aboriginal people in the past. 'With some noble exceptions, we failed to make the most basic human response and enter into their hearts and minds. We failed to ask: how would I feel if this were done to me?'[8]

But at the end of a decade of the Howard Government, a more persistent question had framed itself: 'What if I had to live like that?' It was a change that not only expressed itself in policy terms and attitude but also reached back into the pages of the nation's history, as conservatives challenged what historian Geoffrey Blainey had taught Howard to call the 'black-armband view of history'.[9] The history wars, to borrow from Joshua Foa Dienstag, 'exposed the subterranean connections between history and politics which had existed unseen, like the system of wires and pipes beneath a great city'.[10] And nowhere were the history wars more bitterly contested than in the history of indigenous Australians. First the stolen generations were denied, then the frontier massacres.[11]

Before Howard, Aboriginal rights were more ascendant than they had ever been, following the High Court's recognition of traditional indigenous title to land in the 1992 Mabo decision and the subsequent intense negotiations between the Aboriginal leadership and the Keating Government. Howard's election changed the dynamic. In 1988, Howard had promised to rip up any treaty that might be signed with Aboriginal people. In 1995, as he headed towards government, he said few Australians would dispute that the living standards of Aborigines and Torres Strait Islanders required urgent focused attention but that many were 'exasperated and perplexed that so much could have been spent and apparently so little achieved'.

Howard made it clear that, when he was in government, Aboriginal policy would focus on improving standards and opportunities in health, employment, education and housing, which he called practical reconciliation.

> The whole Aboriginal policy area has been hijacked by the social engineers, the politically correct and other sundry groups more intent on dividing than uniting our community. The actions we take must be within the framework of one undivided Australian nation with a common respect for the one body of law, to which all are equally accountable and from which all are entitled to receive an equal share of justice.[12]

He campaigned on the slogan 'For All of Us'. In 1996, he referred to a black-armband view of history, saying: 'This "black-armband" view of our past reflects a belief that most Australian history since 1788 has been little more than a disgraceful story of imperialism, exploitation, racism, sexism and other forms of discrimination.'[13]

Howard caught the public mood. So too did Pauline Hanson. In her maiden speech to the parliament in September 1996, Hanson claimed that she had won her seat of Oxley 'largely on an issue that has resulted in me being called a racist. That issue related to my comment that Aboriginals received more benefits than non-Aboriginals'. She went on to say that she was 'fed up to the back teeth with the inequalities that are being promoted by the Government and paid for by the taxpayer under the assumption that Aboriginals are the most disadvantaged people in Australia'. In response, Howard said: 'One of the great changes that have [*sic*] come over Australia in the last six months is that people do feel able to speak a little more freely and a little more openly about what they feel.' At the Human Rights and Equal Opportunity Commission, Indigenous Social Justice Commissioner Mick Dodson— like his brother Pat, a major force in the indigenous struggle—accused Howard of pandering to prejudice, bigotry and hatred.

In May 1997, former High Court judge Ronald Wilson and Mick Dodson delivered the National Inquiry into the Separation of Aboriginal and Torres Strait Islander Children from Their Families. The 'stolen generations' report reduced Labor leader Kim Beazley to tears in the parliament, but was howled down by conservative commentators who seized on Wilson's conclusion that the policy of forcible removal of children from indigenous Australians could properly be labelled 'genocidal' from at least 1946 and constituted a crime against humanity.[14] Conservative columnists spent thousands of words describing the stolen generation as a myth and three years later feasted on the defeat of Lorna Cubillo and Peter Gunner's test case in the Federal Court, which former ATSIC chairwoman Lowitja O'Donoghue described as devastating. At a reconciliation convention in Melbourne, a large part of the audience turned their backs on Howard as he lectured them on why there would not be a national apology to the stolen generations, but why there would be a 10-point plan to restrict native title. Howard had travelled to Longreach in Queensland to reassure pastoralists and miners, while his Coalition partner, National Party leader Tim Fischer, promised 'bucketfuls of extinguishment ... on a fair basis'.

In May 2000, more than 200,000 people walked over the Sydney Harbour Bridge in the cause of reconciliation. It brought to an emotional climax the 10-year journey of the Council for Aboriginal Reconciliation, but Pat Dodson, regarded as the father of reconciliation, stayed away in protest. The previous day, during a ceremony at the Opera House at which the Declaration Towards Reconciliation was officially handed to the nation, part of Howard's speech was drowned out by shouts of 'say sorry', which he refused to do. Howard was shepherded on the stage by ATSIC chairman Geoff Clark. Two months later, in July 2000, Clark was arrested and charged with sexual assault.[15] Clark was later cleared but it was the beginning of the agonising demise of ATSIC, which was finally abolished in 2005, and a tipping point—that moment when ideas cross a threshold, tip and spread contagiously like wildfire. Increasingly, the agenda shifted from what Howard called 'symbolic gestures and overblown promises' to the strife of Aboriginal communities: alcoholism, violence, petrol sniffing, child abuse, corruption and illiteracy. Increasingly, the mood was to go beyond sorry.

In September 2000, anthropologist Peter Sutton, in a paper called 'The Politics of Suffering',[16] called for a fundamental rethinking of Aboriginal policy. He wrote:

> The contrast between progressivist public rhetoric about empowerment and self-determination on the one hand, and the raw evidence of a disastrous failure in major aspects of Australian Aboriginal Affairs policy since the early 1970s [on the other] is now frightening. Policy revision must now go back to bedrock questions, with all bets off, if it is to respond meaningfully to this crisis.

Asked what the right question should be in deciding where to take indigenous policy, Sutton subsequently told me: 'I think the right question is always, "How does this affect a two-year-old girl's chances?"'[17] In 1999, a Women's Task Force in Queensland, chaired by academic Boni Robertson, had detailed horrific acts of violence and child abuse in indigenous communities.[18]

In the Pitjantjatjara homelands of South Australia, plagued by petrol sniffing and internal strife, the twentieth anniversary of land rights in 2001 passed without celebration. In the Northern Territory Parliament in March 2002, John Ah Kit, a long-time player in black politics, declared:

> Aboriginal Territorians are facing a stark crisis. To say anything else would be a lie—and I believe that now is the time for the truth to be told … many Aboriginal people acknowledge that the rot lies within their own communities … The simple fact is that it is almost impossible to find a functional Aboriginal community anywhere in the Northern Territory.

A critical convert to Howard's way was Noel Pearson. A young lawyer from Cape York, who was educated by the Lutherans, Pearson came to prominence as an indigenous negotiator on native title during the Keating years and was close to being enlisted into the Labor Party. In 1997, he described the Howard Government as 'racist scum'. But the Howard years saw Pearson emerge as a charismatic conservative. Where many other Aboriginal leaders remained contemptuous of Howard, Pearson broke ranks. He attacked what he called 'passive welfare' and attacked 'progressivist' thinking that excused the state of indigenous Australia as a product of historically derived disadvantage, instead of changing it. He spoke of crying infants being silenced with petrol-drenched rags on their faces. While he continued to advocate for native title, which he saw being whittled away by hostile court judgments, he spoke of the need to restore an indigenous society based on work and family.[19] Pearson attracted condemnation from the Left, but he had Howard's rapt attention. Pearson became a key government adviser and the instrument through which Howard could engage with Aboriginal people on his own terms. In August 2003, Howard travelled to Cape York. At Aurukun, a young woman, Tania Major, told him that she was one of only 15 pupils to finish school, that all the other girls in her class were pregnant at 15, that seven of the boys had been incarcerated, that four had committed suicide, and that almost all were alcoholics.

Howard's stubborn rejection of 'black-armband' symbolism had earned him the distrust of Aboriginal leaders during his first five years in power. But the misery of life in indigenous communities—and his constant re-election—gave a weight to Howard's policy of 'practical rec-onciliation' that would not be denied. Controversially, the Government introduced shared responsibility agreements in which indigenous com-munities undertook responsibilities, such as raising school attendance, in return for services. In the remote West Australian community of Mulan, Aboriginal people undertook to wash their children's faces to eradicate the eye disease trachoma in return for the installation of petrol bowsers. Indigenous senator Aden Ridgeway called it 'petrol sniffing at discount prices'. Pat Dodson called it 'lunacy' that 'smacks so much of the old days when the superintendents of missions lined people up and checked whether they'd cleaned their teeth or put their rubbish bins out on the right angle'. But many more shared responsibility agreements followed. Magistrate Sue Gordon, chairwoman of the National Indigenous Council, said she saw nothing paternalistic in ideas instigated by indig-enous communities.

Federal, state and local agencies were brought together in a whole-of-government assault on Aboriginal living conditions that Peter Shergold, Secretary of the Department of Prime Minister and Cabinet, called a 'new world of bureaucratic connectedness'. Programs previously administered separately by ATSIC were taken up by mainstream departments. Vanstone declared that the Government's commitment to communal ownership of Aboriginal land was 'rock solid' but it encouraged private ownership and long-term leases. There was no romance, she said, in communal poverty. In December 2004, as Mundine prepared to take his seat on the National Indigenous Council, he said that, after a lifetime of support for Aboriginal land rights, he had changed his mind and no longer supported communal ownership of land, which he said was retarding indigenous economic development. Accepting his Bennelong medal, he remarked: 'It was Charles Darwin who said: "It is neither the strongest nor the most intelligent species that survive; it is the species that is most responsive to change." How very true those words are to the situation of indigenous Australians.' Mundine also attacked Northern Territory Chief Justice Brian Martin, who had handed down a one-month jail sentence to a man who had anal sex with a 14-year-old girl who had been promised to him as a wife when she was four. Mundine said the decision was a disgrace.

Conservatives hailed a new dawn in indigenous affairs. But it was a dawn with uncertain features. In July 2005, the Productivity Commission reported that between 1994 and 2002 there were some improvements in indigenous employment, home ownership and post-secondary education participation. But it found that many of the social indicators showed little or no movement. A large gap remained between indigenous people and the rest of the Australian population, the most damning and unmoving of which was that Aboriginal people continued to have a life expectancy 20 years lower than non-Aboriginal people. Academic Marcia Langton spoke of extraordinary efforts that were being made to build 'pathways into equitable and sustainable economic participation', with hundreds of agreements across the industrial landscape. But at the Centre for Aboriginal Economic Policy Research at the Australian National University in Canberra, director Jon Altman said the Howard Government, by continually avoiding an infrastructural backlog that required 'billions of dollars of intervention', had done 'less than tread water'. More young indigenous people than ever before were going to university and graduating, but at the same time there were more who could not read or write. After 10 years of Howard government, Boni Robertson, whose report on indigenous domestic violence had done much to change the nature of the discussion, felt that Aboriginal people had arrived at a new isolationism.

In November 2004, Noel Pearson and Pat Dodson reconciled the divergent tracks of rights and responsibilities and, publicly at least, veered towards the Howard agenda of mutual obligation. At a meeting in Port Douglas, Pearson likened Howard's role in reforming indigenous Australia to Richard Nixon's engagement with China, saying, 'It had to be Nixon that went to China and we have a Nixon who can help us and we need to respond to that', while Dodson said Howard's policy of mutual obligation had 'a grounding within our culture and society'. Pearson suggested it was the beginning of a 'radical centre' in black politics. The vehicle for delivering this message to Howard came in the unlikely figure of former AFL champion Michael Long, who set off on a Quixotic walk from Melbourne to talk to Howard about indigenous suffering. Long said he was sick and tired of attending funerals. As Long approached the NSW border with his feet blistered and bandaged, his message gradually crystallised into a question, quietly asked: 'Where is the love?'

13

THE DOCTRINE OF CHOICE

Samantha Maiden

'There are many hundreds of thousands of people in this community who are prepared to make additional sacrifices to exercise a freedom of choice.'
—John Howard, MP for Bennelong, 1974

JOHN Howard's agenda on health and education demonstrates his life-long commitment to the politics of choice, social conservatism and individual responsibility. It is also the story of his evolution as a political salesman. After the failure of his agenda to inspire voter loyalty during the wilderness of the Hawke–Keating years, the Prime Minister has found a formula that works. Howard's doctrine of choice, nurtured throughout a 30-year political career, has reshaped the debate over public and private funding of health and education.

As Prime Minister, Howard has fostered the notion that aspirational families should invest in private health insurance and private schools. By providing taxpayer-funded grants to allow them to exercise choice, he has diverted federal funding away from universal healthcare, free university degrees and public schools and into the hands of private providers. In a speech in 2004 outlining his fourth-term priorities, Howard spelt out the twin benefits of a system governed by choice: quality and efficiency.

'Just as patients have a right to choose between different health-care providers, parents have a right to choose the type of education that best suits the needs of their children,' Howard said. 'I am proud of the fact that more than 300 new, independent schools have opened in Australia since we came to office, the bulk of which are low-fee schools. On average, every time a parent chooses to send their child to an independent school, they save Australian taxpayers at least $3000 per year per child.'[1]

The way Howard applies his philosophy of choice to health and education is both aspirational and egalitarian. It provides the political framework to sell a user-pays model as a message of personal empowerment while at the same time appealing to the Australian notion of a fair go. The choice between the public and private systems is a universal right, not the privilege of a wealthy few.

Traditional boundaries between public and private funding are collapsing. In health, the 30 per cent private health insurance rebate has pumped $17 billion of government money into the private sector. Billions of dollars have also flowed to private schools, triggering an inevitable debate about giving parents vouchers to increase their freedom to choose.

Howard's radical agenda of choice has presented a serious challenge for the Labor Party which for decades had been the party voters trusted most to take care of hospitals, schools and universities. Newspoll surveys show that Howard has narrowed the gap on these issues at critical stages of the electoral cycle. In March 2005, 43 per cent of voters surveyed believed that Howard was the leader more capable of handling education, while 39 per cent thought Labor leader Kim Beazley more capable. On Medicare, the Prime Minister successfully narrowed the huge lead the ALP opened up in 2003 over the decline in bulk billing in the lead-up to the last election. Labor has lost its natural advantage in the policy areas that were once it strengths, allowing the Prime Minister to push the national debate back towards his own key strengths: the economy and national security.

'Traditionally,' says Newspoll chairman Sol Lebovic, 'health and education are Labor's territory. This year [2005] the Coalition has managed to get closer on education. I think the issues—health and education—largely have been neutralised. They are still among the most important issues to voters but they didn't seem to be the driving force for voters at the last election. They don't come into play unless you've got major differences in policy.'

In the 1980s Howard was a Medicare-sceptic, describing the scheme as 'a human nightmare', 'a financial monster' and 'an administrative quagmire', 'a scandal' and a 'miserable, cruel fraud'. In June 1987 he told radio presenter John Laws: 'The second thing we'll do is get rid of the bulk-billing system. It's an absolute rort. We will be proposing change to Medicare which amounts to its de facto dismantling ... we'll pull it right apart. Bulk billing will be abolished, except for people such as pensioners who really need it.'

His views were reflected in John Hewson's Fightback! manifesto, which proposed that Medicare be curtailed and largely confined to pensioners and health-care cardholders only. The policy proved a disaster for the Coalition and arguably cost Hewson more votes in the 'unlosable' 1993 election than Fightback's consumption tax.

From the wreckage of Fightback the doctrine of choice emerged. Choice was the missing link between a policy that appealed to economic rationalists and middle Australia. Fightback was perceived as regressive. Choice, on the other hand, was progressive, the democratisation of privilege, putting everyone on an equal footing.

Liberal MP Andrew Robb, who was the Liberal Party's federal director and campaign director in 1993, says:

> Fightback was an 800-page document. Some people unfairly called it an 800-page suicide note but it has provided a lot of the agenda. The choice framework grew out of this. Howard and the party learnt that you can offer what we were offering in 1993 without necessarily ditching what was there. Choice is a key part of a philosophical basis. You could provide choice between public and private that benefits both. That's the evolution in health and education and it's now gone into superannuation and workplace relations.
>
> I think the Labor Party still see their working class base in the traditional factory fodder image. That's not life any more. For a government to pat them on the head and say 'just give us the tax dollars and we will work it all out in health and education' doesn't work these days.[2]

Howard, who was educated in the state school system and sent his children to state schools at a primary level, did not mention education policy in his 1996 campaign speech. But his reforms in education are far-reaching. Australia's public schools, attacked by Howard as too 'politically correct', have moved to the centre of the Government's values debate. 'New-age curriculum' in schools and 'cappuccino courses' taught by baby boomer academics remain within the Government's sights.

Today, federal spending on private schools outstrips grants to publicly funded universities. Almost 40 per cent of teenagers attend private secondary schools and one in three Australian children do not attend public schools. Howard sees a direct link between the cultural values of public schools and the growth of private education. Parents are exercising choice. As Howard said in 2004:

> They feel that government schools have become too politically correct and too values-neutral. It's a reflection of the extent to which political correctness overtook this country. Particularly through the teachers' unions, which I think are a bit out of step. Some schools think you offend people by having nativity plays. You know, the increasingly antiseptic view ... taken about a whole lot of things.[3]

Howard's first choice as employment, education and youth affairs minister was senator Amanda Vanstone, who angered vice-chancellors in her first months in the job when she hinted at savage budget cuts for universities and restricted eligibility for Austudy payments. 'Education has had it too good for too long. Why should the taxpayer on $400 a week pay for somebody to go to university to get a higher paying job?' Vanstone declared.[4]

Ten years on, Vanstone is proud to have introduced the first full-fee degrees, allowing students to buy a place if they missed out on marks.

> Look at what we did. Australian students are in the same position that overseas students were in. If they want to invest in themselves, they can pay for the cost of a place in an Australian university. What does that mean? This costs the taxpayer nothing and frees up government-funded places for others. We allow overseas students to buy a place. Why on earth wouldn't we allow domestic students? There is a public and private benefit from education and they were getting a bigger share of the benefit than they were putting in. Yet these kids were complaining about paying more when other kids at the same school were going to get a trade certificate and not be given anywhere near the assistance.[5]

The junior minister in the education portfolio, David Kemp, who was responsible for schools when the Howard Government was first elected in 1996, extended the choice doctrine under his funding reforms for private schools introduced in 2001.

'Under Labor a "new schools" policy restricted the right of parents to establish a new school if it would attract students from a state school in the same area,' he says. 'We abolished Labor's system for funding non-government schools. John Howard very quickly appreciated that this policy would be very important to aspirational voters and gave it strong support.'[6]

Kemp's new funding arrangement, known as the socio-economic status (SES) model, abolished the link between a private school's wealth, in terms of fees and endowments, and the public funding it was eligible to receive. His reforms replaced the Education Resources Index system, a needs-based funding model, with a new measure of the socio-economic status of parents. By matching parents' addresses with Australian Bureau of Statistics Census data, schools were ranked on an SES index so that those that drew students from areas of high SES would receive less government funding than schools that drew students from areas of average or low SES. As a means test for parents, SES is a rough and ready measure that takes no account of anomalies in ABS data and gives relatively generous funding to some wealthy schools, particularly boarding schools attracting students from rural areas. Cabinet ministers recall that the arguments over a new schools funding model was among the most passionate debates of 2005. Kemp was forced to make the schools package even more generous and include a 'no losers' policy for private schools under pressure from cabinet colleagues, including Peter Reith. In 2004, the SES system was extended to capture Catholic schools.

But, as Mark Latham discovered at the 2004 election, reforming the system is fraught with danger. Any threat to government funding for private schools becomes divisive, regardless of the fact the ALP's schools policy at the last election guaranteed the overall level of funding to private schools and increased grants to struggling low-fee independent schools.

Kemp's other main attempt at reform—his radical higher education reform plan—ran aground when a cabinet briefing paper fell into the hands of the Opposition, a leak that sparked a police investigation. The plan called for deregulated course fees and a voucher system but the outcry that followed prompted the Prime Minister to affirm the Government's election promise not to introduce either. Howard also uttered the words that would come back to haunt him. 'There will be no $100,000 university fees under this Government,' he pledged. While the Prime Minister now argues that he was referring to HECS degrees, Australia today has more than 50 courses charging upfront fees of more than $100,000.

In late 2001, Kemp's switch to the environment portfolio allowed the Prime Minister to promote Brendan Nelson to the education portfolio and straight into cabinet. Nelson tied the Government's $31 billion schools funding package to plain-language reporting to parents and, in a flourish of patriotism, ensured that schools had a functioning flagpole to fly the Australian flag. A review of the Government's university policy led to the 2003 Nelson reforms, which granted universities the freedom to set their own HECS fees within a capped range. The new freedoms for universities to set fees were accompanied by widespread complaints that the Government was providing a declining share of funding but demanding a greater say in course content and curriculum. The Howard Government contributed 53.8 per cent of universities' revenue in 1996 and just 40.75 per cent in 2004.

Howard has also challenged the 'university or bust' culture, championing the debate over technical training at a time of skills shortages. He has called for 'a change in the Australian mindset' so that 'a prized technical qualification is as valued as a university degree'.

I think we did as a nation go through a stage when we downgraded apprenticeships. When we thought that the only path to a satisfying, rewarding career was to go to university. Some people have suggested that I'm denigrating university education, but what I am doing is extolling high-quality and flexible technical qualifications as the right training path and the right career path for many young Australian men and women.[7]

After years of threatening to demolish Medicare, Howard's first choice as health minister, Michael Wooldridge, was charged with repairing the damage. Wooldridge cites the introduction of the private health insurance rebate in 1999 as a classic example of Howard's pragmatism. By pledging to cover 30 per cent of the cost of private health insurance, the Prime Minister provided billions of dollars in taxpayer assistance to the private sector, his preferred means of service delivery. However, as critics of the scheme have noted, it was later reforms to introduce financial penalties for those that failed to join a scheme after they reached their thirties that prompted membership to lift substantially.

'Lifetime health cover managed to keep premium increases flat between 1999 and 2001,' Wooldridge says.

> The end result was that in February 2002, for the first time in 25 years of Newspoll, the Coalition was equal to Labor on health. What the polling would show after five years was the public said: 'We still don't really trust them. We think they're going to do things to Medicare, but they are good at fixing problems.'[8]

Wooldridge also confirms that the Medicare Gold policy put forward by the then Labor leader Mark Latham at the 2004 election had previously been offered to and rejected by the Coalition. The plan, which would take over-75s out of the private health insurance pool, was seen as unsustainable. 'People tried to sell that to me. I said don't be silly. I think it's a crazy idea,' he says. 'It would just be enormously expensive. It was never going to be something that was going to float.'

However, he concedes there were also losses. 'It took me five budgets to get the bowel cancer screening program. I don't think they thought paying someone to have something stuck up their bum would be politically popular,' he admits.

When Wooldridge retired in 2001, his replacement was Victorian senator Kay Patterson, a former gerontologist with an eye for detail and a passion for strategies to respond to the ageing of Australia's population. She struggled in the portfolio. Her tenure was marked by health insurance premium increases and a sharp decline in the number of GPs bulk billing, sparking a public debate over the private health insurance rebate and the universality of Medicare.

Tony Abbott, Howard's Mr Fix-It, was given the portfolio, with cabinet backing to spend on health in the lead-up to an election year. The result, after several false starts, was Abbott's Medicare Plus. The centrepiece of the Coalition's health pitch during the 2004 election—the Medicare safety net—allowed taxpayers a refund of 80 cents in the dollar once they reached a 'threshold'.

Howard, the man who had once called Medicare 'an unmitigated disaster', was sold to voters at the 2004 election as—to borrow Abbott's phrase—'the best friend Medicare ever had'. Medicare Plus, however, turned into a case of policy overstretch after the election. When costs blew out by more than $1 billion, the Prime Minister forced Abbott to break his 'rock-solid, iron-clad' promise on the safety net and scale back the rebate just a year after it was unveiled. Once again, Howard the political pragmatist was at play, even if it meant dumping a promise that was the centrepiece of his election strategy for Medicare.

'There's a sense in which, probably, the Medicare Plus safety net issue was a bit akin to losing your political virginity,' Abbott noted. 'I've had a very smooth run through the senior reaches of political life so far. So it just happens.'

Howard has preached an agenda of choice on health and education that has underpinned a dramatic collapse in the traditional divide between public and private funding. During the Government's fourth term, the last bastion of the education system largely untouched by competition reforms, the nation's TAFE and training schools, will be thrown open to market forces under reforms designed to establish new technical colleges and encourage private training providers. The Government has entered into a new deal with the states over recognition of trade qualifications across state borders. The Prime Minister has also signalled a willingness to debate federal–state relations in the health portfolio after years of cost shifting and playing the blame game over responsibilities.

The evidence that Howard has succeeded in changing the political landscape on health and education was underlined by voter reaction to Labor's Medicare Gold policy at the 2004 election. The Whitlamesque notion of unlimited free health care for over-75s generated scepticism and suspicion among voters who had come to believe, under Howard, that the best things in life were not free. Latham badly miscalculated, too, with his schools policy, which threatened to cut government subsidies to 67 'elite' private schools and freeze funds to 111 more. Latham's pledge to guarantee overall funding to private schools and boost funding to poorer private and public schools was drowned out by the politics of class warfare.

Labor must now come to grips with both the extent and the permanence of the Howard revolution, which has rendered much of the ALP's weaponry redundant. In education, as with health, the philosophy of choice neutralises any attack based on the politics of envy. Rolling back the policies that have been embraced by aspirational middle Australia has become unthinkable. Howard has trip-wired the political agenda.

14

JUMPING THE WHITE PICKET FENCE

Kate Legge

THE WHITE picket fence dreamt up by a pony-tailed Sydney advertising executive for a 1988 Liberal policy brochure is one of the most enduring pieces of political iconography in Australian history. The strip of white pickets fencing off a nuclear family of four on the front cover of the Liberals' 'Future Directions' manifesto was dubbed 'Back to the Future' by feminist critics and political opponents who saw the symbol as a retreat to the social conservatism of John Howard's hero, Robert Menzies.

Weeks after the launch, Andrew Peacock stole the leadership crown from Howard but the white picket fence stuck fast in the public mind and helped define Lazarus with a triple bypass[1] when he reclaimed the Liberal leadership in 1995 and went on to defeat Paul Keating a year later.

The fence became shorthand for traditional family values. It promoted male breadwinners and the importance of mothering over career-centred feminists and, by anointing one model brood, appeared to reject alternatives such as gay couples or blended households of children. Although the 'Future Directions' brochure was short-lived, the fence defined Howard as patron saint of the stay-at-home mum.

Women on the political Left feared they would be sent back to the hearth. They warned of childcare cuts, tax changes to enshrine men as sole earners, even a return to fault-based divorce. None of these grim scenarios has come to pass. Childcare places fall short of demand but continue to multiply; gay marriages have been outlawed federally but these are occurring in record numbers; and mothers of young children are returning to the workforce earlier than ever before, some of them kicking and screaming as a result of the Coalition's welfare to work reforms.

In 2003, when Howard opened the Liberal Women's Conference in Adelaide, he finally laid the picket fence to rest by declaring that the typical Australian family was a two-income household, giving the example of a policeman and a part-time sales assistant. Gone were the days, he said, when the norm was two full-time highly paid professionals or a family with a sole breadwinner once children arrived on the scene.

Take note of Howard's furphy. The two highly paid professionals were never a norm but he had long played on perceptions that Labor favoured this group for political gain and in this christening ceremony for the new Australian family he had to bury the bogey as well as the old statistical mean.

'It is a very different society, not a worse society—in so many ways a much better society than what it was years earlier,' he said. 'And our responsibility is to deal with life as it is … rather than according to either an idealised paradigm or indeed an unduly elitist paradigm, but rather something that represents the average life experience of millions of our fellow Australians.'

So what happened to Howard? Did he evolve as the social and cultural landscape shifted around him or was the white picket fence always a clever piece of electoral positioning to win the hearts of conservative men and women? Was he ever a crusty ideologue or merely a crafty political operator?

* * *

Human Rights Commissioner Pru Goward, a personal friend of Howards, whom he chose to oversee women and family issues, recalls running into Keating while working for the ABC in the Canberra press gallery in the late 1980s when she was heavily pregnant with her third child. The treasurer of the day stopped her in the corridor to ask how she planned to manage her high-profile job and a newborn.

'I told him I was going to take as much time off as I could and that my mother was coming to help. He said: "Good on yer love. Much better than hiring a Karitane nurse." Some other female journalist had hired a full-time nurse so that she could come back to work and he disapproved of this,' she says. 'Howard, however, had every opportunity to express his private views and he never did. I never heard him say to me: "You should be home with the kids."'[2]

The founding director and conservative think tank of the Sydney Institute, Gerard Henderson, who was Howard's chief of staff in the 1980s, also cannot remember ever hearing his boss pass judgment on mothers who work. 'He never raised it. If he had real concerns about mothers being at home he would have said so privately and he never uttered a word. He never criticised any woman who worked,' Henderson says. 'But he was very conscious that Labor's Catholics were conservative on this issue and he also sensed that many stay-at-home mothers felt devalued or disparaged and he knew that a lot of them lived in suburbs and regional centres where the Liberals needed votes.'

In 1969 Keating, as the newly elected Labor member for Blaxland, gave a maiden speech that applauded the traditional female roles of mothering and homemaking. Twenty-four years later he led a Labor government that focused on childcare and measures to assist a new breed of highly educated and career-centred mothers into work. Supported by Australia's leading feminist Anne Summers and a coterie of women ministers, Keating presented a public face of a reconstructed new-age guy. But in private his views had not advanced much beyond his parliamentary debut.

Annita Keating did not return to paid work after her marriage to Paul. Paul Keating defied convention and moved his wife and children to Canberra so that he could see more of them. He was the family man par excellence. He did not want the fleeting weekend glimpses that satisfied every other male MP. Since the couple's separation Annita Keating has spoken critically of her husband's control over the domestic sphere. He did not want her to learn English and lose the foreign Dutch accent. He loved the European elegance. She wanted to be understood. Moreover, she revealed that her husband's growing agitation over her efforts to develop a public role as first lady became a source of friction that contributed to their split.

Janette Howard, on the other hand, who seemed to epitomise the white picket fence model, has told Goward that she had intended returning to work as a teacher part-time when her children were young but the plan was jettisoned by them both when her husband was promoted to treasurer under Malcolm Fraser, which effectively made her a single mother. Although Howard made a point of flying home for his children's Saturday sport, he put his politics first.[3]

What an exquisite irony, then, that Keating, a closet believer in motherhood, was perceived publicly as embracing feminism while Howard wrapped himself in the white picket fence for electoral kudos and managed to out-family-man the father of them all.

* * *

The openly gay British-born Liberal strategist Graham Wynn is credited as the brains behind the 'Future Directions' manifesto, which Howard's former chief of staff, Grahame Morris, says became the template for Liberal policy. The white picket design was an agency concept that appealed to the party's engine room because of its association with home, comfort and family values, according to the then federal Liberal director Tony Eggleton. It accentuated tradition at a time when Labor support for working women was creating a backlash among stay-at-home mothers and social conservatives. Keating's 1993 non–means-tested childcare policy, which handed dollars to every two-income family regardless of household wealth, generated political opposition from mothers not in the paid workforce. They felt undervalued and left out and Howard moved quickly to be their new best friend.

In columns for *The Daily Telegraph* Howard attacked the universal nature of this support, calling it 'a glaringly inequitable proposal' with nothing at all for single-income families. Single-income families became part of his disenfranchised constituency, voters who were vulnerable to Howard's claims that two-income professional couples were another of Labor's wealthy elites. A decade later, in 2003, Howard had moved to reconcile these warring camps with talk of the typical two-income family and a universal childcare rebate of his own.

The Australian's George Megalogenis believes Howard changed his mind on women when working mothers took advantage of rapidly growing part-time employment opportunities in the pink-collar service industries. Housing prices also forced the policeman's wife into the retail sector. In his book *Faultlines: Race, Work and the Politics of Changing Australia*, Megalogenis argues that Howard is a social conservative who sought to benefit single-income families with tax changes but these fistfuls of dollars were ultimately too small to keep mothers at home. 'Howard,' he says, 'is an economic liberal and social conservative, a free marketeer and an occasional social engineer. The times have suited him politically at the start of the new millennium, but the hard numbers of working families didn't vindicate his social agenda.'

But those who have advised Howard throughout his career resist the idea of his surrender to the inevitable. They insist that the Prime Minister was motivated always by the Liberal mantra of choice and his uncanny ability to swoop on political advantage. 'As long as I've known him,' says Grahame Morris, 'he has been big on choice.'

> What annoyed him was that the social trend seemed to value women at work and almost denigrate women who stayed at home to look after the children. But it was choice for all that motivated him. Thou shalt stay at home was never his stance. He just did not like the fact that all the financial help went to women who chose to work.[4]

Research by the Canberra-based economic modelling group NATSEM into how families fared between 1982 and 1995 showed that the losers during this period were children living in couple families with one breadwinner. Here was a constituency ripe for Liberal courtship, and the white picket fence imagery with its lament for an earlier epoch won Howard votes. But the women who felt marginalised were already on the move. The 1976 census shows that women waited until their youngest child had reached primary school age before returning to work. Flash forward to 1996 and the typical mother returned to work after her youngest turned three. By 2001 the majority of women took jobs when their youngest was one to two years old. Ever alert to seismic social shifts, Howard was ready to jump the fence.

Social commentator Bettina Arndt was delighted to attend a private dinner with Howard at The Lodge in 2001 for a wide-ranging discussion on women and in particular the views of controversial British economist Catherine Hakim. Arndt had written about Hakim in articles for *The Sydney Morning Herald* canvassing the economist's thesis that modern women fell into one of three groups. Women, according to Hakin, were either work centred, home centred, or part of a new majority of 'adaptive women' who moved in and out of employment as family circumstances evolved. Arndt says that Hakim's research confirmed Howard's broad-church approach, which was anchored to the pillar of choice and not driven by any desire for social engineering.

Goward agrees. 'I always thought that he was very open and driven by the data, which was showing that most women work part-time. As a prime minister he is a great listener. He loves new facts. He loves new information. He keeps a very open mind.'[5]

Howard's realisation that juggling work and family had become 'the great barbecue stopper' was the result of listening to men and women on his trips around Australia. By 2004 Howard's family policies became centred on that policeman and his part-time working wife.

Government sources say that Howard was not all that opposed to the maternity leave that Goward put up for cabinet endorsement. The most vocal critic was Health Minister Tony Abbott, who rallied against a measure he said would reward working women. Abbott is an ideologue who makes Howard seem progressive by comparison. NSW Liberal MP Barry O'Farrell, who worked for Howard in the 1980s, says his former boss spoke in parables, not through the prism of hard-and-fast rules. 'For someone who's always worn that tag of ideologue, when you push your way back through the fog of memory it is hard to find an angular shape. The impressions do not match the words and maybe that is his political masterstroke.'

The white picket fence served him remarkably well at a critical turning point in Australian political history. Far from making the electorate cringe at its sepia-tinted vision of family life, voters liked this comfy reference to the bosom of our being. As Grahame Morris says: 'The public perception of John was of a good family man. Out of all the images you could craft for a future leader, this one takes some beating.'

V

HOWARD ABROAD

15

ALL THE WORLD'S A STAGE

Greg Sheridan

JOHN Howard is an unlikely revolutionary, perhaps an unlikely international statesman. But he has revolutionised Australian foreign policy and become one of the most formidable and senior statesmen in the Asia Pacific. It is, as with most things involving Howard, a story of extraordinary ordinariness, a series of deep-rooted convictions, several dollops of good luck and a superb opportunist's ability to take advantage of opportunities as they arise.

The Howard decade in foreign policy describes an arc that starts with awkwardness in the region, low ambition, unfamiliarity with Asian leaders and poor acceptance in Washington and London. It rises through periods of deep uncertainty, notably the challenge of Pauline Hanson, but then ascends through a series of opportunities taken to arrive at inclusion in the East Asian summit, unprecedented intimacy with Washington and a renewed partnership with London. Howard, dismissed by his legions of critics as the ultimate provincial, the small-town solicitor, the Poujadist pretender, arrives in the end as a formidable figure abroad and a prime minister at home whose tenure is identified with national security as much as with good economic indicators—the two great buttresses of the entire Howard edifice.

How did it happen? Why did it happen? What does it mean? To understand the Howard ascendancy in foreign policy, it is necessary to understand Howard the politician and then to look at the interaction of a series of completely unpredictable events with his core beliefs as Prime Minister. It is a story that is both more complex and simpler than most commentators allow. It is more complex because Howard has shown increasing dexterity, sophistication and shrewdness in his responses. And simpler because, with all that governmental virtuosity, Howard has not strayed much from the core beliefs he has been developing all his adult political life.

In foreign policy Howard's decade has been dominated by four seminal events: the East Asian economic crisis in 1997, the rise and demise of Pauline Hanson in the late 1990s, Australian intervention in East Timor and the 11 September 2001 terror attacks on the United States. In response to each of these, Howard has both developed and refined his foreign policy approach. He has done so in a way that has transformed Australian foreign policy, rebuilt bridges to Asia, intensified our relationship with the United States and, critically, won broad public support.

Howard has been animated by a series of ideas that he has refined and developed in office but which in essence have retained the core of their integrity throughout his prime ministership. He believes that his predecessor, Paul Keating, over-emphasised the new turn towards Asia, which frightened and alienated the public and wrongly downgraded our traditional ties with the United States and Britain. In Howard's view, the US alliance remains as vital to Australia as ever, and the United States generally will grow more important to Australia, and to Asia, in coming decades. He believes foreign policy must generally run in accord with public opinion and the national character and that no element of the national identity should be amended to satisfy foreign policy impera- tives. Howard prefers bilateralism to multilateralism and believes that effective working relations with Asian nations are best developed prag- matically around issues of common concern rather than symbolically around grand gestures and sweeping rhetoric. Good relations in Asia are enhanced, not complicated, by a close Canberra–Washington connec- tion. Finally, Howard also believes that Australia's respect internationally is generated not by windy rhetoric or politically correct obeisance to United Nations pieties but by the strength of the Australian economy, the social cohesion and tolerance of Australian society and the perform- ance of the Australian Defence Force.

These beliefs, in all their particulars and in their cumulative generality, are more or less the exact opposite of the beliefs of the general foreign policy academic and commentator class in Australia, but they seem well accepted by the public. As a result, foreign policy academics and commentators have seldom had less influence on, or found themselves less able to analyse or explain, Australian foreign policy.

Within the grid of Howard's beliefs and the defining events that have allowed him to express them in national policy, several international themes have pervaded his decade: the emergence and travails of the Bush administration, the political evolution of Indonesia, the economic rise of China and latterly India, the strategic emergence of Japan, and the 'war on terror'—prosecuted in both the Middle East and South-East Asia. A lesser theme has been the emergence of new Asian regional structures.

There is no doubt that as a foreign policy prime minister, Howard started poorly after his election in 1996. This is not because he had an unsophisticated or provincial mind, or indeed even a lack of interest in foreign policy. He had, after all, been federal treasurer for nearly eight years in the late 1970s and early 80s, with all the international exposure that brings. He had been a part of all the big foreign policy decisions of the cabinet of Malcolm Fraser's government. He had a mind well schooled in the power realities of the Cold War and had long been interested in defence policy and Australian military history. To this day he can point out subtle differences between different biographies of the great Australian general from World War I, Sir John Monash.

Howard started as Prime Minister in 1996 with several distinct disadvantages in foreign policy, not the least of which was that his party had been out of office for 13 years. He lacked first-hand knowledge of the contemporary crop of international leaders with whom he would deal. He deliberately eschewed the ways of his predecessor. Keating's obsession with the 'big picture' and his love of grand symbolism and soaring rhetoric were anathema to Howard, who felt such behaviour was electoral poison. In his first months, therefore, Howard lacked a positive agenda in the region and his first visits to Asia, especially to Indonesia, were marked by a certain clumsiness. He repeatedly told Indonesians how different their society was from Australia, a statement that was true, but unbalanced by any positive message.

The rise of Pauline Hanson exacerbated every damaging dynamic at work in Australian politics. Howard's initial response to Hanson was clumsy and ineffective. He recognised that she represented some serious sentiment in parts of rural and regional Australia—not so much anti-Asian sentiment as anti-elite, and to some extent anti-globalisation at a time of rural economic distress. Howard adopted a softly-softly approach to Hanson, defending her right to raise issues while not embracing her views. This dismayed many Australians, who were looking for forthright rejection of the racism inherent in her appeal. It also played very badly in South-East Asia. Every nation is to some extent a prisoner of its stereotypes and the chief stereotype concerning Australia in South-East Asia is a memory of the White Australia policy. Hansonism, while it lasted, raised a political cost to any Australian politician of taking any positive initiative towards South-East Asia.

Eventually Howard recognised Hansonism as a threat not only to Australia's interests in Asia but to the Coalition's electoral interests and he committed the Liberal Party to placing One Nation candidates last in how-to-vote cards in all elections. This virtually guaranteed the electoral eclipse of One Nation, which now has not a single representative in the national parliament. Nonetheless, while it lasted, One Nation did great damage to Australia in Asia.

However, Howard never held the view that Australia should or could walk away from Asia. But he was looking for new terms on which to make the engagement. Oddly, unpredictably, the East Asian economic crisis of 1997 gave him that chance. It was initially a currency crisis, which spread first from Thailand throughout South-East Asia and then into South Korea. There were International Monetary Fund bail-out plans for each of Thailand, Indonesia and South Korea. Japan and Australia were the only nations to contribute to all three IMF plans. In each case Australia contributed $1 billion. This was money used as a currency guarantee and Australia ultimately recovered its funds, as expected. Nonetheless it was a powerful sign of commitment. Just as many in the region were coming to the view that Canberra, under the influence of Hanson, was walking away from Asia—a view reinforced by listening to the bitter denunciations of Howard by Keating and his former ministers—Canberra took a great big step back into the middle of the region's affairs.

The crisis also changed the dynamics of the relationship between Australia and South-East Asia. Until the crisis the South-East Asian economies had been among the fastest growing in the world, out-paced only by China. Their collapse brought an end to the illusion of straight-line projections of compound high-rate economic growth.

The South-East Asian economies had built up dangerous imbalances but their underlying real economies were sound and they recovered in time. Nonetheless, things had changed. Australia no longer looked the laggard. Now its stability—the strength of its economic institutions—was prized. Australia was seen no longer as a slow-growth, small and old economy but as a regional strongman that weathered the regional crisis and went on to post impressive growth rates of its own. This changed the way South-East Asians, and others, looked at Australia and it also changed the way Australians looked at themselves. While these changes suited Howard, it would be wrong to suggest that he experienced any schadenfreude at East Asia's discomfort. He has always recognised that a stable South-East Asia is in Australia's interests.

Similarly, and this is far too little remarked, the Asian economic crisis led to sharp differences between Washington and Canberra over regional policy. Howard and his Foreign Minister, Alexander Downer, felt that Washington paid too little heed to the danger of instability in Indonesia in particular. In truth the idea that Canberra is Washington's poodle is wildly exaggerated for every period of Australian history. Canberra is always pushing its own interests. The closeness of the alliance with the United States allows it to influence US Asian policy. Canberra and Washington, although joined in common aims, naturally saw the South-East Asian crisis differently.

East Timor proved to be Howard's biggest challenge in his early years. The highly eccentric and unpredictable B J Habibie had succeeded Suharto as president of Indonesia. East Timor was a roiling issue of controversy in Australian politics. Howard wrote a letter to Habibie, urging him to offer much greater autonomy to East Timor and ultimately to hold a referendum on independence. It is often forgotten that at this stage the public and private purpose of Australian diplomacy was for East Timor to remain a part of Indonesia. Howard's diplomacy was directed at finding a way for this to happen that would be internationally acceptable.

The underlying strategic purpose of Howard's initiatives was to remove the thorn of East Timor from the Australia–Indonesia relationship. Ever since the Indonesian invasion of East Timor in 1975 and the deaths of six journalists working for Australian news organisations, this had been a matter of contention between the two neighbours. The Australian Government's analysis was that if East Timor could be removed from the bilateral equation, the quality of the relationship could be vastly improved. Eventually, that is exactly what happened, but it did not look possible at first.

In 1998 the East Timorese voted overwhelmingly for immediate independence. Pro-Jakarta militias undertook savage killings and destruction of East Timor's scanty infrastructure. Under huge public pressure, the Howard Government was forced to respond. It quickly organised a United Nations mandate and led a peacekeeping force, the International Force in East Timor or Interfet. Much has been made of the US refusal to commit ground troops to serve in Interfet. In fact, while the administration of Bill Clinton was undoubtedly slow to respond, it did three things that were critical and without which the Interfet mission could not have succeeded. The US provided crucial logistic support that Australia could not supply itself; it provided navy and marine backup on ships stationed off East Timor, which acted as a critical deterrent to any Indonesian military that might have been tempted to actively oppose Interfet; and it put massive diplomatic pressure on Indonesia to accept Interfet in principle. Far from illustrating the limitations of the US alliance, as is often said, the episode illustrates exactly the opposite: that the US alliance is indispensable to most things Australia wants to achieve, even in its nearest region.

Australian forces were seriously ill-equipped for the mission in East Timor because of the pernicious effect of the 'Defence of Australia' doctrine, which held that the Australian Defence Force should be configured purely to repel an attempted invasion or attack on Australian soil, which would inevitably come through the 'sea–air gap' to our north. This short-sighted and foolish doctrine led to the monstrous neglect of the army, which in 1998 had too few soldiers even for so modest a commitment as East Timor. The troops who were available were woefully ill equipped. Consequently the East Timor campaign marked the beginning of the Howard Government's move away from the anachronistic defence doctrines of its predecessors and towards a more realistic doctrine that acknowledges the importance of coalition operations and the ability to project force, including infantry force, over distance.

In spite of the problems, the Australian troops, led by General Peter Cosgrove, performed magnificently in East Timor. Cosgrove himself became a national folk hero. Howard basked in Cosgrove's glory. But, initially at least, the outcomes were not what Howard had wanted. Australian policy had been to keep East Timor part of Indonesia and improve relations between Canberra and Jakarta. Instead we got an independent East Timor and a poisonous relationship with Indonesia. Once again Howard's adaptability and shrewdness as a politician came into play. He quickly capitalised on the overwhelmingly positive domestic and international sentiment towards East Timor and claimed Australia's military role there as a reflection of our national character, helping the weak against the strong.

At the same time he began the long task of repairing the relationship with Indonesia. Jakarta's hostility to Canberra over East Timor, though intense for a time, was remarkably short-lived. Successive Indonesian presidents, through all their travails, and not without many false steps, came to the view that Australia could be a useful friend. The tragic terrorist bombings in Bali in 2002, which killed 202 people, 88 of them Australians, brought the two countries much closer together. By 2002 Howard and Downer were experienced regional politicians. They responded with grace, dignity and compassion to the Bali bombings, mourning not only the Australians killed but also the terrible blow to the Balinese. The Indonesians showed maturity and common sense in welcoming the assistance of the Australian Federal Police in the investigations, which were successful in tracking down the perpetrators.

From the point of view of foreign policy, this had almost infinite benefits for the Howard Government. It brought forth a process of the most sustained and transparent trials of terrorists in any Muslim nation, which had a bigger impact in educating Indonesians about the terrorist threat than anything else could have done. It pioneered a partnership between the Australian Federal Police and the Indonesians that was to flourish. And it produced a special relationship with Susilo Bambang Yudhoyono, then the co-ordinating minister for security and later Indonesia's most pro-Australian president ever.

Tragedy would again bring the two nations closer together with the tsunami that struck on Boxing Day 2004, bringing terrible devastation and loss of life to the province of Aceh. Howard's response was swift, with a commitment of immediate assistance followed within 10 days by an aid and rebuilding package of $1 billion. Howard's lead role in the tsunami relief effort was to boost his stocks throughout the region, but nowhere more so than in Indonesia. When Howard visited Jakarta on 6 January 2005 he was thanked profusely by an emotional Dr Yudhoyono.

It would be rash to predict that there are no troubles ahead, but Howard can now look at the Indonesian relationship as an unmitigated success, an astounding turnaround from 1996, or even 1998. Howard has been to Indonesia more often than any previous prime minister. Downer has been there more often than he has to any other country. The fact that so much of the public business of the relationship has been combating terrorism means that there is no difficulty selling it to the Australian public.

The so-called 'war on terror' has also been central to Howard's other great international success: the relationship with the Bush administration. Howard came into office wanting to intensify the United States–Australia partnership. As the East Timor episode shows, on issues of substance Howard could get results from the Clinton administration. However, he never enjoyed good personal rapport with Clinton. When Howard first visited the United States as Prime Minister, Clinton gave him barely 20 minutes in their main meeting, did not hold the customary joint press conference or even appear with Howard in a standard rose-garden photo-opportunity. Clinton had been engaged by Keating on APEC issues and felt no affinity for Howard.

Howard and Downer believed that George W Bush would offer something much better for them, and for Australia. They both desperately wanted Bush to beat Al Gore in 2000. Howard had spoken to Bush on the phone before the election and Downer had travelled to Texas to meet him. Many of Bush's cabinet officials and senior staff had good Australian connections. Nonetheless it was the terror attacks of 9/11 that drove Howard and Bush together. Howard was in Washington when the attacks occurred and within a few days had invoked the ANZUS Treaty to offer assistance to the United States.

While Howard committed Australian troops to the military operation to topple the Taliban Government in Afghanistan, from where al-Qa'ida leader Osama bin Laden had operated, it must be said that the most crucial decision Howard made was to commit Australian troops to the military operation to dislodge Saddam Hussein from Iraq. This was the seminal event that bonded Bush and Howard forever. Only Britain and Australia joined the United States in sending significant combat troops—a tiny number of Poles also participated. This led to an exceptionally close three-way relationship between Bush, British Prime Minister Tony Blair and Howard.

Again, in foreign policy terms, while Howard would have preferred a broader coalition, this allowed him to intensify the US relationship exactly as he wanted. Howard believed the cause of toppling Saddam was justified. Virtually every intelligence agency in the world believed Saddam had weapons of mass destruction—and that was the clear advice Howard was receiving. He also believed it was crucial that the United States not be left alone to do the hardest work in providing international security.

But he also believed that Australian participation would pay dividends in terms of the United States–Australia relationship. He wanted this for strategic purposes, and he got a more intimate military and intelligence relationship. He wanted it for economic purposes, and he got a free trade agreement that was of immense value to Australia and a defensive position should the United States ever veer towards protectionism. Finally Howard wanted the relationship for prestige to boost his stocks with his own electorate and the region.

Howard got these, too, handsomely winning the first post-Iraq election with an increased majority against Labor's unstable leader Mark Latham who had engaged in wild anti-Bush rhetoric before keeping an almost total silence on the subject of Iraq during the 2004 election campaign. Howard also believes closeness to Washington helps Australia in Asia, because influence in the most powerful capital in the world is another card Canberra can bring to any table in Asia.

In taking this view Howard was actually being very East Asian. Alliance management was the key consideration for all of the US's friends in East Asia. While none of them committed troops to the combat phase in Iraq, US allies such as South Korea, Japan, Thailand and The Philippines offered political support and then committed troops to the reconstruction phase. The most important East Asian leader, Japan's Junichiro Koizumi, was the furthest in front in support of Bush. Thus Howard was ahead of, but in synch with, majority East Asian government opinion on Iraq. It was a perfect fusion of his US and Asian priorities. Indeed the Japanese troops now in Iraq are protected by Australians—another seamless example of US and Asian relationships working together.

The one area where this has not always been the case has been with China. In his early days in office Howard had some rough patches with China, which conducted a series of live missile firings into Taiwanese waters to intimidate Taiwan's voters in a presidential election. Bill Clinton responded by sending a US aircraft carrier battle group to deter China from military adventurism. Rightly, the Howard Government backed the US move. The Chinese were furious and for a time ran a press campaign against Australia. The Chinese decided to take offence over a series of other quite minor incidents, such as Howard receiving Tibet's Dalai Lama after the Chinese had told him not to. The incidents reflected Beijing's clumsiness in handling public opinion in a democracy rather than inexperience on Howard's part but they were interpreted to Howard's disfavour in Australia.

Howard and his government worked out a series of neat and, up to the time of writing, effective formulas for dealing with China. Howard stuck rigidly to his government's formula on Taiwan, which is that Australia has a one-China policy but would oppose the use of force to resolve the issue, thus satisfying both the Americans and the Chinese. It means Australia opposes any formal independence for Taiwan but also opposes any thought on China's part of using force.

Similarly Howard demonstrated to the Chinese that he would make a serious effort to establish good relations. There was no question of ever diminishing the US alliance to accommodate Beijing. By taking this completely off the table Howard has removed one point of potential Chinese bullying of Australia. Similarly, while Howard will naturally not speculate about a hypothetical conflict between China and the United States, there is no doubt that Howard would place the US alliance above the relationship with China. If China were ever the aggressor against Taiwan and the United States took action to defend Taiwan, there is little doubt that Australia would back the United States.

Downer, in a rare gaffe, said in Beijing in 2004 that the ANZUS Treaty would not necessarily apply to a conflict over Taiwan. Downer insists that he was doing nothing more than state in a different way that he would not speculate about a hypothetical conflict. But Howard issued a correction, making it clear that Australia's alliance with the United States was paramount. There are naturally differences between Canberra and Washington over China but these are easy to exaggerate. Everything Howard has ever said about China could easily have been said by the United States State Department.

Howard gives the Chinese as much face as possible—for example, inviting Chinese President Hu Jintao to address the Australian parliament. At the same time he accepts straightforwardly that there are differences between Australia and China over issues such as human rights but says that the two nations should concentrate on the things they agree on, rather than those they disagree on.

Beijing, the most unsentimental capital in the world, wants Australia as a trade partner because it needs secure energy supplies. Thus Howard has been able to manage a booming resources trade with China. Similarly Howard has forged an intense relationship with Japan's Koizumi. Howard's comments on Japan are often under-reported because of the obsession of many foreign policy commentators with China. Howard has repeatedly and explicitly supported Japan's much more assertive foreign and military policy, a policy to which Beijing strongly objects. Also he has elevated to foreign minister level the trilateral security dialogue between the three great Pacific democracies: the United States, Japan and Australia.

As the years have gone by, Howard has become more and more personally involved in foreign policy. National security has been a great poll strength for him. He has identified closely with every Australian troop deployment and with the Australian military more generally. He has consciously brought the military, the army especially, back to the heart of Australian national life. Even when deployments have been controversial, such as in Iraq, the public has maintained its strong support for the troops and this has been a political plus for Howard. He has increasingly personalised control of the 'war on terror', especially through the National Security Committee of cabinet and its supporting bureaucratic structures.

It is an open question how much all of this will survive Howard. It is difficult to imagine a future Australian prime minister as close to a US president as Howard is to Bush. But Howard has forged a strong synthesis of the US and Asian dynamics of Australian foreign policy. The United Nations is not a significant factor in Australian foreign policy. The final proof of Howard's effectiveness in Asia is his inclusion in the East Asia summit. Howard believes he gives expression to Australian interests and values. Much of his strength flows from the length of his incumbency. His journey as Prime Minister, like that of his nation, is absolutely remarkable.

16

AT WAR WITH TERROR

Patrick Walters

IN LATE 2005 John Howard compared the current global terrorist threat to the apprehension felt by an older generation of Australians at the height of the Cold War in the 1950s and 60s. 'This is the modern equivalent of that period that we lived through with the threat of nuclear annihilation,' he said. 'It's something that I factor in to our existence. And what I encourage my fellow Australians to do is to live their lives.'[1]

It is not just the fear of another bomb blast in Bali or a home-grown attack at Bondi. Inside the minds of the Prime Minister's security advisers in Canberra lurks a deeper fear: the threat of a nuclear detonation by a terrorist group in a major city. Howard argues that Australians must accept that they are now living in a new era. He and his senior ministers believe that Islamist terrorism has thrown up a fundamental new challenge to liberal Western societies. The new age of terror has already dictated drastic changes to the law and the expenditure of billions of dollars to pay for additional security measures.

It is impossible to understand Howard's approach to terrorism without an appreciation of the dramatic personal impact the events of 11 September 2001 had on the Prime Minister. The day before the cataclysm, Howard, who happened to be on an official visit to Washington DC, met US President George W Bush for the first time. The auspicious encounter marked the 50th anniversary of the ANZUS alliance, Australia's most important security treaty. The two leaders spent three hours together that day and forged a close rapport.

When the White House discussion turned to global security, Bush and Howard concentrated on ballistic missile proliferation and weapons of mass destruction as well as the challenges posed by rogue states such as North Korea. The emerging threat posed by Islamist terrorism, including Osama bin Laden's al-Qa'ida and Abu Bakar Bashir's Jemaah Islamiah, did not rate a mention.

The next day everything changed when Islamist terrorists turned four passenger jets into missiles to attack New York and Washington. That afternoon a shocked and emotional Howard told journalists at the Australian embassy how keenly he felt for the American people in the wake of the traumatic attacks. 'We will stand by them. We will help them. We will support actions they take to properly retaliate in relation to these acts of bastardry against their citizens and against what they stand for. They are an open, free society and they have this outrageous act of war on them.'[2]

Within days the US war machine began intensive planning for retaliatory strikes. Afghanistan became the prime target, while privately Bush mused about Iraq and Saddam Hussein. In Canberra on 14 September, Howard invoked the ANZUS treaty for the first time, obliging Australia to 'act to meet the common danger' with its US ally—in this case international terrorism. Howard's statement on ANZUS anticipated a wider Australian involvement in future military operations alongside the United States. 'The Australian Government will be in close consultation with the US administration in the period ahead to consider what actions Australia might take in support of the US response to these attacks,' the Prime Minister said.

Since 2001 the challenge posed by Islamist terrorism has generated major changes in Australia's national security landscape. The Government may have failed to anticipate the scope and nature of the emerging terrorist threat but Howard, a consummate pragmatist, has deftly managed the national security debate to his political advantage. This in turn has steadily reinforced his prime ministerial authority.

For John Howard the new global challenge has reinforced the primacy of the US alliance as the bedrock of Australia's national security. The terrorism challenge has led Howard to agree to far-flung military deployments in coalition with US forces and bound the two defence forces even closer together in their operating procedures and choice of major equipment. It has also changed the tenor of Australia's security relations with Indonesia and South-East Asia as well as the South Pacific. Paradoxically Islamist terrorism has brought us closer to Indonesia—the world's largest Muslim country. Finally it has had significant implications for Australia's domestic security environment. Combating terrorism has re-ordered the priorities of our defence force, police and intelligence agencies, and generated sweeping changes in counter-terrorism laws. In the domestic political arena the immediate impact of September 11 regained political momentum for the Coalition and exercised a decisive influence on the 2001 federal election. Ever since then Howard has enjoyed a consistent lead over Labor in polls measuring community attitudes to the Government's handling of national security issues.

Howard's friendship with Bush has seen the emergence of arguably the closest ever high-level defence links between Canberra and Washington. This liaison has directly influenced defence decision-making, including intelligence sharing and purchases of major equipment such as the army's new Abrams tanks.

Within days of September 11, Howard announced plans to double the counterterrorist capability of the special forces and bolster the Holsworthy-based Incident Response Regiment designed to handle chemical, biological and radiological attacks. He signalled that the Australian Defence Force could soon become involved in counterterrorist operations in Afghanistan, the home base of al-Qa'ida. He also announced a raft of domestic counterterrorist measures, including plans to give ASIO wide-ranging questioning and detention powers, as well as new criminal offences dealing with terrorism, including financing of terrorist groups. Air marshals would also be placed randomly on domestic and international flights.

Asked in October 2001 whether Australia could become a terrorist target, Howard responded with language that has remained remarkably consistent ever since: 'I want to say to the Australian people ... we are not as vulnerable as other countries. We should not be alarmed but nor should we be complacent. Nor should we lazily assume it can't happen here.'[3]

Australia's initial military contribution to the counterterrorism response involved sending a taskforce to the Afghanistan theatre, including a 200-strong special forces team that tackled remnants of Taliban and al-Qa'ida forces until its withdrawal in late 2002. The war in Afghanistan led to the capture of two Australians—David Hicks and

Mamdouh Habib—both of whom were later incarcerated in the US military prison at Guantanamo Bay, Cuba. While Habib eventually returned to Australia, Hicks has been charged by a US military commission and remains in prison awaiting trial.

But by the middle of 2002 Afghanistan had become a sideshow. Australian military planners were already deeply engaged in preparing for a much bigger event: war in Iraq.

* * *

We do not know exactly when Howard determined that Australian forces should join a US-led invasion of Iraq but there is no doubt that support for the US alliance weighed heaviest in the Prime Minister's decision to commit to war. The publicly advanced justification for the war—the threat posed by Saddam Hussein's alleged arsenal of weapons of mass destruction—proved to be groundless and the intelligence on Iraq turned out to be plain wrong. Howard and his ministers trusted the assessments provided by Australia's intelligence agencies, which in turn relied heavily on their US and British counterparts for evidence of Iraq's weapons programs.

In early 2003 Australia sent a 2000-strong joint task group to the Iraq theatre, with the SAS again the military spearhead. Australia's participation in the US-led war without United Nations sanction deeply divided the electorate. Ironically, Howard, unlike George W Bush and British Prime Minister Tony Blair, has got through the difficult business with his personal approval rating virtually undiminished. Howard has also been extraordinarily fortunate. Australia's extremely modest military contributions to the 'war on terror' in Afghanistan and Iraq have been carefully orchestrated by the Government. By the end of 2005 they had resulted in but a single operational fatality—SAS Sergeant Andrew Russell killed in Afghanistan in 2002. By contrast, US and British forces in Iraq have suffered a steady stream of casualties ever since the war began in March 2003, with the United States alone suffering more than 2000 dead and 12,000 wounded.

In a pre-war decision that superbly anticipated the post-war chaos in Iraq, Howard told Bush that Australian special forces would stay in the country only for the 'sharp-end' or combat phase of the war. The fact that not a single Australian has been killed on combat operations in Iraq is a tribute not just to the professionalism of the defence force but to their carefully circumscribed roles, which have rarely taken our troops into combat zones.

By late 2005, as the insurgency continued to take a heavy toll of both Iraqis and US forces, two-thirds of Australians thought it was not worth going to war in Iraq (compared with 45 per cent in February 2004).[4] Iraq has become the central front in the war against Islamist terror but Australian's military involvement has not involved the hard slog endured by US and British ground forces in central Iraq. A 450-strong taskforce remains in the relatively peaceful southern province of al-Muthanna, helping guard Japanese troops, while about 200 security guards and headquarters staff are based in Baghdad. With the al-Muthanna group due to be withdrawn in mid-2006 John Howard and his senior ministers face new demands from Washington for a fresh ground commitment to Iraq. This will come on top of the defence force's current mission to Afghanistan, which includes a 300-strong special forces team and possibly a 250-strong provincial reconstruction team within months.

Closer to home the October 2002 Bali attacks killed 88 Australians and exposed a more damaging analytical failure by Australian intelligence agencies, including ASIO, ASIS and the Office of National Assessments (ONA). Our best intelligence efforts failed to provide an early alert of Jemaah Islamiah's plans to attack bars frequented by Westerners in Bali.

'We now understand, after the events in Bali and those of 11 September 2001, that we are living in a world where unexpected and devastating terrorist attacks on free and open societies can occur in ways that we never before imagined possible,' Howard told parliament on 4 February 2003.

The shock of Bali prompted the Government to redouble its efforts to deepen counterterrorism co-operation with South-East Asian neighbours. Paradoxically the Bali outrage paved the way for a remarkable new era of bilateral co-operation between the Indonesian and Australian police, with Australian police hunting for terror suspects with their Indonesian counterparts in the kampungs of Java. Australian signals intelligence provided by the Defence Signals Directorate (DSD) also proved instrumental in the arrests of the Bali bombers.

Fighting the terrorism scourge since Bali has spawned a whole new web of police, defence intelligence and surveillance links with South-East Asian nations, including The Philippines, where Jemaah Islamiah operatives continue to find safe haven. It has also been the means by which Canberra and Jakarta have re-established close official ties in the aftermath of the Australian-led 1999 intervention in East Timor, which threatened a severe rupture in the bilateral relationship. It was the Bali bombings that first brought John Howard and Susilo Bambang Yudhoyono together. Since then Yudhoyono has become Indonesia's first democratically elected president and the pair have worked cooperatively on a range of issues, including the $1 billion Australian-funded tsunami relief fund. Foreign Minister Alexander Downer's setting up of a regular inter-faith dialogue involving regional religious leaders has been enthusiastically endorsed by Jakarta.

Howard, more than any of his predecessors, has taken an extraordinarily close interest in defence and national security. After almost 10 years in office the Prime Minister has become a de facto national security supremo. Cabinet's powerful national security committee is chaired by the Prime Minister. As well as its ministerial representation—including the Treasurer, Attorney-General and Defence and Foreign Affairs ministers—senior bureaucrats also attend. They comprise the heads of Defence, Foreign Affairs and Prime Minister and Cabinet together with the chiefs of ASIO, ASIS, ONA and the Australian Federal Police. The National Security Committee in tandem with the cabinet policy unit located in Howard's office has enabled the Prime Minister to exert tight control over the bureaucratic machinery responsible for security policy. The making of defence and national security policy is no longer the preserve of the departments of Defence and Foreign Affairs. National security issues have become a 'whole-of-government' priority, reinforcing the influence of the Department of Prime Minister and Cabinet in key decision-making.

Howard has created a national security division in PM&C staffed by security experts and now led by former special forces chief Major General Duncan Lewis. The federal government has spent more than $5 billion in the past four years countering terrorism. Since 2001 Howard has doubled the budgets of Australia's principal intelligence agencies—ASIO, ASIS and DSD as well as the federal police. For all of these agencies counterterrorism has become the top priority.

The introduction of tough new counterterrorism laws began soon after September 11. In 2002 six separate terrorism bills were introduced into the federal parliament, creating a range of new terrorism offences under the criminal code. Five were passed into law within months, while the bill giving ASIO special questioning and detention powers finally was given royal assent in July 2003. The federal government also established, in 2002, the National Counter-Terrorism Committee chaired by the Department of Prime Minister and Cabinet to co-ordinate state and federal counterterrorism responses.

The arrest and subsequent deportation of Frenchman Willie Brigitte in 2003, underlined ASIO's assessment that Australia remained at risk of a terrorist attack. According to ASIO, Brigitte was an al-Qa'ida operative determined to create a terrorist cell in Sydney with the objective of mounting an attack. Australia has yet to experience a major terrorist attack on home territory. A succession of bombings, including the September 2004 attack on the Australian Embassy in Jakarta, the July 7 London bombings, and the second Bali bombings of October 2005, reinforced for Australians the global reality of Islamist terror. There has been at least one aborted, disrupted or actual attack in Australia or against Australian interests abroad every year since 2000.

But it was the 7 July bombings in London and the threat of 'home-grown' terrorism that prompted Howard to introduce the Government's most far-reaching set of counterterrorism measures in September 2005. At a special Council of Australian Government (COAG) meeting on 27 September 2005 he won the unanimous backing of state and territory leaders for the far-reaching changes. 'In other circumstances I would never have sought these additional powers,' Howard conceded immediately after the COAG meeting. 'But we do live in very dangerous and different and threatening circumstances and a strong and comprehensive response is needed.'

Police forces have now been given tough new powers of preventive detention of terrorism suspects for up to 14 days and control orders in circumstances where a person is deemed a security risk to the community. They have also been given 'stop, question and search' powers where there are reasonable grounds for assuming that a person might be about to commit a terrorist act. New sedition laws targeting persons inciting violence against the community and strengthened offences dealing with the financing of terrorism have also been passed by federal parliament.

Leading up to all of these changes, Howard had been deeply influenced by events half a world away. Visiting London two weeks after the bombings had a telling effect on him. At a press conference held after COAG, he said:

> I think the chilling reality that home-grown terrorists exist—a
> lot of Australians, I guess all of us, found that a bit hard to
> accept. We tended, because of the experience of September
> 11 to see a possible terrorist threat being executed by people

flying into the country covertly and attacking us in a devastating way and then trying to escape ... And the reality is that we are worried there are people in our community who might do just this.[5]

Within days of special amendments to counterterrorism legislation being passed by parliament, ASIO and state and federal police mounted their biggest ever counterterrorism operation in Australia, swooping to detain 17 suspected terrorists in Sydney and Melbourne in early November. Government counterterrorism policy has also ensured that the defence force continues to play a highly visible role. The defence budget, particularly the new special operations command created in 2002, has received a significant boost. In December 2005 Howard and Defence Minister Robert Hill released the latest defence update paper, which examined changes to Australia's security environment. The document concluded that 'for the foreseeable future' it remained unlikely that Australia would face conventional military threats. Instead it nominated terrorism as Australia's number one security challenge. 'Defeating the threat of terrorism, countering the proliferation of WMD and supporting regional states in difficulty remain of the highest priority,' the update concluded.[6]

Launching the update at Sydney's Victoria Barracks, Howard announced a billion-dollar plan to upgrade and enlarge the army. The army must have the capability to play a role not just in the defence of Australia and its immediate neighbourhood but in continuing coalition operations such as Iraq and Afghanistan. 'I have to say on behalf of the Government that we will need to commit ever-increasing amounts to defence in the years ahead,' the Prime Minister warned. 'That [increased spending] remains a very strong commitment and belief of the Government,'[7] he said.

Howard has been a consistent supporter of higher defence spending ever since he assumed the prime ministership and the global terrorism challenge has simply reinforced his view of the need to invest more in the defence force. After years of zero real increases in the defence budget, the Government's 2000 defence white paper outlined a long-term plan to lift spending by $32 billion, or 3 per cent a year in real terms, over the decade to 2010. It is a commitment that the Government has so far honoured and is expected to continue to meet up to and beyond 2010 in the face of rapidly rising real increases in capital equipment as well as personnel.

The 2000 white paper remains the only substantial statement of defence policy produced by the Howard Government. Notwithstanding the new military demands posed by the global struggle against terrorism, it remains the key intellectual foundation of the Government's defence policy. The white paper identified three priority tasks for the defence force: the defence of Australia, contributing to the security of the immediate neighbourhood, and supporting Australia's wider interests and objectives 'by being able to contribute effectively to international coalitions of forces to meet crises beyond our immediate neighbourhood'.[8]

It is the third of these priority tasks—contributing to coalition operations—that has been the focus of government defence policy in a new era of unconventional, asymmetric conflict. Howard's decisions to send troops to Iraq and Afghanistan in support of US-led coalition forces ensured that the army has become the prime focus of political attention.

The global assault on terrorism has led the Government to demand far more of our land forces—demands that were anticipated by the 2000 white paper but will take the best part of a decade to achieve. 'The emphasis will be on a professional, well-trained, well-equipped force that is available for operations at short notice, and one that can be sustained on deployment over extended periods,' the white paper concluded presciently. 'This type of force will provide the flexibility to deal with operations other than conventional war and contribute to coalition operations.'

The Government has promised major new investment in combat forces, logistics, and transport for the land forces. For the army this means being able to sustain a brigade-strength force (3000) on operations for extended periods, and at the same time maintain at least a battalion-sized battle group (750 to 800) available for deployment elsewhere. The latest defence update says the defence force must now be prepared to operate in more complex and ambiguous environments where 'adversaries, including non-state adversaries, have increasingly lethal capabilities'.

Howard accepts that military force alone will not defeat Islamist terrorism. But he is determined that the defence force will become more versatile and better equipped for a broader range of operations than defence planners could have conceived only a decade ago. Since 2001 he has consistently argued that Australia cannot remain immune from a possible terrorist attack. While billions of dollars have been spent upgrading security across Australia, the Government has been slow to devise a comprehensive strategy for engaging the country's 400,000-strong Muslim population.

As prime minister, Howard has changed the dynamics of national security policy-making in Australia. As national security supremo, he has more effectively mobilised the resources of federal and state governments to counter terrorism. He utterly rejects the charge that he has manipulated and exploited the threat for political purposes.

Howard argues that the new reality facing Australia dictates a need for continued vigilance. According to the Prime Minister, the fight against terrorism around the world and 'particularly here in Australia, will be long and hard'. It is an assertion that Howard's political opponents are not prepared to challenge.

17

TEAM AMERICA

Roy Eccleston

At 8.46 a.m. on 11 September 2001, as John Howard prepared for a press conference at the Willard hotel in Washington, 19 men on four planes in the flawless autumn sky above prepared to change the world. At that moment, 330 kilometres to the northeast, American Airlines flight 11 slammed high into the north tower of New York's World Trade Centre, beginning a cascading nightmare of collapsing skyscrapers, a blazing Pentagon, a new terror named al-Qa'ida, and a US roused from its post-Cold War delusion that the world was no longer threatening.

Howard, in the US capital for his first meeting with President George W Bush, felt the full shock of the attack as he witnessed first-hand the confusion and trauma. Across the Potomac River, clearly visible from his hotel, smoke soon billowed from the Pentagon. It blackened the bright-blue sky; and it cast the suddenly long shadow of terrorism over the United States and its allies.

For Australia the terrorist strike brought its own changes: the beginning of a new sense of insecurity—later rammed home by the Bali bombings—and an ever-tighter embrace with the United States on foreign and defence policy. The 1951 ANZUS treaty has never been more closely nurtured by Canberra, and the US has never been more anxious for Australia's support.

Before Howard's first meeting with Bush that week, few Americans had heard of the Australian Prime Minister, although he had been in the job for more than five years. *The Los Angeles Times*, in an editorial, called him John Hunt.[1] But Howard's ambition was to be recognised elsewhere: in the White House, by the President of a country he saw as Australia's ultimate security. That desire was dramatically and emotionally reinforced by what he saw in Washington that day.

Eighteen months after the attacks, when Bush invited Howard to his ranch in Crawford, Texas, it was clear that Howard had succeeded. Bush noted how they had stood together on 10 September at Washington's naval yards to commemorate the 50th anniversary of ANZUS. And 'the next day Australia and the United States began writing a new chapter in the history of our alliance,' Bush said, standing by the man he then described as 'a man of steel'. 'Australia came to America's aid in our time of need, and we won't forget that.'[2]

Howard is counting on it. He has made the United States his prime foreign policy focus in defiance of critics who argued it would damage relations with Asia and encourage terrorists to attack Australians. The onetime foreign policy novice and his Foreign Minister, Alexander Downer, have decided that stronger US ties in a volatile world will make Australia safer and a more relevant player in a region increasingly focused on China.

There has really been only one public disagreement between the two leaders, and that came when Bush called Australia the 'sheriff' of the Asian region.[3] Howard quickly rejected the tag. 'I don't see this country as being a sheriff, a deputy sheriff, as having any kind of enforcement role in our region,' he said.[4] But there is no doubt Howard chose the way of devoted junior partner, strengthening Australia's links with the United States, binding it to the US 'war on terror', but also tying himself to the flawed intelligence—and the failure or success—of the war in Iraq. On some issues, like global warming and protection of citizens such as accused terrorist David Hicks, he has been more in tune with Bush than even Britain's Tony Blair.

In early 2006, then, Howard was in lockstep with the polarising US president, backing him with troops in Afghanistan and Iraq and having used that relationship to secure a (less-than-ideal) free trade agreement, signed in 2004. That Howard has become such a favoured US ally with a relatively small military commitment is testament to his political skills, simultaneously playing to Washington and the home audience, whose unhappiness with the troubled campaign in Iraq is tempered by the very low number of Australian casualties—one death in a training accident. It was not as close under Bill Clinton, who was US president when Howard was elected in 1996. Howard's bid to boost the alliance struggled under the Democrat who showed sporadic interest in Asia and too often was mired in domestic issues. Howard did not have a bad relationship with Clinton, who visited Australia in 1996, but it was not a warm one. It cooled markedly in mid-1999 when Howard visited the White House soon after Clinton decided to impose tariffs on Australian lamb imports. The lamb decision, later ruled illegal by the World Trade Organisation, prompted a furious response in Australia at such shoddy treatment for an ally, but it underlined the crucial importance of US domestic politics in presidential decision-making. Howard was also given pretty poor hospitality—no stroll for the cameras, no joint press conference with Clinton.[5]

A few months later, as the situation in East Timor became more and more unstable in the wake of the country's vote for independence, Australians found there was more to be upset with the United States about than lamb. Howard, under public pressure to come to the aid of East Timorese attacked by Indonesian-backed forces, worked to secure international support for a peacekeeping force to restore order. But his calls for the US to help with troops at first won lukewarm support in the Clinton administration. Australia was seeking 500 US troops to back its own pledge of 2000 to lead the force as the situation deteriorated.[6] But as negotiations continued, Howard warned that the 'extent of any ground force commitment from the US at this stage is unclear'.[7] Later, Clinton called and promised a 'tangible' US contribution, to Howard's relief.[8]

The Americans provided a maximum of 235 troops on East Timor in support roles such as communications and transport, and a few hundred more in Australia. In all, with a Marine expeditionary force, the total was around 3000.[9] US officials felt they had been unfairly made to look unresponsive and were privately critical of Australia, claiming it lacked foresight and contingency planning.[10]

Regardless, the messy handling left a bad impression. *The Weekend Australian* editorialised on 11 September 1999 that Australians now knew that they could not take for granted the security relationship with the United States. 'There was a view that our support in the Gulf and in Vietnam might have resonated in Washington,' the newspaper said. 'But the US has made it clear that it will not risk American lives on the ground in East Timor.'

Bill Hayden, the former Labor leader and former foreign minister, claimed that East Timor showed Australians that 'we're pretty much alone', and that 'the only thing that made us important in the past, the US presence under ANZUS, is behind us, a washed out shadow at best'.[11]

Howard did not agree, and when Bush was elected in the controversial 2000 election, the Australian leader set about building relations with a US leader who was ideologically more in tune with Australia's coalition government. The new Republican President showed every sign that he was more likely to see the importance of the Australian alliance. Right from the start, Bush made clear that he would not be doing foreign policy in the same way as Clinton, who he believed had weakened US power by ignoring allies, especially in Asia.

Bush assumed a go-it-alone approach. He rejected the Kyoto global warming pact, announced that he would abandon the anti-ballistic missile treaty with Russia to allow development of a missile shield and put a stop to US support for increased diplomacy with North Korea. But he had also made two vows that were music to Howard's ears. 'We must show American power and purpose in strong support for our Asian friends and allies—for democratic South Korea across the Yellow Sea ... for democratic Japan and the Philippines across the China seas ... for democratic Australia and Thailand,' he said. And he also insisted that a US priority would be to push for free trade in the world.[12]

Howard and Bush were always going to get on personally. Meat-and-potatoes types, proud family men, they saw themselves as plain-spoken and straightforward. Both liked to quote the conservative philosopher Edmund Burke; both were socially conservative but economically adventurous, with free market philosophies that embraced bold tax reform agendas. And circumstance provided Howard with good reason to refocus the United States on the ANZUS treaty, an alliance born out of a reluctant post-World War II realisation by Australia that its future security lay more with the United States than Britain. Howard's initial meeting with Bush on 10 September 2001 commemorated the 50th anniversary of that alliance. He believed that Bush, by inclination (and, as it turned out, circumstance), would be a stronger supporter of ANZUS. The pivotal moment was September 11, after which it took Howard just three days to invoke the mutual security clauses of the ANZUS Treaty for the first time in order to pledge Australian military support in what Bush was calling the 'war of the 21st century'.[13]

Howard had shared the horror with Americans and was deeply moved. But he saw that invoking this treaty, conceived in the Cold War, could bring fresh relevance to both it and the alliance. The enveloping sense of crisis created by the attacks also helped Howard politically, allowing him to build up his image of strong leadership two months ahead of a federal election.[14] Howard believed the attacks showed the vulnerability, even fragility, of nations.[15] And as he said much later, in late 2004: 'America has no more reliable ally than Australia and I'm not ashamed to say that, because in the long run it's only America that could be our ultimate security guarantee.'[16]

Bush wanted Australian support for a missile shield. He got it. In May 2000, asked to name countries that had given support to the idea, the Pentagon could name only two: Australia and Poland.

Australia's initial foreign policy priority with the US under Bush was very different: a free trade deal. Inside the administration it had a keen supporter in US trade representative Robert Zoellick who had proposed a similar plan in 1992. Howard's former foreign policy adviser, Michael Thawley, sent to Washington as ambassador to replace Andrew Peacock in early 2000, began lobbying the Bush administration as soon as it was elected.

The Free Trade Agreement (FTA) idea was opposed by influential Australian foreign policy analysts such as Stuart Harris, a former head of the Department of Foreign Affairs and Trade, and former ambassador to China Ross Garnaut. Both worried that it would send the wrong signal to Asia. This was an important theme of Howard's critics—that in focusing on the US relationship, Australia was neglecting China and the broader Asian relationship.

The FTA was on the menu when Howard met senior Republicans at Thawley's residence in Washington for a pleasant Sunday afternoon barbecue on 9 September 2001. Inside the grand house, a TV showed young Lleyton Hewitt whopping an aged and slow Pete Sampras in the final of the 2001 US Open in New York. Howard dashed to catch glimpses of the tennis between hobnobbing in the garden.

The last time Howard had been in town, to visit Clinton in 1999, the only top cabinet guest was secretary of state Madeleine Albright. This time there was a virtual who's who of the conservative power elite, from the hawkish Vice-President, Dick Cheney, to secretary of state Colin Powell, Defence Secretary Donald Rumsfeld, the soon-to-be chairman of the Joint Chiefs of Staff Dick Myers, and the man who has been called Bush's brain, Karl Rove.

Also in this new administration was a second tier very familiar with Australia, including deputy secretary of state Richard Armitage, deputy defence secretary Paul Wolfowitz, and Zoellick.

Howard certainly missed some schmooze time thanks to his tennis watching. But the to-ing and fro-ing was symbolic of how he has ended up playing the relationship with Bush—a loyal ally but always with an eye on his domestic interests.

When the terrorists attacked, Howard felt that the United States' peril was also Australia's. If al-Qa'ida could strike the United States, and be actively seeking chemical, biological and nuclear weapons, Australia as a Western nation and US ally was also at risk. But he had another reason for action. Like some other Australian leaders before him—Robert Menzies in the case of Vietnam is an example—Howard believed Australia had to back the US when others would not, to win future support should the nation's security be threatened.[17]

It was a belief that led Howard to send the SAS to Afghanistan to strike at al-Qa'ida and the Taliban, and eventually to support the invasion of Iraq on the grounds that Saddam Hussein had weapons of mass destruction that he might provide to terrorists. Howard insisted that Hussein had to be disarmed but rejected the ALP argument that UN weapons inspectors could do that. It was also a logic that led Howard, in late 2002, to state that Australia had the right to strike at terrorists plotting an attack in another country, prompting some outrage in the region. Former Malaysian prime minister Mahathir Mohamad said he would consider it an act of war.[18]

But Howard believed the Bali bombings of October that year, in which 88 Australians died in a toll of 202, justified pre-emption. He said later:

It stands to reason that if you believed that somebody was going to launch an attack against your country, either of a conventional kind or of a terrorist kind, and you had a capacity to stop it and there was no alternative other than to use that capacity, then of course you would have to use it.[19]

This was essentially the Bush Doctrine. At all costs, terrorists had to be stopped firstly from getting their hands on weapons of mass destruction and secondly from using them. In Iraq, though, the weakness of this doctrine became obvious—it depended on good intelligence. No WMD were found and no link to al-Qa'ida was proved. If Iraq was not training

Islamic terrorists before the invasion, it soon was. Australia was in Iraq, but Iraq was a mess, with at least 30,000 Iraqis killed since the conflict began.

Yet, for all his tough talk, Howard ensured that Australia's contribution was carefully measured. The SAS and RAAF jets were used in the dangerous opening days, but by late 2005 Australia had about 200 troops in Afghanistan and 1300 in the Iraq region, including navy and air force personnel. (The US had 160,000 in Iraq and 18,000 in Afghanistan.)

It is fair to ask why Australia—one of the original invading powers—did not contribute more troops to try to maintain vital security in Iraq those first few years. Howard did not appear to buy the 'you break it, you own it' rule about invasion espoused by Powell.[20] While Iraq remained dangerous, Australian forces were less involved in the deadliest areas and missions. Combined with good luck and training, the resulting lower casualty figure was one reason why, as Bush and Blair were suffering badly in opinion polls at the end of 2005, Australia's Iraq role was not a hot political issue.

Even so, critics said Howard made Australia more of a target for terrorists. Former Labor prime minister Bob Hawke described Iraq—as he once had Vietnam—as a 'bloody, senseless and immoral war' that had made Australians more vulnerable.[21] With a higher profile among Islamic radicals, Australians may well be more at risk—yet Australia had been singled out for retaliation well before Iraq. Australia's crime, according to al-Qa'ida leader Osama bin Laden, was an action widely supported by Australians: leadership of the United Nations peace-keeping mission that helped East Timor move to independence from Indonesia. 'The crusader Australian forces were on Indonesian shores, and in fact they landed to separate East Timor, which is part of the Islamic world,' bin Laden railed in a video sent to the Arab broadcaster al-Jazeera in November 2001, when he also called for holy war on the West. And the Bali attacks, perhaps partly inspired by this sort of propaganda by al-Qa'ida, were also before Australia's involvement in the attack on Iraq.

In contrast to Howard's pro-Bush line, the ALP denied that the case had been made for war. Labor continued to view the alliance as one of the central pillars of security policy. Without it, argued Labor foreign affairs spokesman Kevin Rudd, Australia would need to spend at least a further $13 billion on defence.[22] Where Labor differed with Howard was in its belief that a true ally did not always need to agree with Washington.

Tensions rose with the rise of Labor's Mark Latham, who personalised the anti-US rhetoric when he called Bush 'the most incompetent and dangerous president in living memory'.[23] Trouble with the Bush administration was clearly on the cards when Latham became leader in December 2003. According to his book *The Latham Diaries*, Latham saw the alliance as 'just another form of neo-colonialism' that produced a 'timid insular nation too frightened to embrace an independent foreign policy'. 'Look at New Zealand,' he wrote, 'they have their foreign policy right, and it's the safest country on earth. The US alliance is a funnel that draws us into unnecessary wars; first Vietnam and then Iraq.'[24]

Bush feared that a Labor Government would weaken the coalition in Iraq if it pulled out Australia's troops. He lashed out at a press conference with Howard in the White House Rose Garden in June 2004, warning that a fulfilment of Latham's pledge to withdraw forces by Christmas would be 'disastrous', 'dispirit those who love freedom in Iraq', and 'embolden the enemy'.[25]

Not surprisingly, Latham's election defeat was cheered by Bush, who took time out from his own campaign to hail Howard as 'the right man to lead that country'.[26] Yet when it came to the free trade agreement the Americans did not give much away—even to Bush's 'man of steel'. The deal provided only incremental increases in access to key farm products such as beef and dairy, and nothing extra at all in access to sugar. The US spin was that it would be a US$2 billion boost for manufactured exports to Australia, which dropped a five per cent tariff.

A hint of what the US really thought came when Zoellick appeared before a Senate hearing to boast about how little the US had given away in the sensitive agriculture area. He boasted about the fact that no sugar was included and was mocking in his description of the 'huge' concessions on dairy products. Zoellick told senators that Bush had not been moved by Howard, who had made several appeals on greater access to farm products such as beef. 'And frankly, in terms of dairy I think we've increased our quota ... the huge amount of maybe $30–$40 million a year,' he said.[27]

So Howard got an FTA but Australia's interests came a long second to US domestic politics. And there are no guarantees of US support in the ANZUS pact either. There is a requirement to consult, and in the event of an attack each side would 'act to meet the common danger in accordance with its constitutional processes'. That provides an expectation, not a certainty, of US support for Australia—and also of Australia's backing for the US in places such as Iraq.

It is a two-way street. And to switch metaphors, in the case of Asia it is a double-edged sword as well. ANZUS provides Australia with access to the US political and military leadership, intelligence, equipment, and ever-closer interoperability and training with US forces. Australian troops are increasingly equipped to fight overseas with the US. This makes Australia more influential and makes any potential aggressor more reluctant. But ANZUS could also embroil Australia in a military conflict between the US and China, since it identifies a nation's ships and aircraft as territory. If China attacked Taiwan, and the US defended Taiwan as it is obliged by treaty to do, Australia could be hard-pressed to stay out of it. After all, Australia likes to boast it has fought beside the US in every major military conflict in a century.

Downer stumbled over this problem in Beijing in August 2004 when he suggested that ANZUS might not be invoked in a dispute over Taiwan. 'The ANZUS treaty is invoked in the event of one of our two countries, Australia or the United States, being attacked,' Downer said. 'So some other military activity elsewhere in the world, be it in Iraq or anywhere else for that matter, does not automatically invoke the ANZUS treaty.'[28]

It went down very badly in Washington. The US ambassador in Canberra, Tom Schieffer, issued a reminder that ANZUS included assets such as ships. 'We are to come to the aid of each other in the event of either of our territories are attacked, or if either of our interests are attacked, our home territories, or either of our interests are attacked in the Pacific,' he said. In correcting Downer's error, Howard was more specific than the treaty itself: 'We have to consult and come to each other's aid when we're under attack or involved in conflict.'[29] Downer's trouble illustrates the tension Australia has experienced balancing its close links with the US while strengthening relations with the emerging dominant power in Asia, China. The clearest signal of Australia's dual focus came in October 2003 when the Australian parliament hosted addresses on consecutive days by Bush and Chinese President Hu Jintao—an honour British and Japanese leaders have not had. And, after a stumbling start, Australia also found itself in late 2005 with a seat at the table at the first meeting of the East Asia Summit, a new regional grouping including China, Japan, South Korea, the Association of South-East Asian Nations, India and New Zealand.

The United States is not included. At the beginning of 2006, Howard and Bush were closer than any leaders of the two nations have been. But the relationship necessarily has a use-by date. Howard's real achievement has been to strengthen the formal connections. Invoking ANZUS, whether it was necessary or not, gave the old treaty a new relevance. And securing a free trade agreement, however incomplete, sets out new economic, trade and business links that will broaden the relationship and give Australia a wider sphere of support and influence inside the US. Whether this translates into future security for Australia, or whether the next US president in 2009 will have much interest at all in this country, is impossible to know. When Australia opted to send troops to Vietnam, it thought it was buying a guarantee of future US military help on tap. The difficulties with Clinton over East Timor proved the danger of such assumptions.

VI

HEARTS AND MINDS

18

LOSING THE PLOT

Steve Lewis

PERCHED in the shadows of Queensland's Glasshouse Mountains, Steve Irwin's Australia Zoo is one of the best-known landmarks in the federal seat of Longman. On a good day, a couple of thousand people walk through its gates in search of the Crocodile Hunter, whose business skills and international fame saw the zoo named Australian Tourism Exporter of the year in 2004.

The corporate success of Irwin, an effusive fan of John Howard, has a neat political parallel. Mal Brough, a former army officer who has been the federal Liberal Party MP for Longman since 1996, has known Irwin for years, often dropping in from his electoral office just minutes away. His career success under Howard has been in tandem with Irwin's: a happy synchronicity.

Before Howard came to power in 1996, Brough's seat would have been regarded as a marginal seat, with its working class hamlets of Donnybrook and Toorbull once considered Labor strongholds. Only 7 per cent of the population of Longman have a tertiary education, well below the national average of 12.9 per cent, while a third falls into the lowest income bracket. So it is a measure of the distance Howard has advanced on the electoral landscape in the past decade that Brough is sitting comfortably on a two-party-preferred margin of nearly 8 per cent.

It also represents a classic lost opportunity for the Labor Party—the case of an electorate chock-full of blue-collar voters that has turned its back on the century-old political force. In October 2004, Labor's primary vote collapsed to just over 35 per cent. After preferences, it could muster a paltry 42.34 per cent of the two-party preferred vote. Thank you, Mark Latham.

The Howard years have been a decade of retreat for Labor. Seats such as Longman were within sight for the ALP in 1998 and 2001 but turned back to Howard in 2004 and now appear out of Labor's reach. The pattern is repeated across the country. Electorates that previously rested on a wafer-thin margin now require swings of 5, 6 or 7 per cent in Victoria and Western Australia. This is Howard country now and Labor's 13-year dominance under Bob Hawke and then Paul Keating seems a distant memory.

Labor has been frozen out of office as a result of a multitude of factors. Rather than reinventing itself and presenting a fresh facade to an electorate yearning for political change, modern Labor has resisted a necessary makeover. When ad man John Singleton claimed in October 2005 that most punters did not know what Labor stood for, he summed up the dilemma for a political party that has failed to embrace an agenda in tune with changing Australian society. Like a sporting team lacking direction, it has struggled to adapt to changed playing conditions. Federal Labor has failed to capture the loyalty of the new class of independent contractors and consultants, the stay-at-home business entrepreneurs who have infiltrated the workforce in recent years. Too often, Labor has played the politics of envy without realising the changing nature of the base vote it used to represent. The party has not been able to successfully plough a middle ground in policy, instead adopting a scattergun approach that has left voters confused about what it stands for.

At the same time, Labor has been outflanked by Howard who has combined conviction politics with a skilful pragmatism the likes of which Australia has rarely, if ever, seen. Crucially, Howard has seized the economic agenda and Labor has struggled to respond. As Opposition Leader Kim Beazley concedes, Labor has tried to fight the battle on too many fronts, instead of focusing on the issue that concerns voters the most. 'In a curious way there were too many targets,' says Beazley. 'You had too much that was out there that you were arguing about.'[1]

Beazley's intention to confine the party to a more coherent policy agenda of perhaps 10 or 12 big-ticket policies may allow the party to better address the most significant reason why it remains out of office: failure to reassure voters on its ability to manage the economy and keep interest rates low. It has never really recovered from the blow it was dealt by the '$10 billion black hole' attacks aimed at Labor after the 1996 campaign. Neither has Labor successfully countered Coalition claims that a vote for the ALP is a vote for a return to the high interest rates of the late 1980s and early 1990s. (Never mind that the 90-day bank bill rate hit a near record 21.4 per cent in April 1982, when Howard was Malcolm Fraser's treasurer.) The potency of the Coalition's interest rate campaign was driven home during the 2004 campaign when Mark Latham, portrayed as an L-plate leader by the Government's political machine, resorted to signing a giant cardboard interest rate 'pledge' to keep interest rates low.

Latham's campaign failed to make any headway in the brick-veneer suburbs that Labor once claimed as its own but which are now Howard's territory. As the first results trickled in on election night, it was clear that the Coalition had been returned with an increased majority, securing its biggest swings in the mortgage belt seats. In the middle-class enclave of Aston, for example, in Melbourne's outer-suburban south, the Liberal Party's Chris Pearce doubled his margin, increasing his two-party preferred vote from 56 per cent to 63 per cent. Considered a marginal seat just a few years ago, Aston is now a safe haven for Pearce. Highly geared families were not willing to take a risk on Labor and its highly combustible leader. The ALP simply had not done enough to respond to the unrelenting campaign on interest rates waged by the Coalition and its super-efficient campaign machine.

Evan Thornley, the multi-millionaire founder of internet search engine LookSmart and an influential figure within Labor ranks, summed up the party's dilemma this way:

> The problem is the punters don't trust us with the keys. They want to know we care and we can manage the economy. But what they've seen is disinterest [sic] from the intelligentsia and empty lip service from the machine. Our people don't trust us with their jobs, mortgages, taxes or whatever else they consider 'economic management' to be.[2]

Labor's failure to weave an economic narrative through its policy agenda can be traced back to 1996, right at the start of its decade in the wilderness. It can be traced back to its failure to understand why it now found itself in Opposition, blaming a 'reform-weary' electorate for its defeat. When Beazley became leader, a shocked and demoralised Labor turned its back on the reform agenda and legacies of 13 years of Labor government and abandoned the hard-line rhetoric adopted by Keating when he was opening the economy to foreign banks and tearing down protectionist walls.

Spooked by the hammering dished out by voters, Labor sought to differentiate itself from the Government by opposing its big-ticket reforms. In response the Coalition's senior figures argued that Labor was locked in the past and was the enemy of any reform that would generate national prosperity. Labor MPs were suffering from post-Keating traumatic shock, trying to distance themselves from what they perceived to be the negative aspects of the former prime minister. The irony was that Howard understood Keating's failure better than his former Labor colleagues. While Howard was wary of economic reform in his own first year, he rightly perceived that what the electorate really disliked about Keating was the perceived arrogance and pomp of a Labor Government that was out of touch with the aspirations of mainstream voters. Under Keating Labor had come to be seen as the party of chardonnay socialists rather than the battlers.

Beazley, after frontbench stints in both the Hawke and Keating governments, was elected unopposed after the 1996 debacle, after narrowly scraping home in his own seat of Brand. Affable and decent, Beazley has led Labor for about six-and-a-half of the 10 years it has spent in Opposition. In his first term, he performed a solid managerial role, preventing the party from descending into endless recrimination and factional paybacks. He also benefited, during Howard's first term, from a series of ministerial scandals and resignations that unsteadied the Government. He admits that Labor was guilty of distancing itself from the Hawke–Keating reform agenda. 'Yeah, possibly. I defended the Hawke and Keating governments all the time with pride. I am not going to trash my own historical legacy. But did we make a point of trying to get a narrative based on the processes of the Hawke and Keating era into a structure of policy for the next decade of governing Australia? No, we didn't.'

There is the nub of it. Labor failed to grasp the great reforms from its predecessors while in Opposition and to build on these to present an attractive outlook to the electorate. Labor thought its biggest gift ahead of the 1998 election was the Prime Minister's announcement of the introduction of a goods and services tax. Beazley turned the subsequent election into a de facto referendum about the GST and voters were *almost* swayed to put Labor back into office. Howard's great tax adventure *nearly* backfired, with Labor securing a 4.61 per cent swing, two-party preferred. The Coalition's preferential vote actually dipped below 50 per cent, but it managed to cling to power.

The damage done to Labor was twofold. First, Labor was now confirmed as no longer the party of reform. Second, whereas Howard was prepared to stick with an unpopular policy because he believed it was necessary, Labor cast itself in the role of a Cassandra, preaching economic doom as confused consumers and businesses tried to deal with the complexities and inequities of the new tax system. When these prophecies failed to materialise, as anyone who had studied the introduction of consumption taxes in dozens of countries must have known they would, Labor's credibility as a sound economic manager took another body blow. Labor compounded its problems by promising to roll back key aspects of the GST, without taking account of the budgetary situation.

In his second term as Opposition Leader Beazley began casting around for an election theme and commissioned several people to work up ideas. The result, Knowledge Nation, was released in July 2001 as the centrepiece of Labor's bid for re-election, attempting to lay out a big-picture reform agenda for the next 10 years. It sought to join the missing links between private and public investment in education, training and research: the things that underpin a prosperous economy. Knowledge Nation sank like a stone, a victim of appalling presentation and marketing. The Government lampooned the manifesto and its Barry Jones-inspired cadastral diagram as 'noodle nation'.

Beazley now describes Knowledge Nation's failure to take off as his 'profoundest political regret'. He remains wedded to the principles that underpinned Knowledge Nation and he argues that it was one of the few genuinely fresh ideas to emerge in federal politics over the past decade. The view from the electorate, however, was that Knowledge Nation was a campaign aimed at intellectual elites that failed to speak to the ordinary voters, with whom Howard so instinctively connects.

Early in 2001, with an election a matter of months away, the tide appeared to have turned for Labor. The Coalition lost power to Labor in Western Australia and a week later Queensland Labor Premier Peter Beattie was returned with a massive swing. In March retiring defence minister John Moore's safe seat of Ryan fell to Labor in a by-election with a swing against the Government of almost 10 per cent.

While many in Labor believed that the federal election was as good as won, Howard had already started listening and responding, changing the compliance rules on the GST, cutting fuel excise and delivering a carefully targeted, big-spending budget in May. By August, when the Norwegian vessel *Tampa* rescued more than 400 stranded asylum seekers, Howard had already clawed back to level pegging with Labor in the opinion polls. Howard had drawn crucial conclusions from the performance of One Nation in state elections, which was splitting the conservative vote and punishing the Liberals, the Nationals and the CLP. His response to the *Tampa* incident was a rallying cry to conservative voters who were tempted to vote One Nation. And it was spectacularly successful. One Nation's vote never recovered.

Federal Labor's failure to capitalise on the collapse of One Nation as Beattie had done in Queensland, and as Howard was about to do nationally, was a crippling failure. While Beazley supported the Government's 'Pacific solution', he found himself uncomfortably wedged between his two constituencies: the majority who wanted strong border protection and the vocal inner-city socialists who objected passionately to dangerous and embarrassing standoffs at sea. In any event, the September 11 attacks in the United States, which put national security at the top of the agenda, were always going to favour the incumbent prime minister. Labor went into the 2001 election well behind and stayed there. The subsequent inquest followed the familiar pattern established in 1996 and 1998. Labor seemed blind to its own failings, preferring to believe that it was robbed of the 2001 election. Blaming Howard's manipulation of the electorate's xenophobia hid from the party its own failure to connect with ordinary people.

* * *

Rather than using the 2001 election loss to bring a new face to the parliamentary party, Labor chose Simon Crean as its new leader. Crean's trade union pedigree won him no points with the electorate and his approval ratings struggled to rise above 30 per cent. He was little match for Howard and led a divided party until he was eventually persuaded to resign, in late 2003. Mark Latham, a protégé of Gough Whitlam, whose use of crudity in the parliament had gained him as much notoriety as a fresh approach to policy, was the surprising choice as Crean's replacement. For a time he seemed to have the measure of Howard, wrong-footing him on his proposal to cut back MPs' generous superannuation payments and forcing the Prime Minister to match the commitment. He seized the initiative on the free trade agreement with the United States, forcing the Government to introduce some minor but highly symbolic amendments to the legislation in return for Labor's support. But Latham was to stumble, badly, when he committed to bringing Australian troops home from Iraq by Christmas of 2004. The leadership neophyte was pursued relentlessly by the Government and never quite recovered his self-assurance.

Ignoring calls to focus more avidly on economic management, Latham instead sought to impose his own political ideas on the electorate. It worked well for a while, with Latham and Labor gaining solid approval ratings. The Coalition's relentless attack on the Labor Party's record on interest rates took its toll. With record household debt, Australian voters were not prepared to take the risk of electing Latham as the country's leader. Labor's support went backwards, slumping to its lowest primary level since 1906. The Coalition not only increased its majority in the House of Representatives but gained a slim majority in the Senate for the first time in two decades. Labor's despair was overwhelming. In the wake of its fourth straight defeat, the party leadership determined to forge ahead with a program of restoring the party's economic credibility. Latham bolstered his frontbench team and reshaped it to place a stronger emphasis on economic development, industry, innovation and infrastructure.

Latham's messy departure in early 2005 brought Beazley back into the leadership. After the crazy/brave Latham experiment, there was little appetite among the Labor caucus to blood another new-generation leader, such as Kevin Rudd or Julia Gillard.

The tragedy of the 2004 election for Labor is the blow-out in margins in seats such as Longman and Aston, Canning in Western Australia and Eden-Monaro in the southwest of NSW, all of which have turned a deep shade of Liberal blue.

What have 10 years out of office really taught the Labor Party? There is certainly a stronger focus on developing sound economic policies and ditching some of the class-war antics of the past. Beazley is defensive when challenged over Labor's inability to win over middle Australia, at least in sufficient numbers to deliver him the keys to The Lodge. 'In terms of the two-party-preferred vote, actually our vote has been going up since '96 but it hasn't been going up enough.'[3]

Realistically, Beazley accepts that Labor could have done much better with the presentation of its policies, not just Knowledge Nation. But he must also accept a large part of the blame for Labor's failure to present a sufficiently attractive alternative to the person in the street. And as Singleton puts it, Labor's message had to be clear enough to be understood by the man with seven schooners under his belt.

* * *

Howard has mastered, better than any other political figure since Robert Menzies, the art of reflecting the values and aspirations of suburban Australia. In the process, he has left Labor in his wake, a damaged political machine that still relies too heavily on the union movement for its financial and political underpinnings. When asked to analyse how the past decade will be remembered Beazley reverts to his academic training. 'I am a historian by profession so I will make a calculated guess that in 20 years' time, historians will write up this period as a waste of space.'[4] The Hawke–Keating period will be seen as the era of reform, but Beazley argues that the Howard era will be seen as one of 'reaction and ideology'. The assessment is hardly surprising, as is Beazley's tendency to gloss over the reasons why he remains on the Opposition benches. The Coalition has ruthlessly exploited the benefits of incumbency, certainly during the 2001 and 2004 campaigns. Howard the ideologue has become far more pragmatic in his pursuit of power.

Two of the biggest spending advertising programs ever seen—the GST and last year's WorkChoices campaign—involved vast sums, all paid for by the public purse. Almost in awe, Beazley describes the Liberal Party's political machine as the 'masters of spin, the masters of presentation'. At the same time, he argues that the Coalition has adopted an unprecedented shamelessness about using public funds to support their position. But Howard has effectively spooked Labor through the course of the past 10 years. He has articulated deeply held beliefs, outflanking Labor time and time again. He has become the master of presenting a simple proposition that best reflects the prevailing public view. 'Then he has the physical discipline to carry it through,' says Beazley. 'I have not seen in politics a man work so hard on presentation [yet be] so soft on administration.'

It is not an unreasonable judgment by Beazley. But he should also engage in a fair degree of self-analysis to determine why Labor's primary vote has slipped back to well below the critical 40 per cent mark. A stronger focus on developing centrist policies that appeal to the aspirational strains of middle Australia and reassuring voters that Labor is as able as the Coalition to keep interest rates low is paramount for the party's future success. The size of Howard's majorities in seats such as Longman is an indication of just how tough that task will be.

19

READ MY LIPS

Bill Leak

'I'm tired of all this nonsense about beauty only being skin deep. That's deep enough. What do you want, an adorable pancreas?'
—Jean Kerr[1]

MARCH 2, 1996 marked the start of 10 long years of struggle for the nation's cartoonists. John Howard's ordinariness is one of his most effective electoral attributes, but it is almost impossible to capture. It's a bit like having to draw something that's not there. As someone once said of British politician Gordon Brown, 'when he leaves a room the lights go on'. Howard seemed to us like that—or, as Paul Keating put it, 'like a lizard on a rock—alive but looking dead'.

Mark Latham, on the other hand, had it all: a big boofy head, as flat at the back as it was bulbous at the front; a nose in the middle of it as formless and as formidable as a boarding-house pudding; little gimlet eyes sparkling away behind small rectangular glasses; the kind of tight lips that can be rendered with just one squiggly line; and only two chins between his mouth and the collar of his shirt, both almost as big as each other. The man who told us 'politics is Hollywood for ugly people' summed up in his whole being why it is that most politicians are a delight to draw.

We look for big noses like Peter Costello's magnificent proboscis, big ears like Tony Abbott's or Billy McMahon's (who was famously described as looking like a Volkswagen with the doors open), or big droopy eyes the size of ping-pong balls like Philip Ruddock's. Politicians like Rob Kemp, Bob Hawke and Robert Menzies did the decent thing by cartoonists by allowing their eyebrows to sprout in much the same way as other men disfigure themselves with handlebar or Zapata moustaches. Bronwyn Bishop and Graham Richardson gave us bouffant hairdos that endeared them both to us forever, while—perhaps most generously of all—Alexander Downer donned fishnet stockings and stilettos just to give us a trademark to run with and enjoy. What we need is a feature to exaggerate to the point of absurdity, something—anything—to get a grip on … but, please, not ordinariness.

From his first days in parliament in 1974 right up to his ascension to the prime ministership, Howard was known as either 'Little Johnny' or 'Honest John'. Both soubriquets were equally ironic. He earned the first because he's one of those men who looks small despite being of above-average height, and he became lumbered with the second through the distinctly Australian process of twisted logic that results in redheads being named 'Bluey', bald men 'Curly' and an unfortunate one-legged man I once knew answering only to 'Fred Astaire'.

Journalists as well as cartoonists found it difficult to get a handle on Howard when he first rose to prominence in Malcolm Fraser's ministry in 1977. Fraser himself, with his half-closed eyes lurking somewhere behind the hanging gardens of his eyebrows and his jaw, the length of which was restricted only by the amount of drawing space available, was a gift from God. But his treasurer was a different matter.

Treasurer John Howard as portrayed by Bill Mitchell in The Australian, *22 August 1981*

Howard was mired in the 1950s, a man who came over all misty eyed when recalling those glory days when Australia was still hanging on firmly to Mother England's apron strings, nice people lived in suburban houses on a quarter acre, a wild night was when someone broke free from singing songs around the piano and danced the hokey-pokey, and modern art was a foreign pestilence successfully quarantined from our shores. Cartoonists and journalists alike portrayed him as a man living in the past, defined by a series of tired clichés.

During his never-ending battles with Andrew Peacock in the late 1980s and early 1990s we cartoonists had to study Howard ever harder while drawing him more and more often. He had the petulant look of a little boy complaining to his mum that he was being bullied at school, forever twitching his shoulders, accident prone and devoid of charisma and charm. Few of us dreamt he would one day make prime minister, but Lazarus with a triple bypass was nothing if not tenacious and it was clear that he was in for the long haul.

His bottom lip has always been his most outstanding feature. For some reason it always looks completely white, especially under the lights in the House of Representatives. When he makes his way to the dispatch box, one can't help being reminded of a zinc-creamed cricketer heading out to the crease. I lengthened his lower lip by 10 per cent after he brought in the GST and nobody noticed.

Alan Moir, a cartoonist with an exceptional gift for coming up with just the right image, started drawing Howard with only one eye. When one day, out of forgetfulness, he drew him with two, readers of *The Sydney Morning Herald* complained.

IN THE LAND OF THE BLIND THE ONE-EYED MAN IS KING......

Alan Moir, The Sydney Morning Herald, *12 December 2002*

Thanks to an enormous upper lip, a protruding lower one and the absence of a discernible forehead, it became standard practice for cartoonists to represent Howard as a simian creature who had not evolved as far from the ape as one might expect of a future states-man. Soon after Howard became Prime Minister my colleague Peter

Nicholson started a minor diplomatic crisis with our nearest neighbour by drawing then Indonesian president Suharto as an orang-outang swinging happily through the trees high above a jungle engulfed in flames. Peter tried to defend this highly seditious piece of whimsy by demonstrating to the Indonesians that drawing our political leaders as apes is perfectly acceptable in Australia. He came running in to my office and asked me if I had any cartoons that made John Howard look like a monkey. I was able to oblige with several thousand.

Bill Leak, The Australian, *16 August 1998*

* * *

Oscar Wilde once said it's absurd to categorise people as either good or bad; people are either charming or tedious. The 1996 election came down to a choice between the charming and the tedious. And, to the disappointment of many—and the grim-faced self-affirmation of others— tediousness won on the day.

It was Keating who said 'when the government changes, the country changes'.[2] There are many of us still wondering why he had to squander an election just to demonstrate that it was true.

Howard's victory speech said a lot about our new Prime Minister. The man with the pinched eyebrows and the permanently pleading look on his face waited for the cheering to die down before he dribbled into the microphone: 'The deepest, the most profound emotion I'm experiencing here tonight is … humility'. The contrast with Keating's 1993 victory declaration, 'the sweetest victory of all', could not have been greater. Howard was apparently a man who rated humility as an emotional experience. Nicholson, with his brilliant cartoon The Big Picture showing Howard arriving in his new office as Keating puts a huge work of art through the shredder in the background, summed up what a lot of people feared most about Howard while at the same time capturing what a lot of others had come to loathe about Keating.

Peter Nicholson, The Australian, *9 March, 1996*

Having realised his ambition to become Prime Minister, Howard quickly transformed himself into a creature entirely different from the one most cartoonists had grown to understand. Given his uncanny resemblance to a chameleon, I guess we shouldn't have been surprised. In his 10 years in office, Howard has reinvented himself more times than Madonna. But, like the pop star, the image changes while the music stays the same. Howard has stuck to his ideological agenda with the tenacity that has characterised his whole political career.

In early 1999, while Howard was resisting calls for an apology to the Aborigines over the stolen generation, US President Bill Clinton was trying to quash rumours that he had sired a half-black love child, one of the many stories his enemies were putting about in an attempt to brand him as a serial philanderer. This gave me the opportunity to invent Little Black Johnny, a half-Aboriginal love child of Howard's own, in a cartoon that showed a tearful Janette extracting an apology from her husband. Sitting between the two was a toddler who looked exactly the same as his 'father', only black.

Readers were both outraged and delighted, in roughly the same numbers, and so another Little Johnny was born. For a year or so he kept on popping up whenever I drew a cartoon on the subject of 'the apology'. The little chap symbolised the Prime Minister's conscience and I continued to draw him in the vain hope that he would eventually get his message through. With time he faded away, just another failed attempt by a delusional cartoonist to influence the public debate.

It's a little known but interesting fact that, as we mature, so do our facial features, especially ears and noses, which continue to grow while the rest of the body shrivels. In time we become caricatures of ourselves, and there's nothing we can do about it. In the case of Howard this is a slow process. After four terms he looks neater and fitter than ever. But his capped teeth, new glasses and trimmed eyebrows are only window-dressing. The nose is growing—and not only in those sudden bursts when one of his more shameless lies has us falling back on the old Pinocchio cliché. His ears are growing too, which seems a bit ironic since he's grown so deaf that he hardly needs them anyway.

Liberal senator George Brandis gave cartoonists a bit of a hand in the 2004 election campaign when it was revealed that he habitually referred to Howard as 'the rodent', a nickname that apparently went back to the early 1990s when Howard was gnawing away at Peacock's leadership. Thanks to Brandis, for a while at least, Howard was drawn by most of us with a long tail and unsightly whiskers on his nose.

Howard was right when he said 'the times will suit me'. He has presided over the parliament during a period of historically ineffective Opposition and that, of course, has suited him just fine. It has also suited us cartoonists whose job it is to act as a constant thorn in the side of any government, regardless of its political stripe. We look for hypocrisy and

Bill Leak, The Australian, *25 January 2004*

falsehood with the same eagerness with which we look for big noses and gap teeth, and Howard keeps us busier than ever.

From his 1996 declaration that he would enforce unprecedentedly high standards of parliamentary behaviour (a notion that cost him seven ministers in his first term), through to the spectacular 'children over-board' deception and the subsequent '*Tampa* election', cartoonists have been outraged and grateful in equal measure at the political audacity of this arch-conservative-turned-revolutionary.

And it got worse. Next thing we were being told that a bloke called Saddam Hussein was squirrelling away a stockpile of weapons of mass destruction in a place called Iraq and if we didn't stop him dead in his tracks he'd be on his way across the oceans, hell-bent on testing them out on the likes of us. Cartoonists had a field day pointing out the absurdity of this proposition, but if we presumptuously assumed we were acting as a substitute Opposition, we were soon to realise we were even less effective than the 'real' one in Canberra.

We wore out a lot of pencils expressing our disgust at the treatment of asylum seekers, thinking mandatory detention had to be a temporary aberration, the sort of thing that could never happen in Australia. But here we are, many years and thousands of pencils later, all realising that it's going to take a lot more than a few cartoons to bring about any change in the direction of the ship of state as long as Howard is at the helm. It doesn't matter what uniform we put him in, be it as the seven-million-year-old caveman, Bush's diminutive sidekick, the deputy sheriff or a blundering soldier lost in the minefields of Iraq, Howard is always one step ahead, leaving us to wonder what cliché he is going to demand of us next.

Bill Leak, The Australian, *12 June 2003*

It is often said that Howard is the consummate politician and, if managing to turn around both policy and debate on a wide range of issues is any sort of test, you'd have to say it's true. If longevity in office is anything to go by, Howard comes up trumps on that score too. He also proves time and time again that his ability to read the collective mood of the people is pretty near infallible, as is his skill at leading his party and bending his ministers to his will.

The makeover of Howard's appearance and deportment has been as complete as the makeover he has given the country. Howard has reshaped Australia to conform to his own vision. We love the inflated feelings of international self-importance he has given us and we don't seem to care about all the things he has taken away. Happy to live in an economy instead of a society, we might as well also accept that we are all Little Johnnies now. Smaller, meaner and less attractive, we're looking more like monkeys every day.

Bill Leak, The Australian, *9 October 2004*

20

THE HOWARD IDIOM

Imre Salusinszky

THE CLOSEST I have come to an understanding of John Howard's style, and how it has contributed to his success, came during the 2004 election campaign.[1] I was getting ready for work, with the radio blaring as usual. On the airwaves was a doorstop interview with Howard, and journalists were asking for his view of US film-maker Michael Moore's documentary *Fahrenheit 9/11*. The film portrays both the 'war on terror' and the invasion of Iraq as elements of a vast right-wing conspiracy engineered by the Bush family.

Consider, for a moment, how our two previous prime ministers might have responded, in a similar situation: Paul Keating would surely have unleashed the vitriol, while Bob Hawke would probably have experienced a brain explosion. So what did Howard do? Oozing patience, he reminded the journalists that Moore's film was a work of interpretation, not of accredited fact. And no, he had not seen it yet but, yes, he might— and he might even enjoy it. All delivered with calm equanimity.

'Come around the wicket, or try a short ball,' I thought. 'You'll never bowl him with that one.'

A brief study of Howard's style—of his rhetoric and his idiom—suggests that the very qualities of quotidian evenness that have roused the

Howard-haters to accusations that Howard is a vision-free zone have been integral to his success. Critics less blinded by hostility, including Judith Brett, have noticed that Howard's style is, if not visionary or high-flown, anything but uncreative. Relinquishing, perhaps consciously, any claim to the rhetorical arts that would place him on a pedestal alongside Bob Menzies or Gough Whitlam, Howard has instead perfected the tone of the cautious, understated, suburban man and elevated it to an original, inclusive and—above all—successful political lexicography.

The roots of this style lie, no doubt, in the plain-speaking Methodist tradition in which Howard was raised; in his training and work as a solicitor; in his study of the style of Australian cricket leadership; and, above all, in his lower-middle-class origins. While Menzies spoke *about* the 'forgotten people', or middle class, Howard speaks *for* them, voicing their concerns and values in their own language. His good fortune is that, more than half a century after Menzies' famous speech, they are forgotten no longer. Indeed, in the 21st-century Australian political landscape, they form the basis of any successful electoral coalition. As Brett says,

> Howard is Menzies' successor not because he has gone back to him, to mine his words and images to oversee a return to 1950s Australia but because, like Menzies before him, he has been able to adapt the language and thinking of his party's political traditions to the circumstances of his political present.[2]

Arguably, nothing testifies more powerfully to the success of this style than the fact that, during his brief period of ascendancy over Howard in early 2004, Mark Latham copied it assiduously, prattling on about bedtime stories and jabs for the tots as if he were the kindly neighbourhood paediatrician.

Classical rhetoric recognises a division into three styles of formal elocution. Plain style is for teaching and middle style is for argument, while high style is reserved for poetic embellishment. It can be seen that John Howard has shifted the style in which Australian political leadership is conducted downwards—not towards the demotic or colloquial, which fall outside the art of elocution entirely, but towards the plain end, precisely where it merges with the middle. Words chosen from this band on the elocutionary dial are neither ornate nor technical nor colloquial or slangy. And talking of the dial, plain-to-middle style is the closest of the elocutionary modes to conversation, which has allowed

Howard to make unprecedented use of that medium so despised by the people at ABC television's *Media Watch*: talkback radio.

After 32 years in parliament and a decade in The Lodge, Howard has made more speeches accessible to political historians and the public than any other figure in our political history. But he is also our most accessible public speaker in the sense of having opened out the rhetoric of Australian political debate to the broad mainstream. This is a stylistic achievement, but also a strategic one, in Howard's continuing rejection of those he repeatedly calls our 'cultural dietitians'—people who think they know what is best for us. Howard, even his enemies will concede, is a conviction politician. His language flows from a fairly narrow set of core convictions, even as its simplicity reinforces their claim to truth.

So let's look at some specific features of the Howard style.

First, of course, it is 'relaxed and comfortable'. When Howard used this phrase to outline his vision for Australia in the run-up to the 1996 election, the mockery from within the political class was shrill. As usual, I believe, hostile commentators were doing Howard's work for him. Was 'relaxed and comfortable' really a slip? Was it a tacit admission by Howard that he lacked 'the vision thing'? If we look at his keynote speech to the Menzies Research Centre a year earlier, we can see how the ground for 'relaxed and comfortable' had been carefully laid: 'Building a lasting and fruitful relationship with the region involves achieving a unique synthesis between a comfortable acceptance of Australia's past, a confident assertion of its ongoing values and traditions, and a positive readiness to understand, accept and embrace new associations.'[3]

Comfortable acceptance is Howard's politically astute response to what he described in 2003 as the 'seemingly perpetual symposium on our self-identity'[4] that occupied the Keating years and to the anxieties it aroused within the electorate surrounding key symbolic issues discussed elsewhere in this book. When Howard uttered the phrase 'relaxed and comfortable' it was marked down as a win for *Four Corners* journalist Liz Jackson—when it was of course a win for Howard. (It is worth remembering that, eight years later, the same journalist and the same program found the proposition that voters might put interest-rate stability high on their list of priorities so peculiar that a young mum from the suburbs was plonked under the spotlight in front of her McMansion and displayed before viewers as if she were an exotic item.)

If 'relaxed and comfortable', as politics, means the rejection of the new 'cultural cringe' of the 1980s that saw more shame than pride in Australia's values and history, then as style it involves a rigorous avoidance of invective, admonition or wilful embellishment. It is, above all, a style that soothes rather than hectors or challenges. The one-time Howard departed from script was at the 1997 reconciliation convention: when indigenous leaders turned their backs on him, he abandoned his conciliatory remarks and instead shouted about his 10-point plan on native title. He has not repeated the mistake. Voters recognise that Howard's relaxed style betrays a high level of self-control, and an equally high level of self-knowledge. Contrary to Keating and Hawke, respectively, there is neither hatred nor hysteria bubbling beneath the surface.

Second, Howard's is a style designed to avoid the classic mistakes of Australian public life. Given his relentless media exposure, Howard's lack of stuff-ups during his decade in government is surely one of the notable features of his performance. A cautious, moderate style is the perfect resource of a cautious, moderate politician. Australians, it is well known, hate hubris and shrill aggression—both more or less out of reach of the plain style of speech. Keating's parliamentary invective played well in the press gallery, but Howard knew what he was doing when, instead of returning it in kind, he branded Keating 'the arch-perpetrator of personal abuse in this parliament'.[5] Howard, famously, appears to have undergone a hubris bypass, and this is reflected everywhere in his language. 'The Government will use its majority in the new Senate very carefully, very wisely and not provocatively,' he averred after the 2004 election.[6] As he told his colleagues in the partyroom when they convened after the election, this was a moment 'which we are entitled to savour, however soberly and carefully and privately and non-triumphantly'.[7]

But useful as the plain style can be for political persuasion, a third feature is that, in the hands of a highly articulate exponent such as Howard, it can also be extremely useful for obfuscation or vagueness. Witness Howard's highly anticipated statement on the leadership in June 2003: 'I have given a lot of thought to my future. The Liberal Party has been very loyal and generous to me. I'll always put it first. Whilever it remains in the party's best interests and my colleagues want me to, I'd be honoured to continue as leader.'

As a working journalist to whom it fell to interpret this piece of Sphinx-like wisdom, my first response was: 'That's *it?*' My second thought was to note the slight archaism 'whilever', which took me back soothingly to the 1960s. But the real point about the statement, a masterpiece of plain speaking, is how much it avoids. Howard, for example, says he'll be 'honoured' to continue as leader for as long as the party wants him to, which is subtly different from saying he will, in fact, do so.

And last, I identify in Howard's style a feature that I call 'constitutional'. At every point, Howard's form and content are driven by a recognition that he has been elected firstly by the voters of Bennelong to represent them in the federal parliament and secondly by the Liberal Party caucus to lead the Government: if he is supposed to talk like a head of state, nobody told him about it. In other words, Howard's style is pointedly non-presidential, and this is reflected as much in what he refuses to articulate—including an apology to the stolen generations—as in what he says. The plain style is not appropriate for the poetic articulation of the collective dreaming, and Howard has little interest in stretching it to fit the purpose. The desire for a strong leader, who can emerge to refine the national soul and burnish it until it glows like something pure and noble, betrays an undertow of fascism. Howard-haters such as Phillip Adams and Bob Ellis, who accuse Howard of failing them on this point, show a complete lack of appreciation of his sense of his role within a constitutional monarchy.

In case anybody should think the plain style takes less skill to manage than the middle or the high, the opposite is the case. Howard is a fiercely articulate politician who, unlike Hawke, never leaves a journalist in the position of wanting to scream: 'Sir, we need a verb!' And Howard can be eloquent when called for. At the opening of the new Parliament House in 1988, he began in almost Dame Edna mode ('This is a very special occasion') before venturing an extremely succinct summary of the strengths of Australian democracy as 'part of 900 years of parliamentary tradition'.[8] On the many occasions where he has solemnised the sacrifice of Australian Diggers, Howard has been direct and moving. The same style has emerged when he has been called on to mourn with the families of Australian victims of terror, as he was in Bali in 2002:

> As the sun sets over this beautiful island, we gather here in sorrow, in anguish, in disbelief and in pain. There are no words that I can summon to solve in any way the hurt and the suffering and the pain being felt by so many of my fellow countrymen and -women and by so many of the citizens of other nations. I can say, though, to my Australian countrymen and -women that there are nineteen-and-a-half million Australians who are trying, however inadequately, to feel for you and to support you at this time of unbearable grief and pain.[9]

If the plain style has been developed by Howard as a response to domestic political challenges, it has not damaged his credibility in international affairs. At a joint press conference in London with Tony Blair, immediately following the 'second wave' attacks on the London Underground in July 2005, Howard responded in his classic style to a question about the link between terror attacks in the West and the war in Iraq. As the rhetorically gifted Blair looked on 'in clear admiration and respect'—to quote Dennis Shanahan in *The Australian*[10]—Howard said:

> Once a country allows its foreign policy to be determined by terrorism, it has given the game away, to use the vernacular. And no Australian government that I lead will ever have policies determined by terrorism or terrorist threats, and no self-respecting government of any political stripe in Australia would allow that to happen. ... The objective evidence is that Australia was a terrorist target long before the operation in Iraq, and indeed all the evidence, as distinct from the suppositions, suggests to me that this is about hatred of a way of life, this is about the perverted use of the principles of a great world religion that at its root preaches peace and co-operation.[11]

Blair's response was simply: 'I agree 100 per cent with that'.

Finally, let me state succinctly what I take to be the valuable aspect of Howard's legacy. If Howard, as Prime Minister, had not taken the economic reform project, initiated under the Hawke–Keating governments of the 1980s, and married it to a set of conservative social values, I believe the project would inevitably have lapsed or simply retreated into the museum of elite obsessions alongside identity politics. The difference and the cost, of course, would have been that, unlike identity politics, economic reform has been the spark plug for the vastly increased prosperity of Australians over the past 15 years. By the late 1990s, reform was under comprehensive assault from populism and had been abandoned by Labor in favour of Kim Beazley's 'small target' strategy for reclaiming government. By reassuring the electorate that its traditional values have been reclaimed from the social engineers, Howard has created the climate in which potentially unsettling liberal economic policies could proceed. As Judith Brett puts it: 'When Howard became leader in 1995 he faced the task of recreating a language of social unity and cohesion for the Liberals after their 13-year association with economic liberalism and the language of competitive, market-based individualism.'[12] This is the key to the Howard settlement. And Howard's use of the plain style—suburban, direct and articulate—has played no minor part. It seems to me unlikely that, in our time, we shall see a return to the high style in Australian political discourse, whether in the form of the classical references of Whitlam or the satirical flights of Keating. If I am right, this would indicate that Howard has converted the linguistic currency of Australian politics.

Whether commentators love Howard's ends or loathe them, they need to understand how, in his hands, the plain style has become a robust, supple and creative instrument to achieve those ends.

21

HOWARD'S SOUTH PARK CONSERVATIVES

Caroline Overington

> *'The man who is not a socialist at twenty has no heart,*
> *but if he is still a socialist at forty he has no head.'*
> —Aristide Briand

IT is a hundred years since Aristide Briand's expulsion from the French Socialist Party prompted him to utter words that have become part of the received wisdom of politics.

Before John Howard, the notion that young people leaned to the left was largely unchallenged. The youth vote was the dominant force that propelled Gough Whitlam into power in the 1972 'It's Time' election and stayed with Labor throughout the Hawke and Keating years. By 2004, however, when Howard won his fourth election, the ground had shifted dramatically. Less than a third of young people—32 per cent—voted for Mark Latham, while 41 per cent went with Howard. Even allowing for the 17 per cent of 18- to 24-year-olds who voted for the Greens, the uncomfortable truth for the Opposition was that, for the first time since reliable age-specific polling began, less than half of young people were voting for candidates from the Left.[1]

Howard's policies were hardly tailored to young people. He spoke for the middle class, caring more for business than for endangered marsupials. Young people would be expected to work for the dole, and Howard was stridently opposed to student unionism—indeed, to all compulsory unionism—and to the Republic. Under Howard's government HECS fees have doubled. Yet Howard has, over the past 10 years, been utterly transformed in the eyes of the young. To the horror of many baby boomers, Howard's new constituency, the 'young fogies', adore him the way their parents loved to smoke dope.

Howard's position as prime minister of choice for people aged 18 to 24 became apparent during the 1998 election, when Labor arguably misread the mood of the electorate on such issues as immigration. Many voters, particularly in Queensland, abandoned the ALP (and the Nationals) for Pauline Hanson's One Nation. In the aftermath, some in Labor concluded that the result was an aberration but, in a Newspoll taken in June 1999—a year after the election—young people confirmed their preference for conservative politics. *The Australian*'s political editor Dennis Shanahan wrote that the 'young fogies' had poured across to the Coalition 'and deserted Labor so dramatically that there has been a complete reversal of support for the ALP'. 'The youngest voters are now the Coalition's second-strongest area of support, behind its traditional powerbase of the over-50s,' Shanahan noted.[2] The results were confirmed in the 2001 election when a Morgan poll found that 18- to 24-year-olds voting in that election gave Labor their primary vote at a rate of only 1.2 per cent more than the general population. By comparison, in 1990, young people gave Labor their primary vote by 10.4 per cent more than the general population.

In October 2004—the election that would give the Coalition historic control of both chambers—the 'young fogies' of generations X and Y again deserted Labor. Clive Bean of the Queensland University of Technology—one of the principal investigators in the Australian Election Study of voting behaviour conducted after each poll—told *The Australian* in 2005 that it might have been the first time more young people voted Liberal than Labor.[3] The trend was particularly noticeable among young men, 49 per cent of whom voted for Howard, compared with only 28 per cent who voted Labor. In the 25 to 30 age group, an overwhelming 62 per cent of men voted for Howard, compared with 27 per cent for Latham.

The rise of conservative youth under Howard mirrors a similar movement in the United States, where blogger Andrew Sullivan coined the term 'South Park Republicans' in 2001 to describe young iconoclasts who 'see through the cant and the piety' of the Left 'and cannot help giggling'. The term comes from the anti-establishment television cartoon series *South Park* whose heroes are four, foul-mouthed fourth-graders who gleefully lampoon the sacred values of the Left. In his US bestseller *South Park Conservatives*,[4] Brian C Anderson says the program is the 'number-one example of the new anti-Liberalism'. He notes that the show's single black person is called 'Token'. Anderson describes how the show lampoons the boomers, who championed individual happiness over familial responsibility and promoted no-fault divorce.

In Australia, recent studies have shown Australian young people reacting against the liberal–progressive values of their parents in much the same way. Clemenger BBDO's 2005 survey 'Tomorrow's Parents Today' found that young people were significantly more conservative than their parents. They were more likely to volunteer, to give to charity and to go to church. They are also more likely to marry, and there is already evidence that they plan to have their children earlier.

According to Ian Manning of National Economics:

> You do get the feeling that forgoing worldly ambition for the sake of having kids is gradually coming back into favour. In the past, people have said, 'Oh, I can't have a baby yet, I've got to pursue my career'. But maybe it's become socially acceptable to say, 'No, I'd rather have a family'.[5]

The Democrats' 2005 youth poll, based on a survey that is distributed to secondary schools, TAFE, universities, youth and church and community groups across Australia, found that 64 per cent of students viewed 'family' as the most important issue in their lives, ahead of health, education and money. Compared with earlier polls, there was a significant drop in the number who had tried marijuana (from 43 to 33 per cent in 10 years) and much less support for the decriminalisation of drugs. Young people were also increasingly backing the Howard Government's policy of mandatory detention for asylum seekers, with support rising from 41 per cent in 2002 to 58 per cent in 2005.

Education Minister Brendan Nelson, who deals every day with young Australians, is not surprised. He points to some of the obvious factors: the economy has boomed under Howard; there are plenty of new jobs, especially for young people; interest rates have stayed low; school retention rates have increased; and there are more opportunities for travel. Young people, in particular, have never had it so good. But he adds: 'Young people are also much more educated than they have ever been, and they have become much more sceptical and cynical about the attempted manipulation of them.' Nelson says Howard's critics made a fundamental mistake when they mocked the Prime Minister for wanting to return to the 1950s and the era of the white picket fence.

> It's backfired because actually, young people, they are reassured by that. They like the fact that with John Howard, there is a sense that he knows what he is doing. They know the bus is driving along uncertain ground, but the driver has experience. I'm not sure they feel that way about Bob Brown, and especially not about Mark Latham, who just didn't inspire any confidence.[6]

On the other side of politics some of the smarter politicians have noticed Howard's takeover of the youth vote—and are troubled. Labor's Nicola Roxon was just 31 when she was elected to parliament for the Victorian seat of Gellibrand in 1998 but she is not deluded about how old that made her in the eyes of the truly young voters. 'Go and talk to students, and you are double their age. They look at you like you're some amazing authority because you're a member of parliament. But they are really quite perplexed that you might be described as young.'

For several elections now, Roxon has analysed and agonised over the voting trend among the young, 'which is not a positive one for us'. Roxon concedes that 'when the economy is going well—and largely on the back of reforms that we [Labor] brought in, by the way—and you have new people going into the labour market, they aren't that concerned about the issues they might have to confront when things aren't so rosy'.[7] 'Also, increasingly,' she says, 'there's no memory of these things that we did—like save the Franklin Dam—so we're thinking we've got runs on the board, but I'm not sure young people know it.'

During the last election, some within Labor expressed the deluded hope that recruiting rock star Peter Garrett to stand as a Labor MP would appeal to young people, but Roxon disagreed.

> We have to remember he was a hero when we were younger, so we think he has youth appeal, and it's true, to some extent, he does, but if you asked a 19-year-old, they might not even know who Midnight Oil was.
>
> He recently came to speak at a function for me, and he was fabulous but the people who wanted to come were 40- and 50-year-old men. He gave a very passionate and interesting

speech, and people were really engaged, so that really is our key. We've got a perfectly good message, if people listen to it.

Roxon's candid remarks illustrate Labor's critical failing over the past decade. While Howard has been promoting the benefits of a healthy economy, Labor has been diverted by issues such as the republic, the symbolism of Aboriginal reconciliation and opposition to the war in Iraq, which may be important to some young people but are low on their list of priorities.

In 1998, after Howard decided he would not support the Yes vote in the constitutional referendum for a republic, Labor decided to embarrass him. They enlisted the support of young role models such as Jason Yat-Sen Li and the lipstick princess Poppy King, adopted youth-orientated slogans such as 'Give an Australian the Head Job' and distributed condoms marked 'Rooting for a Republic' in the hope they would appeal to young people. In the end, only 46.5 per cent of voters voted Yes to a republic and there was scant evidence that young people backed it more firmly than others.

Labor saw a chance to win back the young vote when Howard backed the US-led war in Iraq. In some of the largest demonstrations since the Vietnam War, young protesters led a cardboard puppet of Howard up the street making it lick the bottom of a cardboard George W Bush. More than 25,000 students took part in the 'Books not Bombs' protest. Yet, as the 2004 election showed, anti-war feeling did not translate into votes. It was another disappointment for Labor, after the Sorry Day march for Aboriginal reconciliation across the Sydney Harbour Bridge in May 2000, which delivered no measurable swing to Labor in the November 2001 election.

These carefully staged events were in any case aberrations to a general trend, in Australia and most other Western nations since the end of the Cold War, away from student and youth activism. The Palm Sunday peace marches, which once were dominated by young people, are essentially dead and even protests against voluntary student unionism in 2005 attracted nothing like the crowds of protesters that once routinely gathered on university campuses.

In part, that's because young people do not have time to paint slogans on to protests signs. They work an average of 20 hours a week, on top of full-time or part-time study, and they leave university with HECS debts worth $30,000 or more. Since the collapse of communism, young people are less likely to adopt the Marxist view that capitalism contains the seeds of its own destruction. To them the fruit of capitalism is new cars, plasma TVs and trips overseas. They have grown up in an age of prosperity in which the welfare state appears redundant. While boomers complain that Howard does not care enough about refugee rights or the environment, their children are more in tune with Howard's focus on the labour market and the creation of more and better jobs. A vibrant economy has emboldened young people to create small businesses of their own.

Together, these factors have meant that Howard—straight-laced, conservative Howard—has been responsible for something that smells suspiciously like teen spirit. He has encouraged the young to rebel.

VII

THE HOWARD DECADE

22

THE STORY SO FAR

Compiled by Rebecca Weisser

1996—Changing the Guard

'If I am wrong and you are right then the democratic processes of Australia will vindicate you and condemn me.'
—John Howard, 16 May 1996

March 1996

2: John Howard leads the Coalition to its first federal election victory in 13 years with a landslide two-party-preferred vote of 53.9 per cent and a 45-seat majority, one of the biggest wins since World War II. 'The government that I will lead will be a government not only for the people that voted for us but also for the people who voted against us,' says Howard.

4: Howard outlines his reform agenda, declaring he has been given an emphatic and unambiguous mandate for the partial sale of Telstra and industrial relations changes. 'There are no circumstances for people to try and frustrate, hinder or torpedo the implementation of our program,' he says.

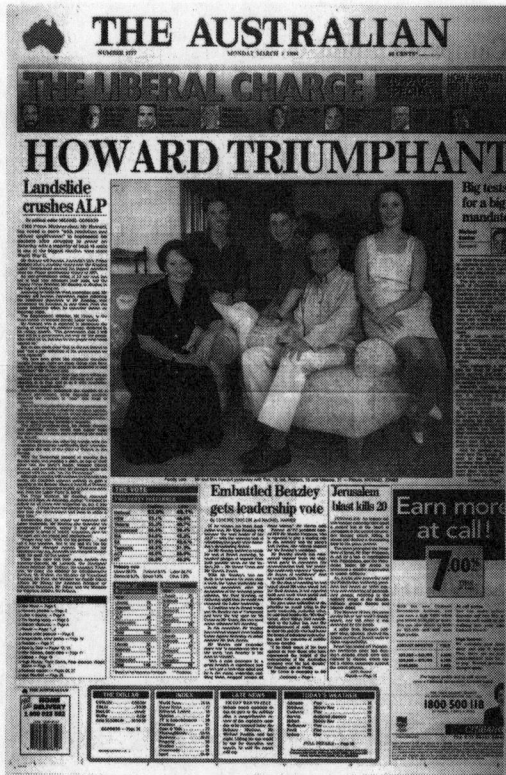

THE AUSTRALIAN

THE LIBERAL CHARGE

HOWARD TRIUMPHANT

Landslide crushes ALP

Big test for a big mandate

Embattled Beazley gets leadership vote

Jerusalem blast kills 20

Earn more at call! 7.00%

7: Howard tells Liberal MPs they could lead Australia into the next millennium if they deliver good government to all Australians.

8: Howard announces cuts to the ministry (from 31 to 28) and dismisses six departmental heads.

11: Howard restores the Queen to the oath of allegiance and the Australian flag to his official car.

12: Peter Costello says the 'days of sloth and waste are over' and pledges to cut $8 billion from the budget over the next two years.

15: Malaysian Prime Minister Dr Mahathir Mohamad agrees to visit Australia for the first time in a decade.

18: Howard announces that he will move his family into Kirribilli House in Sydney, becoming the first Prime Minister since William McMahon not to live at The Lodge.

27: President Suharto invites Howard to visit Jakarta.

29: Howard and Foreign Minister Alexander Downer meet Mahathir, who stops over briefly in Brisbane on his way to New Zealand.

April 1996

28: Martin Bryant murders 35 people and attempts the murder of 20 others in Port Arthur, Australia's worst random killing by a lone gunman. Attorney-General Darryl Williams says he will press for changes to gun laws. 'Gun controls are a state and territory responsibility and some states have been reluctant to impose restrictions that the Commonwealth regards as appropriate,' he says.

29: Howard orders an emergency meeting of state police ministers to toughen gun laws and draw up a national plan for firearm registration. The Port Arthur massacre crystallises resolve for a national approach to the issue.

30: Howard imposes a new code of ministerial conduct on his first day in parliament. It forbids ministers from engaging in any other work, from holding directorships in public companies and from holding shares in companies in the area of their portfolios.

May 1996

10: Howard announces a firearms package, including bans on automatic and semi-automatic weapons, a nationwide register, a requirement for a genuine reason for owning, possessing or using a firearm, minimum standards for storage and mail order sales controls. 'This represents an enormous shift in the culture of this country ... it is an historic agreement. It means that this country, through its governments, has decided not to go down the American path.'

24: Howard indicates he may have to drop some of his election promises because of budget constraints. 'I know the Australian people are very pragmatic ... they understand that changed circumstances can sometimes make the delivery of some commitments difficult, no matter how genuinely made,' he says.

June 1996

16: Howard wears a bullet-proof vest as he confronts an angry crowd of 3000 in Sale on a tour of rural Australia to listen to the pro-gun lobby. 'If I am wrong and you are right then the democratic processes of Australia will vindicate you and condemn me.'

27: Howard rejects claims by Noel Pearson that he does not believe in the spirit of the Mabo decision. 'I have always regarded the Mabo decision itself as being a justified, correct decision.'

July 1996

3: Howard slashes immigration by 10,000 places to 74,000 a year, citing high unemployment. Ethnic Communities Council of NSW Chair Angela Chan says, 'You don't have to come and say we will cut down on Asian migration ... the minister knows where the target groups are coming from.'

7: The Governor-General, Sir William Deane, warns that unless there are drastic improvements for Aboriginal Australians, reconciliation is doomed until well into the next century.

22: Downer tells Asian governments Australia will now fund some development aid projects which were to be axed with the closure of the Development Import Finance Facility (DIFF).

26: Howard bolsters US links by upgrading and expanding Pine Gap and increasing joint military exercises.

28: Janette Howard is admitted to hospital to be operated on for a serious medical condition. Howard cancels his first overseas trip to Indonesia and Japan.

August 1996

9: The Government announces a lowering of the HECS threshold repayment threshold from $28,495 to $20,701 and HECS increases of between 35 and 125 per cent.

13: A $400 million cut to ATSIC is announced.

14: Costello releases the Statement on the Conduct of Monetary Policy giving the Reserve Bank independence ending the need for it to consult with the government before making interest rate changes.

20: First Costello budget provides relief for families and small business, with cuts to unemployment programs, the aged, universities, the

ABC, the Australia Council, ATSIC and foreign aid. Senator Mal Colston defects from the Labor Party to become an independent.

28: Prince Charles and Princess Diana are divorced.

September 1996

1: Senator Richard Alston calls for the full sale of Telstra, drawing a rebuke from Howard the following day.

10: The independent member for Oxley, Pauline Hanson, makes her maiden speech, launching a scathing attack on Aboriginal welfare and multiculturalism and calling for compulsory national service. She claims that Australia is 'in danger of being swamped by Asians … They have their own culture and religion, form ghettoes and do not assimilate.' The Government should 'cease all foreign aid immediately and apply the savings to generating employment here at home'. On Aboriginal welfare she says, 'present governments are encouraging separatism in Australia by providing opportunities, land monies and facilities only available to Aboriginals … I am fed up with being told, "This is our land." Well, where the hell do I go?' There was no official reaction from the Prime Minister but a spokesperson for Immigration Minister Philip Ruddock said: 'The Government has made clear its continued support for multicultural policies.'

16: Howard meets President Suharto in Jarkarta and tells him Australia does not need to choose between 'our history and our geography'. 'Neither do I see Australia as a bridge between Asia and the West, as is sometimes suggested,' he says. 'Rather I believe that our geography and our history are elements in an integrated relationship with our region and the wider world.'

22: Howard makes a veiled reference to Hanson's maiden speech, saying, 'One of the great changes that have come over Australia in the last six months is that people do feel able to speak a little more freely and a little more openly about what they feel. In a sense, the pall of censorship on certain issues has been lifted … I welcome the fact that people can now talk about certain things without living in fear of being branded as a bigot or as a racist … And that freedom of speech carries with it a responsibility on all those who exercise that freedom to do so in a tolerant and moderate fashion.' ATSIC Social Justice Commissioner Mick Dodson accuses Howard of a lack of pandering to prejudice, bigotry and hatred.

23: Hanson says, 'By making the comments he made over the weekend, he is being the leader I am prepared to have.'

24: Holocaust denier and revisionist historian David Irving says he will lodge a new visa application 'because these remarks made by the Australian Prime Minister show a new climate of freedom of speech now applying in Australia'.

25: Howard rejects Hanson's views on Asian immigration and multi-culturalism but defends her right to express them. He supports reductions in the immigration program, saying: 'there is a link between the high level of unemployment among certain groups in Australia and some past immigration levels in the composition of our program in the past'.

October 1996

1: Howard abandons his election promise for a full public inquiry into cross-media ownership in favour of a low-key, internal review.

8: Howard vows always to denounce intolerance and defend the non-discriminatory nature of Australia's immigration policy but questions the value of an inquiry into the stolen generation, saying additional funds would be better spent on improving Aboriginal health, education, housing and employment opportunities.

14: Assistant Treasurer Jim Short resigns after controversy about his ANZ shareholding.

15: Parliamentary Secretary to the Treasurer, Brian Gibson, resigns over share-trading technicality.

19: Liberal Jackie Kelly retains the seat of Lindsay with a primary swing of more than 6 per cent after Labor forces an election re-run on a technicality.

27: Democrats Leader Cheryl Kernot agrees to support the passage of IR legislation after 171 changes.

30: A joint motion opposing racism and re-affirming a non-discriminatory immigration policy attempts to dispel fears voiced in Asia. Howard says the motion 'is an embodiment of certain attitudes and values that both sides of the House in the national Parliament have in common'.

November 1996

19: Howard emphasises the upgraded relationship with the US as President Bill Clinton visits Australia, only the third US head of state to do so. Clinton says Australia could be a 'shining example' of how people could come together as one nation and a 'beacon of hope'.

21: Parliament passes Howard's first major economic reform: the Workplace Relations Bill. Industrial Relations Minister Peter Reith agrees to amendments from the Australian Democrats, including a no-disadvantage test ensuring that employees could not be worse off if they signed a non-union individual contract. Reith says the next step is 'better practices in key industries like the waterfront, construction and meat processing'.

December 1996

6: Minister for Aboriginal Affairs Senator John Herron appoints entrepreneurial Aboriginal businessman Gatjil Djerrkura as the head of ATSIC.

23: The High Court rules on the Wik case that pastoral leases do not extinguish native title.

1997—The Year of Uncertainty

'We are living at the moment at a time of tremendous change and upheaval. When somebody comes along and offers simplistic solutions, and a few scapegoats thrown in for good measure, it's easy to cream six or eight or 10 points in an opinion poll mid-term.'
—John Howard, 30 April 1997

February 1997

9: Howard announces unemployed 16 to 20 year olds will be forced to work up to 20 hours a week on community-based projects in trial work-for-the-dole schemes. Participants will be paid award rates and will be obliged to work only the number of hours that equate to their dole payment.

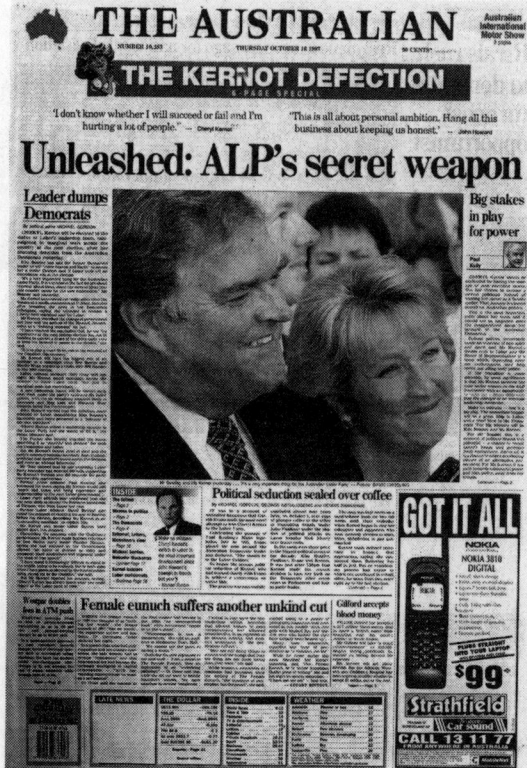

22: Reflecting on his first year in office, Howard talks of a '10-year leadership transition'. 'While my health lasts and I've got my marbles and I'm delivering good leadership and political success, you stay. But when that changes, you don't.'

March 1997

25: Legislation to overturn the world's first euthanasia laws passes the Senate, overriding Northern Territory law.

31: Howard meets Chinese Premier Li Peng in Beijing and proposes a strategic relationship that focuses on trade, with regular military consultation and a human rights dialogue to manage differences between the two countries.

April 1997

2: Governor-General Sir William Deane urges action to address the widening gap in health between indigenous and non-indigenous Australians.

8: Howard refers travel rort allegations against Colston to federal police and calls on him to stand down as Deputy President of the Senate. Liberal Senator Bob Woods and National Party backbencher Michael Cobb are also under investigation for allegedly rorting parliamentary expenses.

9: Colston agrees to stand down as Senate Deputy President but refuses to resign from parliament.

11: Pauline Hanson launches the One Nation party in Ipswich.

16: Howard says he will not accept Colston's vote in the Senate.

17: The Charter of Budget Honesty Act becomes law, setting a framework for sound fiscal management and informing the public about public finances.

21: Former WA premier Carmen Lawrence is charged with perjury over her evidence to the 1995 Easton Royal Commission.

30: Howard says Hanson is 'articulating the fears and concerns and the sense of insecurity that many Australians feel at a time of change and instability'. 'Now it's easy to sort of finger the fact that people feel uneasy and unhappy. The next step is to say, "Okay, you've fingered the uncertainty. What are you going to do about it?"' he tells Radio 3AW.

May 1997

1: Downer uses the launch of *Asialine*, a magazine for Australian business in Asia, to make a strong attack on Hanson, saying her views are offensive to people of all backgrounds. 'Those views promote an insular Australia separate from the region. This is the concept of a little Australia: inward looking, narrow-minded, protectionist and disconnected from our own neighbourhood,' he says.

2: Tony Blair wins a 179-seat majority, to become the first Labour prime minister in Britain for 18 years.

8: Nine months after Hanson's maiden speech, Howard directly attacks her views for the first time. 'She is wrong when she suggests that Aboriginals are not disadvantaged. She is wrong when she says that Australia is in danger of being swamped by Asians. She is wrong to seek scapegoats for society's problems. She is wrong when she denigrates foreign investment, because its withdrawal would cost jobs. She is wrong when she claims Australia is headed for civil war,' he says.

13: Costello's second budget delivers a tax rebate of up to $450 per year on savings and a $1 billion Federation Fund for construction.

15: The Industrial Relations Commission signals the end of the traditional award system by rejecting an industry-wide claim for a wage rise.

21: The Government announces further cuts to immigration, halving the family reunion program and increasing skilled migration, saying cuts are linked to high unemployment.

26: Howard tables Bringing Them Home, the Human Rights and Equal Opportunity Commission's report into the separation of Aboriginal children from their families. Ronald Wilson's inquiry concludes that the forcible removal of children was an act of genocide. Howard says: 'Personally, I feel deep sorrow for those of my fellow Australians who suffered injustices under the practices of past generations towards indigenous people ... [but] Australians of this generation should not be required to accept guilt and blame for past actions and policies over which they had no control.'

At the Reconciliation Convention in Melbourne, some Aboriginals turn their backs on Howard.

June 1997

5: Howard bows to pressure from the car industry to accept a four-year freeze on car tariffs from 2000 to 2004.

July 1997

7: Howard foreshadows a new round of industrial relations reform. 'We have as a nation over the years adopted as part of our ethos a higher minimum wage rate than many other countries. Now, one of the consequences of that is that you do have higher levels of unemployment,' he says.

11: Small Business Minister Geoff Prosser quits, admitting he has become a liability to the Government because of claims that conflicts of interest breached the Ministerial Code of Conduct.

15: Colston is charged with fraud for rorting his travel allowance and frequent flyer points.

25: Howard is admitted to a private hospital suffering severe pneumonia on the eve of his 58th birthday.

31: A landslide at Thredbo kills 18 people, with only one survivor, Stuart Diver. Howard issues a statement from his hospital bed saying: 'The horrifying pictures of the scene at Thredbo are a reminder to all of the fragility of life and reinforce the strength which can be gained from a sense of community in times of national tragedy.'

August 1997

1: Howard is released from Sydney's Mater Hospital but is ordered to spend another week resting at Kirribilli House.

13: Howard returns from medical leave to set the scene for an election to be fought on tax reform. 'Any proper reform package has got to include significant reductions in personal income tax ... There must obviously be a thorough examination of the introduction of a broad-based indirect tax to replace some or all of the existing indirect taxes', he says.

31: Princess Diana dies of injuries sustained in a car crash in Paris. Howard says the 'horrible and tragic accident' would sadden people all over the world. 'I extend my very deep sympathy, particularly to the two young sons [Prince William and Prince Harry], who have suffered the trauma of a marriage break-up and have now lost their mother at the very young age of 36,' he says.

September 1997

10: Howard overrules cabinet and delivers a five-year tariff freeze for textiles, clothing and footwear from 2000 to 2005.

12: After 18 months of Howard Government, unemployment has risen from 8.4 per cent to 8.7 per cent.

24: Transport Minister John Sharp and Administrative Services Minister David Jull are forced to resign over travel rorts.

25: Howard is forced to admit his staff had been told in May of travel rorts that cost Jull and Sharp their jobs. He claimed to know nothing of it himself. A third minister, Peter McGauran, is also alleged to have rorted travel claims.

26: Science Minister Peter McGauran is pressured into resigning over travel rorts. Howard sacks his closest friend and most senior adviser Grahame Morris and removes another staff member, Fiona McKenna, from his office.

30: Minister for Veterans Affairs, Bruce Scott, is alleged to have wrongly claimed thousands of dollars in travel allowances, scotching his chances of a promotion to cabinet.

October 1997

1: ALP Deputy Senate Leader Nick Sherry is revealed to have claimed $43,000 in accommodation allowances while staying with his mother.

3: Senator Nick Sherry attempts suicide over travel claims that were valid but were ridiculed by Peter Costello.

5: Howard announces a re-shuffle to replace ministers demoted in the travel rorts scandal, promoting David Kemp to Education replacing Amanda Vanstone who is demoted to Justice. He promotes Mark Vaile to Transport and Nick Minchin to Special Minister of State.

6: Howard threatens to walk away from the Kyoto climate control conference if it costs jobs and puts a speed limit on economic growth.

13: Workplace Relations Minister Peter Reith sets a provocative new benchmark for the waterfront, calling for a 43 per cent improvement in container handling rates to meet Asian productivity levels.

15: Cheryl Kernot defects from the Democrats to join the Labor Party and is elevated to the ALP's leadership team. Howard says, 'This is all about Cheryl Kernot's personal ambition, nothing else. Hang the principle, hang the Democrats, hang all this business about keeping us honest, hang all this business about being a noble, principled third force. Whenever the Labor Party has wanted her vote on a vital issue, she has been there.'

21: Howard spells out his strategy for beating Labor. 'Governments who win elections will not win another election by simply sitting back. That is a recipe for losing. They must offer the general public something new and better. They must give people new incentives to vote for the Government again,' he says.

24: As the Asian currency crisis spreads to Hong Kong, Howard calls for calm, saying doomsayers are over-reacting to the Asian currency crisis. 'I think words like "meltdown" are quite extreme and not appropriate,' he says from Edinburgh.

26: Howard is optimistic of a good outcome at Kyoto after a CHOGM communiqué fails to specify targets and recognises Australia's position on differentiation. In an allusion to Chamberlain's 1938 Munich agreement Howard quips that the outcome is 'differentiation in our time'.

28: The Australian share market loses 7.2 per cent or $27.4 billion as markets crash around the world in response to the Asian currency crisis before bouncing back the next day.

November 1997

5: Howard scraps his controversial accommodation bonds for people entering nursing homes after Liberal Party polling shows that the policy triggered a backlash from a key Liberal party constituency: people over 55, especially women.

17: In the biggest float in Australian history, more than 1.2 million investors share $1.85 billion in profits after Telstra shares rise by 80 cents on their first day of trading. Howard hails the result as a 'great investment by the mums and dads in the ownership of a great Australian company'.

24: Hanson records a video to be aired in the event of her death. It begins: 'Fellow Australians, if you are seeing me now, it means I have been murdered.'

December 1997

7: Howard floats a possible double dissolution over his Wik legislation but looks at other triggers to avoid a race election. Costello predicts that the Government would use an election to secure the passage of all legislation facing Senate obstruction including small business exemption from unfair dismissal laws, implementing a charter of budget honesty and Public Service reform.

8: Howard commits his government to boosting growth to a sustained level of 4 per cent. 'The overriding aim of our extensive economic reform agenda is to deliver Australia an annual growth rate of over 4 per cent on average during the decade to 2010,' he says.

9: Costello discusses, in a private meeting between business chiefs, a GST of 10 per cent, personal tax cuts of up to $17.3 billion, the abolition of state payroll tax and a crackdown on tax loopholes.

11: Australia signs the Kyoto Protocol, committing it to continue with the treaty-making process but not to be bound by it. Under the protocol Australia would be allowed to increase greenhouse gas emissions to 108 per cent of 1990 levels by 2010. Other developed countries would cut their emissions by an average of 5.2 per cent. Howard says, 'We fought for Australian jobs every inch of the way and the outcome vindicates the Government's stance.'

Howard calls for a debate on multiculturalism with the publication of a discussion paper by the National Multicultural Advisory Council called Multicultural Australia: The Way Forward. Howard says, 'What this discussion paper does is to open up some of the issues, not to call in question the commitment of Australia to multiculturality or to diversity or to the underlying principles.' Describing the paper as hasty and ill-conceived, a member of the council that produced it resigns in protest.

14: Plans to reform the waterfront by using non-unionised labour trained in Dubai collapse after pressure on the United Arab Emirates to prevent the training.

16: The Government gives $63 million in response to the Stolen Generation report but refuses to compensate children forcibly removed from their families or to give an official apology. The Minister for Aboriginal Affairs, Senator Herron, says, 'An apology can really only be given by those that were responsible. Would you ask the British to apologise for coming to Australia with the convicts?'

30: Chinese President Jiang Zemin agrees to visit Australia. Relations had been strained over human rights and Taiwan in 1996 but Australia's abandonment of the co-sponsorship of the annual resolution criticising China in the UN Commission for Human Rights is seen to have contributed to improved relations.

31: Howard says next month's Constitutional Convention is a 'once-in-a-century opportunity for a broad cross-section of the people who comprise modern Australia to examine the relevance of important features of our present Constitution'.

1998—No turning back

'Do you get rid of the deliverers of these results? Do you replace the competents with the incompetents?'
—John Howard, 2 September 1998

January 1998

15: Fifteen-year-old Sydney schoolboy Ian Thorpe emerges as Australia's newest swimming superstar, with a breathtaking gold medal-winning performance in the 400m freestyle at the World Swimming Championships in Perth.

22: US President Bill Clinton faces threat of impeachment proceedings after an investigation was opened the previous day into allegations that he urged 24-year-old intern Monica Lewinsky to lie under oath in denying that she had an affair with him.

26: Hanson attacks Australian of the Year Cathy Freeman and Young Australian of the Year Tan Le, asking 'Why have we got an Aboriginal girl and an Asian girl at this time?' and saying appointments were 'heading down the line of political correctness'. Howard says of Hanson's comments, 'They were stupid, they were petty and they're very divisive remarks being made on Australia Day.'

28: The waterfront is at flashpoint after the nation's second-biggest stevedore, Patrick Corporation, confronts the Maritime Union of Australia (MUA) by striking a deal with a non-union operator backed by the National Farmers Federation. Patrick CEO Chris Corrigan says, 'If war is to come, it's to come from the Maritime Union.' Howard nominates waterfront reform as a priority, saying, 'Internationally competitive maritime and waterfront industries are essential to boosting Australia's trade performance in the current economic environment in the Asia-Pacific region.'

February 1998

10: Howard advises Clinton that Australia will send SAS soldiers and aircraft to fight in a new Gulf War, the first time ground troops would be committed since the Vietnam War.

13: The Constitutional Convention votes in favour of Australia becoming a republic by 89 votes to 52. The nation will vote next year on whether to replace the Queen with a president chosen by a bipartisan parliamentary majority. Howard says, 'Any commonsense interpretation of this convention is firstly that a majority of people have voted generically in favour of a republic and secondly that amongst the republican models, the one that has just got 73 votes is clearly preferred ... it would be a travesty, in commonsense terms, of Australian democracy for that proposition not to be put to the Australian people.'

25: B A Santamaria dies. The Prime Minister says, 'His death has ended the life of one of the most profoundly influential figures in post World War II politics.'

March 1998

5: New stricter travel rules for MPs are brought in, in the wake of travel rorts.

11: Resources Minister Warwick Parer admits he breached pecuniary interest guidelines over a $2 million investment in coal shares.

13: Western Australian Liberal backbencher MP Don Randall is locked out of the party's federal convention for suggesting that Cheryl Kernot was having an affair with Gareth Evans and 'had the morals of an alley cat on heat'. Howard says, 'I have never approved of attacks being made on people's private lives: it has no place in public life in this country.'

15: Howard announces the sale of a second slice of Telstra for $40 billion as the centrepiece of the Liberal re-election platform. Howard says, 'Just as Robert Menzies made Australia the greatest home-owning democracy in the Western world, so it is my goal that my government will make Australia the greatest share-owning democracy in the world.'

24: The Government announces that free-to-air stations will be given free use of high-definition digital television without competition from pay-TV for 10 years from 1 January 2001. The Minister for Communications, Senator Alston, says, 'This government would normally welcome additional competition, in any industry, as healthy and likely to lead to benefits for the consumer. However, Australia's free-to-air and pay-TV industries, in these special circumstances, deserve a degree of special treatment, and the Government makes no apology for this decision.'

28: The Senate's rejection of the Workplace Relations Amendment Bill provides the Government with a trigger for a double dissolution.

April 1998

7: Patrick sacks its entire waterfront workforce, declaring war on the MUA.

8: Non-union stevedores begin work at Patrick after the lockout of 2000 MUA workers.

12: Corrigan claims victory as *Australian Endeavour* is the first Australian ship unloaded using non-union labour.

16: There are violent clashes between locked-out wharfies and police in Fremantle. Howard says the MUA would have to shoulder the blame for any job losses resulting from its dispute with Patrick.

22: Federal Court Justice Tony North orders Patrick to re-instate the 2000 wharfies it dismissed two weeks ago.

29: Howard personally intervenes in the waterfront dispute, seeking to negotiate to bring about waterfront reform.

May 1998

1: ASIO to receive new powers to tap phones, use tracking devices and access computers as part of security preparations for the Sydney 2000 Olympics.

3: A leaked letter from the Minister for Communications, Senator Alston, to the Managing Director of the ABC, Brian Johns, complains of ABC bias in coverage of the waterside dispute.

5: MUA workers return to Patricks in a victory for the union.

12: Costello's third budget has a $2.7 billion surplus, the first surplus in 8 years.

21: President Suharto, Asia's longest serving leader, announces his resignation and steps aside for Vice-President B J Habibie. Howard gives a cautious welcome, saying, 'My government will co-operate with fully with Dr Habibie's administration ... as indeed we will co-operate with any future Indonesian administration.'

27: Howard promises that a GST will not be increased once it has been introduced.

June 1998

2: Hanson says in parliament that 'native title is the precursor to the establishment of tax-payer funded sovereign Aboriginal states'.

3: Howard says Hanson's speech 'is not only an inaccurate dishonest speech, but it verges on the deranged'.

13: The Coalition is battered by One Nation in the Queensland state election. The new party captures 11 seats with more than 22 per cent of the vote in the Queensland state election. Hanson describes the election as a slap in the face for Howard, saying, 'When he called me deranged, he was calling the majority of Queenslanders deranged.'

18: Senior Liberal MP and Parliamentary Secretary, Tony Abbott, challenges Howard's refusal to preference One Nation last by publicly calling on the Liberal Party to 'halt the Hanson contagion'. 'Equivocating over Hanson, whatever the reason, alienates far more voters in the Centre than it conciliates on the Right,' he says.

25: Labor's Peter Beattie becomes Premier of Queensland with the support of Independent Peter Wellington.

29: Howard and Independent, Brian Harradine, come to an agreement on Wik legislation that should see it passed by the Senate.

July 1998

1: Howard claims victory on Wik as he and Senator Brian Harradine broker a compromise on his 10-point plan. The compromise is welcomed by the National Party, the miners and some Aboriginal leaders. Noel Pearson says the Bill remains discriminatory but that Senator Harradine has at least salvaged some rights for indigenous people to protect their heritage on farming land.

2: James Hardie says it will set up a holding company in the Netherlands and relocate its head office to the United States. The company will gradually migrate to the US, where it derives more than 70 per cent of its income.

6: Queensland's Electoral Commission investigates One Nation after an expelled member alleges discrepancies in the party's constitution.

9: Keating denies government allegations that former President Suharto channelled funds to him through the sale of a piggery.

10: Howard meets Colston to secure support for the passage of the Government's Telstra Privatization Bill.

11: Colston scuttles the sale of Telstra in a late-night vote.

21: Costello raises the question of leadership, saying that Liberal colleagues have asked him to replace Howard. 'Look, bear this in mind, I helped John Howard become leader and I did that because I thought he was the right person to lead the party and he has my full support.' Howard says, 'I think people are always after the top job in politics—nothing unusual about that. I'd be the last person to decry ambition.'

22: Howard agrees to limit the sale of Telstra to 49 per cent.

28: Janette Howard reveals she suffered from cancer two years earlier.

August 1998

7: Two car bombs detonated outside the US embassies in Kenya and Tanzania kill at least 66 people and injure more than a thousand.

8: Saudi multimillionaire Osama bin Laden is named by a former CIA counterterrorism agent as the prime suspect behind the bombings of the US embassies in Kenya and Tanzania, which have killed 168 people. He is already suspected of involvement in the 1993 World Trade Centre bombing.

11: One Nation is investigated for fraud after a former member alleges that dues intended for the political party were directed into the commercial entity Pauline Hanson One Nation Ltd without the knowledge or consent of members.

13: Howard offers $17 billion in tax cuts, increased payments or compensation in exchange for the introduction of a GST.

21: The US launches 75 Tomahawk cruise missiles against Osama bin Laden's training camps in Afghanistan and a suspected chemical weapons factory in Sudan. President Clinton says, 'This will be a long, ongoing struggle between freedom and fanaticism, between the rule of law and terrorism.' Some Republican members of Congress question the timing of attacks as a diversion from the sex scandal that has dogged Clinton for months.

30: Howard announces a federal election will be held on 3 October with tax and economic security the main battleground. Howard says, 'The main issue will be whether ... at a time of economic uncertainty, even turmoil in some of the world, whether the Coalition or the Labor Party should be placed at the helm of economic management in Australia.' Beazley says, 'We are going to be talking about security and opportunity for our people. We're going to be talking about the sort of nation we need to be in this new century.'

September 1998

2: Costello announces economic growth in the year to June of 3.9 per cent, showing that Australia has weathered the Asian economic crisis in good shape. Howard describes Australia as 'the economic strongman of Asia' and asks: 'Do you get rid of the deliverers of these results? Do you replace the competents with the incompetents?'

3: Hanson announces a 2 per cent 'Easytax' and massive cuts to government spending to replace the abolition of personal tax and six other taxes. The package is attacked by the major parties, business and community groups.

11: Independent Prosecutor Kenneth Starr finds 11 possible grounds for impeaching President Clinton, claiming he 'pursued a strategy of deceiving the American people and Congress' for seven months over the Lewinsky affair, albeit acknowledging a physical relationship.

18: Democrats Leader Meg Lees announces that her party accepts the principle of a GST but demands that food be exempt and other changes be made to achieve greater fairness.

20: At the Liberal campaign launch, Howard says, 'I have never been more sure than I am today that I am doing the right thing by Australia in pursuing the cause of taxation reform. It is with a sense of excitement that I look forward, and all Australians should look forward, to the 21st century. We have the opportunity to leave a mark as the Australian people in the 21st century. We cannot assume that it will simply fall into our lap.'

October 1998

3: The Coalition wins a second term, with a majority of 13 seats, despite polling only 49 per cent of the two-party-preferred vote. Howard says, 'We won carrying what many people regarded as the electoral liability of a big tax plan … We will get the Parliament back as soon as we can and we will introduce the tax legislation as soon as possible.' Pauline Hanson fails to win the seat of Blair.

7: Mark Latham attacks Kim Beazley, saying 'People think Kim's a big angel but some of this stuff is a bit dirty behind the scenes.' Deputy Leader Gareth Evans says Latham has 'always been more of a solo flier than a team player'. Beazley defends Latham, saying, 'He's been an asset to us and he will be again.'

14: At a joint party meeting Howard tells his colleagues that implementation of the tax package is the Government's first aim in its second term but 'Non-economic issues will bulk large on the political horizon over the next three years, there will be a referendum on the republic, we do need to achieve reconciliation … not necessarily through the eyes of the former government once-removed, but through the eyes of the current government and the leaders of the indigenous people.'

20: Beazley names his shadow ministry, appointing Cheryl Kernot (who only just wins her marginal seat) to Transport and Regional Development and describing her as 'the most able person to come into politics in the post-World War II era'.

November 1998

1: Saddam Hussein forces a showdown with the US and UN by refusing to co-operate with UNSCOM and demanding the resignation of Chief Weapons Inspector Richard Butler.

29: Howard announces that a declaration acknowledging past and present wrongs will be the key to the reconciliation program of the

Howard Government's second-term race policy. The document is to be unveiled on 27 May 2000, six years after the Council for Aboriginal Reconciliation was created.

December 1998

4: Habibie succumbs to the pressure of student protests and brings forward elections to 7 June 1999, also ordering a corruption investigation into former President Suharto.

9: Mark Waugh and Shane Warne admit that they sold information about weather and pitch conditions to an illegal Indian bookmaker. Howard expresses disappointment. 'Australians love their cricket and anything that looks as though it is knocking cricket off its pedestal is something that does deeply disturb Australians,' he says.

10: The Howard Government's $1.4 billion a year rebate for private health insurance passes the Senate with the support of Harradine and Colston. Private fund members will get a 30 per cent rebate on premiums from 1 January.

13: Latham launches a scathing attack on the Labor Party in the *Australian Economic Review*. He writes, 'Labor's flaws in policy-making arise from structural problems in its policy culture.' He says federal Labor needs to 'avoid repeating the mistakes of Bob Carr in NSW; opportunistic in Opposition, followed by broken promises and pedestrian policies in government.' Glen Milne writes in *The Australian*: 'Already reviled inside the Caucus as a philosophical traitor, Latham is regarded as politically unstable as well; a walking time bomb.'

17: Clinton launches a series of air strikes against Iraq the day after a damning report on Iraq was handed to Kofi Annan by weapons inspections chief Butler.

20: Clinton, the second US president to be impeached by the House of Representatives, faces trial on charges of perjury and obstruction of justice.

27: Six die after the Sydney-to-Hobart yacht race runs into horrific, near cyclonic conditions in Bass Strait. Howard says the race is 'part of our way of life and these people have lost their lives following a sport they love'.

1999—Defending what is right

'A small, vulnerable community was about to be denied the freedom they have sought for so long and voted so overwhelmingly to achieve.'
—John Howard, 19 September 1999

THE AUSTRALIAN

EAST TIMOR IN FLAMES

Militias 'cleanse' Dili

- 25,000 herded out
- Belo's home burnt
- 24-hour troop alert

Pleas for help on the darkest day

Tight security cloaks Jiang's arrival

You catch the plane, we'll park the car.

January 1999

11: The Howard Government signals that Australia will for the first time press Indonesia to allow the East Timorese to decide their own future in what Downer describes as an 'historic shift' in the nation's foreign policy. The Opposition supports a referendum on independence.

12: The Indonesian Foreign Ministry says it is 'concerned and deeply regrets' the change in Canberra's East Timor policy.

17: Clinton and other world leaders express outrage at the massacre of 42 ethnic Albanians by Serbian security forces in southern Kosovo.

18: Indonesia begins moves to transfer Xanana Gusmao from a maximum-security prison to house arrest.

26: Sectarian massacres of Christians and Muslims on the Indonesian island of Ambon are estimated to have killed over a hundred people.

27: Indonesia says it will offer East Timor independence if it is backed by the majority of the people. Foreign Minister Ali Alatas says, 'If they want their freedom they are welcome.'

February 1999

5: Three One Nation MPs from Queensland quit the party.

9: Howard waters down his ministerial code of conduct, which forced the resignation of three frontbenchers and the retirement to the backbench of a fourth. 'They are not being softened; they are more commonsense, more realistic,' he says.

11: Indonesia warns it will abandon East Timor if its offer of autonomy is not accepted by the end of the year. Habibie says, 'From 1 January 2000 we don't want to be burdened with the East Timor problem.' Howard says an independent East Timor 'would be more vulnerable, more susceptible to economic pressures, a lot more lonely and a lot more in need of outside help than an East Timor that was part of Indonesia'. Xanana Gusmao says he regrets Australia's opposition to full independence. 'It is what we are fighting for.'

15: Senator Colston pleads that he is too sick with stomach cancer to stand trial on fraud charges but well enough to vote on the GST package by 30 June.

23: The federal Government plans to cut operating grants to universities that collect fees on behalf of student unions. David Kemp says, 'Students should not be forced to join a union to go to university. This legislation will protect their rights.'

26: Fifteen Australian aid workers flee East Timor because of fears for their safety after paramilitary commanders threatened to kill Australian diplomats and journalists, leaving the Australian Government with no representatives in the country.

March 1999

1: Howard announces that Australian troops, police and civilians are likely to be sent to East Timor next year as the backbone of a UN peacekeeping force of up to two thousand people.

5: Costello, Abbott and their wives Tanya Costello and Margaret Abbott are awarded $277,500 after winning a defamation case against author Bob Ellis. Ellis's salacious account of their relationship as students in his book *Goodbye Jerusalem*, which was withdrawn from sale and pulped, recounted a false and damaging story from former NSW Labor minister Rodney Cavalier. Abbott describes the case as a 'terrible ordeal', saying 'Thank God it's over'.

23: Howard releases a draft preamble to the Constitution, saying that it tries to, 'embrace in an appropriate fashion a sense of our history, a sense of who we are, a sense of what we believe in and a sense of what we aspire to achieve'. The preamble is a joint effort by the Prime Minister and poet Les Murray, although Murray says Howard, 'was the boss'. Opposition Leader Kim Beazley says the preamble 'falls short of the mark both in style and substance'.

25: Both sides of Australian politics back NATO air strikes on the former Yugoslavia. Howard says, 'It became unavoidable because of the stubbornness and the intransigence of Milosevic. The determination of the Serbians to pursue continued attacks and reprisals against the ethnic Albanians is really the cause of this action by NATO.'

30: Women will be able to claim a stake in their spouses' superannuation when marriages break down, under reforms announced by the Howard Government.

April 1999

5: *The Australian* reports that Howard has moved former Prime Minister Sir Robert Menzies' desk into his Parliament House office. The desk was used by all Australian prime ministers between 1927 and 1973.

6: Howard offers a safe haven for 4000 Kosovar refugees until they can return to their homes.

9: Australia demands the release of Peter Wallace and Steve Pratt, Australian aid workers in Serbia, after it is confirmed they are alive but in detention in an unknown location. Howard says, 'In a situation like this you try everything.'

11: Serbian authorities accuse Steve Pratt, Care Australia's head in Yugoslavia, of spying.

18: Pro-Indonesia militia open fire on East Timorese in Dili for a second day after 20 are killed on Saturday. Howard says, 'You have to wonder whether these pro-integration militia men are getting some kind of permissive response from the Indonesian army.'

19: Indonesian President Habibie agrees to Howard's proposal to meet him in Bali in an effort to stem bloodshed in East Timor. Howard tells Habibie: 'There was an unmistakeable impression in Australia that ABRI (the Armed Forces of Indonesia) was turning a blind eye'.

21: In America's bloodiest school massacre two disaffected students murder 15 people and leave 22 wounded at Columbine High School before killing themselves.

23: A leaked intelligence assessment details the Indonesian military's complicity in East Timorese killings in the weeks before the massacres in Liquica and Dili. The Opposition claims Timorese lives could have been saved if the Howard Government had acted earlier.

25: Defence Minister John Moore says, 'After the vote, if the United Nations can get agreement with Indonesia, then we would be quite amenable to joining in the United Nations force.'

17: President Habibie commits Indonesia to uphold a UN peace plan for East Timor after meeting Howard for four hours in Bali. The deal offers autonomy for East Timor, a ballot by the East Timorese on their future on 8 August, and a guarantee of security during and after the vote. Howard offers $20 million towards the UN supervision as well as police and civilian personnel. Howard says, 'I don't think any of us should underestimate the significance of Dr Habibie announcing today the approval of the UN agreement by the Government of Indonesia'.

30: Colston's lawyers ask that fraud charges against him be dismissed, citing medical evidence that he will die of cancer before he goes to court. 'I would consider it extremely unlikely that Senator Colston will still be alive in three months' time,' says Dr Stephen Lynch.

May 1999

3: Australia's first drug injecting room opens illegally in the Wayside Chapel in Sydney's Kings Cross. Howard says, 'I'm against heroin shooting galleries. I don't think there is any evidence they are of benefit and they send a bad signal.'

4: In a key speech to the Australia Unlimited conference in Melbourne, Howard sets goals for his second term, promising tighter budgets, more workplace and business deregulation and an extension of 'mutual obligation' in the welfare system. He says the Government's approach is 'founded on a belief that a market economy and a compassionate society are not only compatible but also desirable'.

7: A group of 410 refugees arrive in Sydney on a specially chartered Qantas flight and are welcomed by Howard before being taken by bus to a former migrant hostel. Howard says, 'We want you to be happy, we want you to feel welcome. You will be made to feel very safe here in your safe haven, Australia.'

14: Senator Harradine refuses to support the GST. Howard calls it 'a great setback for Australia'.

28: Democrats Leader Meg Lees agrees to back the GST, ensuring its passage through the Senate. Howard agrees to exempt basic food, restrict diesel fuel excise cuts, boost environment spending and temporarily retain some state taxes. Howard hails the breakthrough as 'a truly historic agreement'.

June 1999

10: The war in Kosovo ends with the first withdrawals of Yugoslav army troops. NATO suspends its 78-day bombing campaign.

21: On the eve of retiring from the Senate, Colston backs the sale of the second tranche of Telstra, leaving 50.1 per cent in government hands.

30: Tim Fischer resigns as Leader of the National Party and returns to the backbench to spend more time with his family and five-year-old autistic son. He is replaced by John Anderson. 'I will miss him terribly,' says Howard.

July 1999

5: Colston escapes all rort charges on the grounds of his terminal illness and collects $1.55 million in superannuation.

National MP Mark Vaile reluctantly takes on the Trade portfolio in the wake of Fischer's retirement.

9: Howard flies to Washington for talks with US President Bill Clinton, infuriated that the US will impose punitive tariffs on lamb imports. Howard says the decision is 'particularly galling and completely unjustified. ... It is hypocritical in terms of American trade rhetoric and sends an appalling signal to those around the world who want to backslide away from more open trade.'

12: The Howard Government persuades the UNESCO World Heritage Committee to give the green light to the Jabiluka uranium mine.

23: A West Australian District Court jury clears Carmen Lawrence of three counts of lying to the Easton royal commission.

25: On the eve of his 60th birthday Howard says, 'I don't have any intention of retiring.'

28: As many as 13 Australians are unaccounted for after a flash flood sweeps through a gorge in Switzerland killing at least 20 people.

August 1999

9: Howard compromises on the wording of the November referendum on the republic, saying, 'I don't want people running around saying after the referendum Howard rigged the question.' The question to be posed is 'Do you approve of a republic with the Queen and Governor-General being replaced by a president appointed by a two-thirds majority of the members of the Commonwealth Parliament?' Beazley says the wording has been chosen 'to diminish the chances of the referendum being carried'.

11: Howard negotiates a new Constitutional preamble, with the Democrats dropping the word *mateship* and including a reference to Aboriginal 'kinship' with the land. Howard says: 'I think we now have an opportunity to unite the country on an aspirational issue in a very positive way.'

17: Bill Kelty announces he will resign as Secretary of the ACTU in February 2000 having worked for the organisation since 1983.

26: Federal parliament passes an historic expression of national regret for all the injustices to Aboriginal people, describing their suffering as the 'greatest blemish' on our history. Howard says, 'It is an honest and sincere attempt on the part of the Government to make a genuine contribution to the reconciliation process.'

30: East Timorese turn out in massive numbers to vote in a largely peaceful ballot in a climate of escalating violence.

September 1999

1: Hundreds of Dili residents flee as armed militia burn houses and shoot independence supporters.

In Serbia, Pratt and Wallace are freed after the original charges against them of spying for NATO are dropped. They are found guilty of passing information to a foreign organisation but granted clemency.

2: Hundreds of people shelter in a school next to the UN headquarters in Dili as armed militiamen roam the streets. Indonesian police fail to act on a promise to arrest anyone carrying a weapon.

4: The UN announces that 70 per cent of the electorate in East Timor have voted for independence. Two militia-dominated towns explode in violence, leaving two UN staff dead. Indonesia deploys 1400 hundred extra troops to the territory and Australian troops are on 30-minute standby to fly to Dili.

6: Thousands of East Timorese are herded out of their homes and independence supporters are massacred by militia working with security forces. Howard says, 'The situation has really got much worse in the last 48 hours.' Australian Ambassador JohnMcCarthy is shot at while Australia discusses with key allies how it could support an international peacekeeping effort in East Timor.

7: Indonesia imposes martial law in East Timor and frees Xanana Gusmao.

10: Hundreds of East Timorese refugees arrive in Darwin. US President Clinton supports Australia's role in building a peacekeeping force but declines to send US troops. Howard says he has told the President that Australians would not understand if America failed to help the peace effort, 'given the depth of the relationship and the contributions we've made in the past'. He says the US has not ruled out contributing troops ('boots on the ground') in addition to their promised logistical support.

12: Indonesia caves in to international pressure to allow peacekeepers to go into East Timor. Habibie says, 'Too many people have lost their lives … We have to stop the suffering and the mourning immediately.' Howard hails the announcement as a tremendous step forward and says, 'Dr Habibie deserves great credit for what he has done tonight'.

14: Australia seems likely to lead the peacekeeping force. Howard says, 'There will be danger, there could be casualties, and the Australian public must understand that. It is a serious, dangerous operation.'

15: President Habibie refuses to take a call from Howard in a sign of the souring relations. Habibie's spokeswoman says, 'There is a very strong feeling of animosity towards Australia, rightly or wrongly, from the pro-integration forces in East Timor. If the UN peacekeeping forces are made up of Australians, they will be singled out. That is my fear.'

Greg Sheridan writes in *The Australian*: 'The deepening tragedy in East Timor represents the greatest catastrophe in the history of Australian foreign policy … the holocaust in East Timor is a direct consequence of the failure of Australian policy.'

16: Senior US officials are highly critical of Australia's handling of the East Timor problem, accusing Canberra of underestimating the depth of the crisis and failing to make the US aware in sufficient time.

18: A backlash in regional Victoria delivers a surprise defeat for Premier Jeff Kennett and the spectre of a hung parliament. Kennett says, 'If I were a betting man, I would suggest you will have a change of government … and if that is the case, I will accept that decision with grace and ride into the sunset'.

19: In a televised address to the nation, Howard says, 'Our soldiers go to East Timor as part of a great Australian military tradition, which has never sought to impose the will of this country on others but only to defend what is right.'

20: Australian combat troops of the International Force East Timor (Interfet) occupy Dili. The International Red Cross estimates that 600,000 people have been internally displaced, with another 200,000 now in West Timor. Howard tells troops bound for East Timor that the nation is confident they will follow in the 'great Australian tradition' of looking after their mates.

21: A package of tax reforms flowing from the Ralph Report receives tentative support from Democrats and Labor, suggesting they will be passed. They include cutting company tax rates from 36 to 30 per cent, halving capital gains tax rate for individual investors and cutting it for small businesses and a crackdown on tax concessions for trusts.

22: In an interview in *The Bulletin* Howard unveils what the magazine calls the 'Howard Doctrine', under which Australia will embrace a new role as the US's peacekeeping 'deputy' in Asia now that it has led a peace force to Timor. 'We have displayed our responsibility, shouldered the burden we should have,' Howard says. 'Australia has a particular responsibility to do things above and beyond in this part of the world.'

24: Howard's doctrine comes under attack from South-East Asian politicians, who brand it racist and a threat to regional ties. Malaysia's Deputy Home Minister, Azmi Khalid, says, 'We are actually fed up with their stance: that they are sitting in a white chair and supervising the coloured chairs.'

27: Howard is forced to clarify Australia's role in South-East Asia. He says, 'The Government does not see Australia as playing the role of a deputy for the United States, or indeed any other country in the region and neither does the Government see the United States itself playing a role as a regional policeman, although continued American involvement in the region is vital to our security.'

October 1999

5: Howard says Keating is undermining the national interest after Keating accuses the Prime Minister of being responsible for 500,000 to 800,000 missing or dead East Timorese. 'The militias are responsible for what's happened in East Timor,' Howard says. Jose Ramos Horta backs Howard as the 'only Prime Minister in Australia in 23 years who has had the courage to respond to the appeals, to the cries of the people of East Timor. They will remember the likes of Paul Keating, who year after year were an accomplice of the Suharto regime.'

14: Howard dilutes a radical reform proposal for Australian universities put forward by Education Minister David Kemp. Howard says, 'There will be no $100,000 university fees under this government.'

19: Steve Bracks forms a minority Labor government in Victoria with the support of three key Independents.

20: Abdurrahman Wahid defeats Megawati Sukarnoputri in Indonesia's first free presidential election. Megawati becomes the Vice-President.

26: Howard enters the republic debate with a detailed defence of Australia's constitutional monarchy. 'I hope [the people] will reject the republic. It will not produce a better Australia.'

November 1999

6: Australians reject a republic, with a vote of 55 against and 45 in favour. Howard tells Channel Nine's Paul Lyneham two days later: 'I didn't knobble the referendum. The Australian people said no. And it's about time all of the participants in this debate accepted that we live in a democracy.'

9: Jonathan Shier, a former pay-TV executive and Coalition government staffer with little public broadcasting experience, is chosen by the ABC board to be the Managing Director of the ABC.

10: Howard bows to public criticism and invites Governor-General William Deane to replace him in performing the opening ceremony at the Olympic Games. 'Ensuring that the Games are a great unifying national event is far more important to me than any personal satisfaction I might get from opening the Games,' Howard says.

11: A group of 170 Iraqi and Afghani boat people are taken to a detention centre north of Broome. More than 700 boat people have arrived in over a week, with intelligence reports expecting up to 2500.

15: Immigration Minister Philip Ruddock claims that 10,000 people from the Middle East are preparing to come illegally to Australia and wants to accelerate debate on his border protection bill. Labor supports the measure in principle.

19: Howard lashes out at multimillion-dollar salaries, saying, 'Examples in the corporate sector of excessive levels of executive remuneration … cause some resentment in the community.'

23: High income earners will pay a special one-off tax to offset the cost of Australia's peace forces in East Timor.

December 1999

9: Unemployment falls below 7 per cent for the first time in nine years.

14: Howard calls on states to abandon safe injecting rooms following UN advice that the plans might violate a convention signed by Australia in 1961 and tarnish the image of the Sydney Olympics.

24: Education Minister Kemp advises that the Government will cut direct grants to universities by nearly $1 billion.

2000—An unstoppable force

'The mood of the Australian community is overwhelmingly in favour of reconciliation. It is and should be an unstoppable force.'
—John Howard, 7 December 2000

January 2000

7: Tech stocks fall after the 'millennium bug' fails to wreak havoc and interest rate fears puncture the Internet bubble.

February 2000

10: Howard denies that the Government's decision to enable a payout of workers and creditors of National Textiles from public funds was influenced by the fact that the company was chaired by his brother Stan.

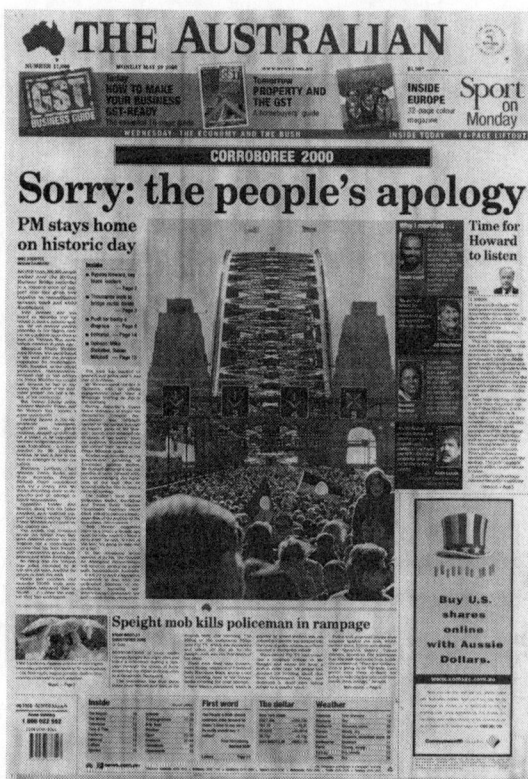

THE AUSTRALIAN

CORROBOREE 2000

Sorry: the people's apology

PM stays home on historic day

Time for Howard to listen

Speight mob kills policeman in rampage

11: Howard rules out further government payouts of workers' entitlements, amid growing concerns in the Coalition about the precedent set by the special treatment granted to his brother's failed textile company. The Prime Minister declares that the Government has 'drawn a line in the sand' on the issue. While sacked workers and secured creditors will be paid in full, unsecured creditors will be paid only 2 cents in the dollar on the $12 million they are owed.

14: The federal Government urges Western Australia and the Northern Territory to amend mandatory sentencing after the death in custody of a 15-year-old boy, jailed for the theft of property worth less than $150. Howard tells Sydney radio that the death of the teenager was 'an awful tragedy' but it was 'preferable' for the Territory Government to deal with the issue.

General Wiranto resigns after a state-sanctioned human rights inquiry finds that he committed crimes against humanity in East Timor.

15: A second group of laid-off workers in regional NSW may be bailed out by the federal Government after Howard pledges to consider their plight in an extension of his safety net scheme covering employees' entitlements.

27: Howard declares that Aboriginal reconciliation will not be achieved by the 31 December deadline and is shifting the Government's emphasis away from the reconciliation document' towards the provision of services.

March 2000

5: Ruddock foreshadows a rise in immigration as early as 2001, the first increase in the migrant intake since Howard came to power.

31: People on unemployment benefits in areas where work is available are warned they will lose the dole if they fail to take jobs on offer. Employment Services Minister Tony Abbott says, 'Unemployed people can't wait for the ideal job.'

April 2000

2: Howard supports Aboriginal Affairs Minister John Herron, who claims there is no stolen generation. 'We're arguing it's not a generation if it was 10 per cent. If it was a generation it means the whole generation, so we think it's a misnomer.' The Council for Aboriginal Reconciliation's Evelyn Scott says the comments raise the likelihood of protests at the Olympic Games.

3: Howard defends his government against charges that it is racist and declares he has not abandoned the reconciliation process. 'The Government is not endeavouring to divide the Australian community on this issue,' he says.

4: During a party-room meeting at least a dozen Coalition MPs and senators demand a more sensitive and more intelligent approach to Aboriginal problems and to social issues such as unemployment, saying that the Government's good economic record is continually being swamped by harsh rhetoric on indigenous and other issues.

6: Howard says sorry to Aborigines offended by his government's refusal to acknowledge the term 'stolen generation' but stops short of indigenous demands to disown a government document that denies the 'stolen generation'. Howard says, 'Let me say very directly to anyone in the Australian community who was in any way offended by that document, I'm sorry about that.'

9: A group of 181 Kosovar refugees fight to be allowed to stay in Australia. Immigration Minister Philip Ruddock refuses to compromise, saying, 'It's time to go.'

16: Howard tells the Liberal Party conference he will target Beazley as a weak leader who 'walks both sides of the street' and is hostage to the unions.

25: Howard addresses a crowd of 15,000 at Gallipoli on the 75th anniversay of the Anzac landings. 'We come to seek the inspiration that stories of compassion and comfort give to others in their time of need, knowing that there are opportunities, in our own lives, to ease the burden of those suffering adversity and hardship,' he says.

May 2000

9: The budget shows an unexpected $2.8 billion surplus, allowing the Government to scrap the proposed Timor levy.

11: Calls are made for Health Minister Michael Wooldridge to resign following a surge of orders for MRI scanners after it is alleged that he leaked a budget decision to limit funding of the scanners.

17: Malaysian Prime Minister Mahathir accuses Australia of reversing its previous policy of engagement with Asia, saying, 'you change your policy because you now feel that Indonesia is weak and you can impose your will ... if you have a policy you should stick to it and not change it simply because you think you can bully others'.

27: Howard addresses Corroboree 2000 at the Opera House but parts of his speech are drowned out by shouts of 'Say sorry'. Howard declares that it is impossible 'to move forward effectively without understanding and acknowledging the pain that was inflicted by the injustices of the past' but says 'part of the process of reconciliation is to adopt practical measures to address that disadvantage'.

28: More than 200,000 people walk over the Sydney Harbour Bridge, giving a new impetus to reconciliation. Aboriginal Affairs Minister

John Herron, one of two official government representatives, along with Philip Ruddock, reveals that he had advised the Prime Minister not to take part because he had to represent 'the whole of the Australian people', not just a section of the community.

29: Howard tells ABC television: 'I know that I have been criticised because the Government won't agree to a formal national apology for past misdeeds. My reason for that and the Government's reason is that we don't believe the present generation should be held accountable for the misdeeds of earlier generations, particularly when those acts were sanctioned by the law at the time.'

June 2000

7: Hundreds of Australians are evacuated from the Solomon Islands by the Australian Defence Force after rebel gunmen seize the Solomon Islands Prime Minister in Honiara.

29: Howard says of the GST, which is to be introduced on 1 July, 'This is the generational change that this country has needed for at least a quarter of a century. It is a change that will immeasurably strengthen the Australian economy.'

July 2000

11: A split emerges in the Labor leadership over the rollback of GST. Beazley sticks to the rollback pledge.

25: Howard considers extending mutual obligation to supporting parents and disability welfare recipients.

26: On his 61st birthday Howard says he will lead the Liberal Party into the next election. 'After that, obviously one has to recognise, I'll then be in my 63rd or 64th year,' he says. 'And nothing is forever.'

August 2000

1: Howard says he will amend the Sexual Discrimination Act to reflect the 'reasonable expectation' that children require the 'affection and care of both a mother and a father'.

10: Howard tells students at Ferntree Gully School in Melbourne: 'I want to see a country where people, irrespective of their background, continue to be treated in a tolerant, decent way ... whatever your background: whether it's Aboriginal or Chinese or Jewish or Muslim; that everybody is treated in a completely tolerant, harmonious way. I think that's very important, I think Australia is very good at that now.'

11: A test case for compensation of the stolen generations fails when a Federal Court judge cites lack of evidence in dismissing the claims of two Aborigines taken from their parents. The judgment dashes the hopes of thousands of others hoping to sue the Commonwealth.

September 2000

1: Howard condemns Mark Latham's 'ludicrous' parliamentary attack on Kerry Packer's gambling losses. Howard says Packer is a good corporate citizen.

4: Nelson Mandela calls on Australia to throw open its doors to the UN. He says, 'I have no doubt that Prime Minister John Howard, if he has a discussion with the Secretary-General, may realise that it is in the interest of Australia to allow any committee of the UN to visit the country.'

11: Thousands of protesters lay siege to a meeting in Melbourne of the World Economic Forum on globalisation. Howard dismisses the protests as 'hooliganism' that offends the Australian way of life and says it is a 'myth' to suggest that rejecting globalisation will help the poor.

15: Cathy Freeman lights the Olympic cauldron in the opening ceremony of the Olympic Games.

October 2000

2: Howard is hoisted on the shoulders of silver medallists from the men's rowing eight as he dances with 150 athletes on the stage of Sydney's Capitol Theatre. One of the rowing eight, Don Burke, says, 'He was at almost every final and everyone in Australia appreciated that.'

10: A $50,000 fraud involving the misuse of Workplace Relations Minister Peter Reith's telephone card sparks an investigation. A total of 11,000 calls from 900 locations around the world have been made with his card between 1994 and August 1999 after Reith breached guidelines by giving it to his son. Howard says he does not think the incident is a 'hanging offence'.

11: Howard asks the Solicitor-General for advice as to the civil legal liability of Reith or any other person for the remaining monies.

12: Howard says that Reith has been foolish. 'As a taxpayer, I am angry and I understand why Australians are angry that $50,000 one way or another should have been racked up and they are left with the bill.'

13: Reith agrees to pay the full amount of $50,000 outstanding on his telephone card bill.

15: Investigation reveals that Reith's breach of guidelines led to subsequent fraud that involved Reith's son's girlfriend, her landlord and his family.

Australia agrees to send peacekeeping forces to the Solomon Islands.

24: Federal cabinet rules out building a second airport in western Sydney, clearing the way for a $4 billion sale of Sydney Airport.

November 2000

15: Costello estimates that the budget surplus could reach $4.3 billion.

22: A federal inquiry is launched into child rape allegations at Woomera as new and substantial information emerges that had been withheld. Ruddock says, 'If there's been some collusive efforts to cover up these matters and avoid reporting obligations and avoid possible penalties, let me say … I'll deal with it.'

27: Councils are given $1.2 billion to repair and build country roads as part of a $1.6 billion project to respond to anger at rising petrol prices. Howard says, 'It is not a pork barrel; there's no room for any sort of claims of undue influence or manipulation. We are going to recognise that local government knows where the priorities are.'

30: Noel Pearson backs the Coalition three years after describing them as 'racist scum' and unleashes an attack on the ALP. He says he shares the Coalition's views about the need to deal with welfare dependency.

December 2000

4: Less than three years after the Maritime Union of Australia said that it was impossible, waterfront workers are achieving 25 crane lifts per hour.

7: Howard describes reconciliation as an 'unstoppable force' in the Australian community and indicates that he will consider calls for a treaty with 'immense goodwill'. He says the Government will provide $5.5 million for a new body, Reconciliation Australia, which will succeed the Council for Aboriginal Reconciliation.

14: Bush claims victory in the US presidential elections.

19: Howard reshuffles cabinet as ministers Herron (Aboriginal and Torres Strait Islander Affairs), Moore (Defence) and Newman (Family, Community Services, assisting on Status of Women) resign, making way for Abbott (Employment and Workplace Relations), Vanstone (Family and Community Services), Reith (Defence) and Ruddock (Immigration, Multicultural Affairs, Aboriginal and Torres Strait Islander Affairs, assisting on Reconciliation).

20: Howard says Australians are living in an era when people 'are faithless about all institutions: not just political institutions. There's criticism of all institutions. It's an era, a period or phase that we're going through. People are very critical of business, very critical of the media. They're very critical of the political system.' He defended most politicians as people who believe in something and try to make a difference.

2001—Whatever it takes
'We are a humane nation but we're not a nation that's going to be intimidated by this kind of behaviour.'
—John Howard, 7 October 2001

January 2001

1: As Australia marks the Centenary of Federation, Howard says: 'A unified, peaceful and purposeful nation has been created by people drawn from the most diverse cultures on Earth. Opportunity and

NEWSPAPER OF THE YEAR

THE AUSTRALIAN

DAWN EDITION

World's worst terrorist attacks paralyse New York and Washington

WAR OF TERROR

■ Thousands feared dead   ■ World Trade Centre destroyed   ■ Pentagon bombed

encouragement exist for any man or woman to achieve their dreams, and yet egalitarianism remains the cornerstone of Australian society.'

8: Latham proposes that long-entrenched welfare safety-net arrangements be abandoned.

26: Lieutenant-General Peter Cosgrove is named Australian of the Year. The Australia Day Council rejects suggestions that Howard influenced the decisions.

February 2001

1: *The Australian* reports that Howard is personally driving a strategy to reach a free trade agreement with the Bush administration, with the aim of announcing negotiations when he visits Washington mid-year to celebrate the 50th anniversary of the ANZUS treaty.

10: Geoff Gallop wins the Western Australian state elections after Pauline Hanson's One Nation Party ran a campaign of 'putting the sitting member last'. One Nation is estimated to have 10 per cent support state-wide in Western Australia and 20 per cent support in the bush.

12: Howard responds to the Liberal defeat in Western Australia, saying a vote for One Nation is a vote for Labor. 'I will be saying repeatedly between now and the next federal election to potential One Nation voters that if you are by normal inclination a Liberal supporter, by voting One Nation and following their preference advice you're voting for Mr Beazley,' he says.

17: Labor's Peter Beattie is returned to office in Queensland with a massive increase in Labor's vote. One Nation's support is reduced but it fractures the conservative vote with the Nationals giving preferences to One Nation.

19: Responding to the Labor victory in Queensland, Howard says social dislocation caused by economic change is the main reason why people are attracted to simplistic solutions. 'Managing the impact of change is the biggest challenge that governments have in a liberal democratic society such as Australia,' he says.

20: Howard takes a personal interest in trying to solve petrol sniffing in Aboriginal communities, committing $1 million over two years to initiatives to a diversionary program for children.

22: Costello backs down and announces that small businesses will not have to file another quarterly business activity statement.

23: Lowitja O'Donoghue concedes that her Irish father may have given her and her four siblings to a missionary-run home. 'I would see myself as a removed child, and not necessarily stolen.' Howard says, 'What she has said is highly significant but I don't want to dwell upon it too much because that would be painful for her … I have never supported the notion of a formal apology because I have never believed the present generation of Australians should be forced to accept responsibility for what happened in earlier times.'

25: Howard refuses to offer motorists relief from the GST impact on fuel excise, saying petrol prices are high because crude oil prices are high.

26: Sir Donald Bradman dies aged 92. Howard says Sir Donald would 'forever be regarded as the quintessential Australian hero who was as gracious as he was valiant'. He says, 'Sir Donald Bradman's contribution was more than to the game of cricket. It was his role in the history and development of Australia that will also be remembered.'

27: Howard signals that he will back down on petrol taxes, saying, 'The Government is currently examining whether there is scope to provide what, against the vast increases that have occurred due to world oil prices going up, would be very modest relief.' The Treasurer also backs down on a two-and-a-half-year-old Coalition decision to tax family trusts more harshly after pressure from the Nationals and Liberal backbenchers.

March 2001

1: Howard cuts the fuel excise by 1.5 cents a litre and abandons further excise hikes. He says, 'I was plainly wrong in not understanding some of the concerns held by the Australian people about the price of petrol.'

7: Howard launches an attack on the Reserve Bank, blaming the fall in economic growth on the bank's 'error of judgment' in raising interest rates in 2000.

17: Labor's Leonie Short wins the formerly safe Liberal seat of Ryan vacated by John Moore, with a swing of almost 10 per cent. Howard concedes that the Government must do better at explaining the advantages of reform but says: 'I reject completely any suggestion that [the result in Ryan] spells inevitable defeat for the Government.'

21: Howard and his ministers launch an attack on banks and credit card companies. 'I'm certainly in favour of any action being taken to prevent the banks charging fees they oughtn't to charge,' Howard says.

28: Howard says Labor's plan to cut the excise on beer is pandering to the interests of Lion Nathan and Labor's refusal to ban online gambling is pandering to Internet gambling operators.

April 2001

6: Natasha Stott Despoja wins leadership of the Democrats, who punish Meg Lees for her support of the GST.

22: Howard announces that Peter Hollingworth, Anglican Archbishop of Brisbane and 'living national treasure', will be the next Governor-General, breaking a pattern that the position should be held by an ex-judge, ex-politician or ex-military chief.

23: The dollar falls as Costello vetoes Shell's hostile takeover of Woodside.

26: Howard clashes with oil companies over the price of petrol. 'I would encourage [Australian Competition and Consumer Commission Chairman] Professor Fels to throw the book at the oil companies if there has been anything untoward done, if there has been any collusion.'

May 2001

1: Howard launches an unheard-of attack on High Court Judge Michael Kirby for intervening in the partisan debate over school funding. 'It's not appropriate for a High Court judge to involve himself in something that is so blatantly and obviously a matter of debate between the two political parties,' he says.

2: A leaked memo from Liberal Party President Shane Stone sheets home part of the blame for the Liberal Party's poor performance in the Queensland state elections to Costello, Anderson and, by association, Howard. The memo says, 'We are seen as a "mean government" ... we have been just "too tricky" on some issues'. Howard brushes it off, saying he has full confidence in both Stone and Costello.

4: Newspoll shows Howard well behind an ascendant Beazley. The Coalition's primary support is just 35 per cent while Labor climbs to 45 per cent.

21: Howard announces a government bailout of victims of the HIH insurance group collapse, including small businesses and thousands of individual Australians. Howard changes his position and announces that a royal commission will be held but stresses that this, 'in no way indicates a lack of confidence in the abilities or the competence' of ASIC to conduct an investigation.

22: Costello spends $1 billion on older Australians, including a $300 bonus and backdated tax refunds in the federal budget.

June 2001

4: After the collapse of One.Tel, Howard turns up the heat on the company's co-founders, Brad Keeling and Jodee Rich, to give back the bonuses they took last year to pay for One.Tel redundancy entitlements, which may be as much as $14 million. Howard says, 'I think everybody who's been involved in this company has some moral obligation to see the workers helped out.'

7: Anglican archbishop-elect Peter Jensen accuses Howard of 'being out of step with God' over his refusal to offer a formal apology to Aborigines. Howard responds by saying that community leaders shouldn't 'presume to interpret God's will too narrowly'.

11: Democrat Senator Aden Ridgeway criticises Noel Pearson, saying: 'Some of us are tiring of this new nauseating and incessant tune that Aborigines ought to get over "victim hood" and that rights alone will no longer do ... Not one notable indigenous leader has come out in favour of Pearson's practical stance and his call for an abandonment of a rights agenda.'

13: Employment Minister Tony Abbott calls for tax credits to boost the after-tax incomes of low-income and middle-income families.

20: Immigration Minister Philip Ruddock rejects as 'extraordinarily naive' a parliamentary committee's key recommendation of a 14-week time limit on the mandatory detention of illegal immigrants.

25: Indonesian President Adurrahman Wahid visits Canberra, the first visit to Australia by an Indonesian leader in 26 years and the first to the capital since 1972.

27: Howard indicates that the federal Government will accept greater control of Ansett by Singapore Airlines. 'If the choice is between the company going out of business or an increase in foreign ownership and saving jobs, then I'd obviously want to keep the company in business and save jobs,' says Howard.

29: Reith decides to retire from politics at the forthcoming federal election. Colleagues suggest that his decision to retire is motivated by the fact that the telecard incident had ended his hopes of becoming Liberal leader.

July 2001

2: Beazley launches the 'Knowledge Nation' plan to boost R&D, education, high tech industries, IT and education. 'This is my political future. I'm staking myself on it,' he says. But a confusing chart used by Barry Jones leads to the policy quickly being dubbed 'Noodle Nation'.

5: Hanson faces charges of electoral fraud in a blow to her bid to win a seat in the Senate.

8: Anderson forces rebel MP Bob Katter out of the National Party.

12: Two days before the Aston by-election Beazley declares that Australians are not overtaxed. Asked whether the voters of Aston were paying too much tax he says, 'No, I don't believe so and I will say that with some vigour.' By contrast, Costello commits to returning to tax payers any revenue gains from faster economic growth.

14: Aston by-election is too close to be called on the day but is retained for the Liberals by Chris Pearce after a detailed count. Howard says, 'I'm not exhilarated by the fact that our primary vote fell, but then Mr Beazley shouldn't be exhilarated by the fact that his primary vote fell, albeit by a much lesser number than did ours.'

23: Megawati Sukarnoputri is sworn in as Indonesian President as Adurrahman Wahid is ousted.

26: Howard announces a royal commission into the building industry to investigate allegations of fraud, standover tactics and violence into dealings involving building workers' retirement funds.

31: Polls show that Howard's standing with voters has bounced back. Newspoll shows the Coalition primary vote at 43 per cent while Labor has fallen to 39 per cent.

August 2001

6: Fugitive failed businessman Christopher Skase dies of cancer. Howard gives the green light for efforts to recover the missing millions. 'There is a legitimate public interest in that, yes,' he says.

12: Howard meets Megawati, the first foreign leader to do so since she became Indonesian President.

16: 351 asylum seekers, including 150 women and young children, arrive at Christmas Island.

18: Labor, led by Clare Martin, wins government in the Northern Territory for the first time in 27 years.

22: A group of 360 asylum seekers arrive on Christmas Island, bringing to 1220 the number of asylum seekers who have arrived by boat this year.

26: The Norwegian freighter MV *Tampa* rescues 433 boat people, most of them Afghanis, from a stricken Indonesian fishing vessel.

27: Australia provides emergency aid to the asylum seekers on board the *Tampa* but Howard refuses to allow them onto Australian soil. *Tampa* Captain Arne Rinnan says he had been forced to head for Christmas Island when several asylum seekers threatened to jump overboard if they were returned to Indonesia. Howard says, 'as a matter of international law, this matter is something that must be resolved between the Government of Indonesia and the Government of Norway'. He says there was a clear obligation under international law for the asylum seekers to be taken to the nearest feasible point of disembarkation: the Indonesian port of Merak. Howard says Australia has to balance its duties of decency and generosity towards boat people with the rights of refugees who seek to arrive legally.

28: The *Tampa* standoff continues as Howard and Indonesia both refuse to accept the asylum seekers. A spokesperson for the Norwegian Foreign Minister says, 'In our view this is quite unprecedented: we have not heard of a situation before in which a vessel has, upon advice, rescued people at sea and been denied access to the port to unload these people.'

29: Howard seeks to have the Border Protection Bill passed to give more options to prevent the refugees landing in Australia. Howard says, 'It is in the national interest that we have the power to prevent, beyond any argument, people infringing the sovereignty of this country.' Beazley accuses Howard of indulging in wedge politics.

31: East Timor offers to accept the *Tampa* asylum seekers but Australia declines the offer.

September 2001

2: Howard comes up with a solution whereby the asylum seekers are taken on board the HMAS *Manoora* to Papua New Guinea to be flown to Nauru and New Zealand for processing. UN Secretary-General Kofi Annan says, 'This is not the way to handle a refugee situation.' Howard stands firm, describing it as a 'humanitarian consideration outcome' and a 'truly Pacific solution'.

4: One Nation offers the Liberal Party a preference deal for the coming federal election on the basis of its handling of the *Tampa* refugees which it says is One Nation's policy towards asylum seekers. Howard refuses.

6: Ansett appeals for a government cash injection of funds as the New Zealand Government and Air New Zealand waver on allowing Singapore Airlines to take a higher stake.

7: Ansett losses of $1.3 million a day force Singapore Airlines to withdraw its original bid for a larger stake.

8: Some 237 asylum seekers plucked by the navy from a small fishing boat are expected to be sent to Nauru.

10: Air New Zealand offers Ansett to Qantas for $1. In the United States, Howard and Bush mark the 50th anniversary of the ANZUS alliance.

11: Two hijacked aircraft plunge into the twin towers of New York's World Trade Centre and another into the Pentagon in Washington. A fourth aircraft crashes. Howard is evacuated from his hotel in the capital. The main suspect is Osama bin Laden.

12: President George W Bush declares war against the perpetrators of the September 11 attacks.

13: Howard commits Australia to providing military support to the US in its retaliation for the September 11 attacks. ' We should stand shoulder to shoulder with the Americans,' he says, 'because this is not just an assault on America, it's an assault on the way of life that we hold dear in common.'

14: Ansett administrators advise the Government that the airline's condition is so bad that it cannot continue to operate. The Government provides funds to enable Ansett to complete its schedules for the day.

Howard invokes the ANZUS treaty. 'Australia stands ready to cooperate within the limits of its capability concerning any response that the United States may regard as necessary in consultation with her allies,' he says. He again says the September 11 incidents were 'an attack upon the way of life we hold dear in common with the Americans'.

16: President Bush issues an ultimatum to Kabul to surrender Osama bin Laden within 76 hours or face a devastating US retaliation for the September 11 attacks.

19: The world aviation industry is in crisis as airlines and aircraft manufacturers cut 80,000 jobs.

23: Some 217 Iraqi and Palestinian refugees refuse to disembark from the HMAS *Manoora* for fear that they will be left in Nauru indefinitely.

24: Newspoll shows that Howard's popularity is at a five-year high.

28: Intelligence sources confirm that associates of bin Laden are active in Australia and raid a property used by suspected militants in the Southern Highlands.

29: Ansett Mark II takes to the skies with a $99 fare from Sydney to Adelaide.

October 2001

4: Howard announces that almost a thousand Australian military personnel—the biggest commitment since Vietnam, and including an SAS regiment and two refuelling jets—will join the US's anti-terrorism force.

5: Howard calls a federal election for 10 November, saying 'This is not a time to change to either a prime minister or to a party that finds it difficult to articulate a clear view on the great issues that challenge the Australian nation.' Mr Beazley cites his five years as Defence Minister saying, 'I have never felt myself better qualified for this position at any time in my life than I feel now.'

7: A dozen asylum seekers wearing life jackets jump overboard with their children wearing life jackets 150 nautical miles from Australian territory. Immigration Minister Philip Ruddock, describes the asylum seekers' actions as 'disturbing and pre-meditated'. Howard deplores the boat people's actions, saying, 'We are a humane nation, but we're not a nation that's going to be intimidated by this sort of behaviour.' Greens Senator Bob Brown says: 'Nobody throws their children overboard unless they're desperate. This is not an exercise in war. It's an exercise in politics.'

8: The US and Britain bomb targets in Kabul and Kandahar in Afghanistan and brace for retaliatory terror attacks.

9: More than 200 asylum seekers, including 54 children, wait aboard the HMAS *Adelaide* and are likely to be taken to PNG as Ruddock adds weight to speculation that the people-smuggling vessels have been deliberately sunk. Howard says, 'I certainly don't want people of that type in Australia, I really don't.'

10: Defence Minister Peter Reith refuses to release a navy video that he says proves children were thrown into the sea. He says the video will not be released while Defence is 'testing the quality for reproduction' but releases a photograph of adults and children wearing life jackets in the water along with navy personnel.

12: Howard talks openly of succession, saying: 'I think the way Hawke and Keating ended up was just so undignified.' Howard says: 'If I go, Peter Costello will become the leader.' He also says, 'You shouldn't assume I will retire. But I'm being very upfront that it's something two years into my term I'll decide: whether I'm going to run again. We have no witnesses. We don't even have a deal. We have nothing of the kind. One of the things you've got to do, which Hawke did not do, though Menzies did, is you've got to think of the medium- and long-term future of the party.'

15: Anthrax hoaxes hit five Australian cities.

18: Costello says Australia ranks third as a terror target.

22: Latham is interviewed by detectives about an altercation with a taxi driver, Bachir Mustafa, in July in which the taxi driver's arm was broken.

23: A group of 353 asylum seekers bound for Australia aboard the SIEV-X drown when their boat sinks in Indonesian waters.

28: Howard launches the Liberal Party campaign for the election, declaring, 'We will decide who comes to this country and the circumstances in which they come.' The centrepiece of the launch is a $1.2 billion 'baby bonus' as a tax rebate of between $500 and $2500 a year for five years for the first child if the child-rearing parent opts to stay out of the workforce.

30: Sailors taking part in the naval blockade of asylum seekers are banned from sending personal e-mail and digital photos after they encounter a suspected illegal vessel.

31: Jonathan Shier is forced to resign as ABC Managing Director on the overwhelming evidence of his having lost the support of the corporation's board and his own executive.

November 2001

3: In a video recording aired on Al-Jazeera TV, bin Laden accuses Australia as an ally of the UN of bringing 'tragedies' to the Muslim world. 'The crusader Australian forces were on Indonesian shores, and in fact they landed to separate East Timor, which is part of the Islamic world,' bin Laden says.

6: Christmas Islanders allege that naval officers told them claims that asylum seekers had thrown their children overboard were lies. One man, speaking on condition of anonymity for fear of reprisals, says he was told by two officers, 'whatever you hear: the asylum seekers did not throw their children overboard'.

7: Howard moves to restore the boat people issue to the centre of the election campaign, saying: 'There is a possibility some people having links with organisations that we don't want in this country might use the path of an asylum seeker in order to get here'.

8: Navy Chief David Shackleton reveals that no children were thrown overboard and that they only advised that there was a threat that children were thrown overboard. Howard, Reith and Ruddock maintain that until today they had no knowledge that no children were thrown overboard. Beazley says, 'You don't have to lie to protect your borders.'

9: Indonesia's chief political and security minister Susilo Bambang Yudhoyono promises that Indonesia will 'put an end' to people smuggling after weeks of mixed signals from authorities over their attitude to asylum seekers using Indonesia as a jumping off point to

Australia. 'We will prevent Indonesia from becoming the transit for illegal immigration activities. We must put an end to that,' he says.

10: The Coalition wins the election with a 2.1 per cent national swing, securing 51.14 per cent of the two-party-preferred vote and a new majority of between 10 and 14 seats. The Liberals win seats from the Nationals and Labor and votes from One Nation whose vote has been halved. Howard says, 'Our mandate is all of the policies we put, and those actions of a government consistent with the philosophy it's enunciated in the five-and-a-half years that it's been in government.' Beazley announces he will stand down as Leader of the Opposition.

12: Australia may be forced to accept refugees it has sent offshore under the 'Pacific solution'. Howard says it would be 'hypocritical in the extreme' to change his position just one day after the election but says, 'Some of the solutions that have been brought up recently are immediate, ad hoc solutions,' and Australia will take its 'fair share' of refugees.

13: Kabul falls to the Northern Alliance as Taliban forces flee to mountain hideouts south of the capital.

22: Simon Crean is elected as the new Labour leader and raises the prospect of processing boat people on the Australian mainland. He says, 'The Pacific solution is not working. They need to review it.'

December 2001

9: Adelaide man David Hicks, who undertook extensive training with al-Qa'ida, is captured in Afghanistan by Northern Alliance soldiers. He is handed over to the US military for interrogation.

18: New counterterrorism measures giving ASIO the power to detain people for up to 48 hours and new terrorism offences carrying a maximum life penalty receive support from Labor but are criticised by Greens, Democrats and civil libertarians.

19: The Governor-General, Peter Hollingworth, claims legal advice constrained him from showing more active concern for the welfare of victims of sexual abuse at an Anglican school while he was Archbishop of Brisbane.

2002—Different times, different circumstances

'You will not escape the reach of terrorism by imagining that if you roll yourself into a little ball you will not be noticed, because terrorism is not dispensed according to some hierarchy of disdain; it is dispensed in an indiscriminate, evil, hateful fashion.'

—John Howard, 14 October 2002

January 2002

14: Pauline Hanson steps down as One Nation's national president in a move that is seen as the death of One Nation as a political force.

23: As hunger strikes continue at the Woomera detention centre, South Australia's Liberal Party Premier, Rob Kerin, calls on Immigration Minister Philip Ruddock to release 'vulnerable' children of detained asylum seekers.

25: Howard brands protesting asylum seekers as blackmailers and rejects all alternatives to the Government's hardline policy. In a major departure from Labor's support for the Howard Government's hard line on asylum seekers, Crean urges the release of children from detention centres, saying, 'it is just plain wrong to hold innocent children behind razor wire'.

28: Catholic Archbishop George Pell says he believes the Government's 'policy of deterrence [of asylum seekers] is being implemented at unacceptable moral cost'. Howard says, 'I respect their views ... but the Government will not be altering its current policy.'

29: Detainees will be relocated to a new detention centre called Baxter near Port Augusta. Ruddock says that 'it's better to have smaller numbers of people in more facilities'. Woomera has 785 detainees.

30: Bush brands Iran, Iraq and North Korea an 'axis of evil'.

31: Afghan officials will visit Woomera within weeks to try to negotiate a cash deal to asylum seekers to return to Afghanistan. Up to 4000 Afghan asylum seekers could return to Afghanistan with a payment from the Australian Government after talks between Howard and Afghan interim Prime Minister Hamid Karzai.

February 2002

9: An inconclusive result in the South Australian election leaves the balance of power in the hands of three Independents. Howard says it is 'not a bad result for the Liberal Party considering where it was six months ago'.

13: An official report prepared by Jennifer Bryant and Major General RA Powell reveals that former Defence Minister, Peter Reith, withheld the truth that asylum seekers had not thrown their children overboard for four weeks of the election campaign.

Labor will form government in South Australia after Mike Rann strikes a deal with renegade Liberal Peter Lewis. It gives Labor control of every state and territory government.

15: Howard urges public servants to tell the 'whole truth' to a Senate inquiry about the children overboard affair.

17: Defence Minister Robert Hill admits photographs showing an asylum seekers' boat sinking were sent to former Defence Minister Reith but were not released. Howard says, 'the people of Australia on the asylum issue voted for our policy, they did not vote according to whether children were thrown overboard'.

18: The Governor-General appears on ABC television's *Australian Story* to rebut charges of covering up the case of a 14-year-old girl who had a sexual relationship with a priest. He says: 'My belief is that this was not sex abuse. There was no suggestion of rape or anything like that. Quite the contrary: my information is that it was rather the other way around, and I don't want to say anything more than that.'

19: Buckingham Palace and Howard distance themselves from the Governor-General. A spokesperson for the Queen, who is due to visit Australia shortly, says that any continuation in office 'would be entirely a matter for the Governor-General's office and not us'. Howard stands by the Governor-General but says he will reassess the situation after hearing the Governor-General's response.

21: Howard dismisses calls for Hollingsworth's removal, saying such a move would trigger a 'constitutional earthquake' but if further claims are made he will ask Hollingworth to respond to them immediately.

27: Chief of the Defence Force Admiral Chris Barrie finally admits there is no evidence that children were thrown overboard from a vessel in waters off Christmas Island on 7 October 2001.

28: Australia signs a bilateral agreement on climate change with the US, raising the prospect that it will not ratify the Kyoto Protocol.

March 2002

5: Ansett's last flight lands in Sydney after all attempts to revive the airline fail.

12: Parliamentary Secretary (Cabinet) Bill Heffernan accuses High Court Judge Michael Kirby of 'trawling for rough trade' in Sydney's Darlinghurst, telling the Senate that Kirby is not 'fit and proper' to sit in judgment on sex offenders.

13: Heffernan stands aside as Cabinet Secretary while police make inquiries about his allegations. Justice Kirby says, 'Senator Heffernan's homophobic accusations against me in the Senate are false and absurd.'

15: One of Heffernan's witnesses is alleged to have been an unreliable witness in a major paedophile court case.

17: Howard terminates former health minister Michael Wooldridge's $5 million grant to the Royal Australasian College of General Practitioners for whom Wooldridge has been working as a consultant since January. Wooldridge diverted $1 million from funds allocated to asthma and $4 million from funds allocated to boost specialist resources in the bush.

18: A Comcar docket used by Heffernan as evidence of Kirby's activities is exposed as a fake. Howard says, 'I've asked Senator Bill Heffernan to resign. I've told him that he owes Mr Justice Kirby an unqualified apology and I've also indicated to him that he should apologise to the Senate.'

19: Heffernan admits he was wrong and says, 'I want to extend to Michael Kirby my sincere apology and deep regret for the allegations that I made in this place. I withdraw them unreservedly.' Justice Kirby replies saying, 'I accept Senator Heffernan's apology and reach out my hand in a spirit of reconciliation. I hope my ordeal will show the wrongs hate of homosexuals leads to.'

April 2002

4: Howard gives the green light to controversial stem cell research using surplus IVF embryos but state premiers say it is too restrictive.

14: Howard says legislation exempting small business from unfair dismissal laws will be returned to the Senate. 'We could have significantly lower unemployment if further changes to the workplace relations were made,' Howard says.

18: Howard presses ahead with plans to give states the power to ban single women and lesbians from accessing IVF after the High Court has refused an application by the Catholic Church to prevent a Victorian woman using IVF.

May 2002

3: In an interview with *The Australian*, Howard regrets questioning the pace of Asian immigration as Opposition leader in 1988, and says for the first time that the warnings of historian Geoffrey Blainey on the issue have been proven wrong. 'Everybody changes, everybody's views mellow and change, and what you might regard as difficult to adjust to 50 years ago is not what you find now.'

7: Migrant intake is lifted to 105,000.

14: Costello brings down a 'war budget' with an extra $524 million to deploy troops to fight terror, $2.872 billion over five years on border protection, $1.3 billion on security and cuts to drug subsidies.

19: The Democratic Republic of East Timor is born. Howard and Crean attend the ceremony in Dili.

Former Australian prime minister John Gorton dies. Howard pays tribute to 'a patriot of incredible fibre and courage'.

28: Cosgrove is appointed to replace Admiral Chris Barrie as Chief of the Australian Defence Force from 4 July.

29: ABC board appoints Russell Balding as Managing Director of the ABC despite pressure from the Liberal powerbroker and board member Michael Kroger to interview Trevor Kennedy.

30: Rodney Adler is banned from being a company director for 20 years, fined $900,000 and ordered to pay more than $5.3 million to HIH creditors for breaching Corporations Law on 185 occasions.

June 2002

3: Immigration Minister Philip Ruddock tells Federal Court judges they should quit and run for parliament if they want to criticise the Government.

14: Bush tells Howard that the US is prepared to begin formal talks on a historic Free Trade Agreement.

18: Howard welcomes a radical reform plan put forward by university vice-chancellors calling for greater flexibility in charging fees. Howard scuttled an earlier deregulation plan by former education minister David Kemp but tells parliament that times have changed.

20: Barry Jones tells the Hawke–Wran review of the ALP that 'in the past six years the Opposition has barely laid a glove on the Government'. He says Howard is a successful practitioner of 'wedge politics' and a 'conviction politician' who is prepared to push ahead on issues which are, on the face of it, vote losers, such as the GST and the sell-off of Telstra. 'But he pushes ahead—and wins.'

Howard defends the navy's reaction to the SIEV-X sinking, saying he is 'perfectly satisfied that the navy behaved honourably, decently and expeditiously'.

25: Sydney airport will be sold for a record $5.6 million to a Macquarie Bank-led consortium banking on traffic doubling in the next two decades to justify the price.

July 2002

3: The Crikey website reveals that Cheryl Kernot and Gareth Evans were in the middle of a five-year affair when she defected to the Labor Party in 1997. Published e-mail messages show that Evans was stricken about lying to parliament over the affair. Labor leader Simon Crean says that if the allegations are true they require a full explanation from Evans and Kernot.

4: Evans says he lied to parliament to protect his family. Howard says he will make 'absolutely no comment whatsoever'.

9: Beazley says Kernot would not have been accepted in Labor if the party leadership had known of her affair with Evans.

15: The CIA claims that Saddam Hussein is no more than three years away from developing a usable nuclear weapon.

18: Two young Woomera escapees, Alamdar and Muntazer Bakhtiyari, aged 14 and 12, are returned to custody after three weeks on the run. Their bid for asylum at the British Consulate in Melbourne fails.

19: Howard vigorously defends the Government's handling of the Bakhtiyari case. 'Anybody who imagines that my government enjoys taking the stance that it does at the present time is mistaken,' he says. 'But we frankly have no alternative but to follow the policies that we are following at the present time.'

20: Labor Premier Jim Bacon is decisively returned in the Tasmanian state election. Howard calls for the Tasmanian Liberals to 'conduct a thorough examination of the reasons for the drop in the Liberal Party vote'.

23: Iraqi Trade Minister Mohammed Mahdi Saleh announces that Iraq will halve imports of Australian wheat in protest against Australia's threat to support future US military action. Downer is defiant. 'Our position simply remains the same. We simply don't support policies of appeasement.'

26: Former Australian Democrats leader, Meg Lees, quits the party. The next day dissident senator Andrew Murray declares himself a 'democrat-in-exile'.

30: Almost a year after Howard declared that the *Tampa* asylum seekers would never set foot on Australian soil, 42 Iraqi refugees whose applications for asylum have been assessed in PNG arrive in the country.

31: A special United Nations human rights envoy declares the Woomera immigration facility 'inhumane and degrading'.

August 2002

2: Howard says that a US military strike is more probable than not.

6: Three ships carrying up to 150,000 tonnes of Australian grain worth $80 million are ordered from Iraqi ports because of Iraqi officials' concerns that the shipments were contaminated with fertiliser and metal filings.

8: After four years of negotiation, Howard announces Australia's biggest export deal, worth $25 billion to supply China with liquefied natural gas. Howard says: 'Of all the world leaders I have met since becoming Prime Minister I have met none more frequently than the president of China [Mr Zhu], despite what is occasionally said about my so-called lack of interest in this part of the world.'

14: Former East Timor governor Abilio Soares is sentenced to three years' jail for human-rights crimes in East Timor: the first verdict brought by an Indonesian court against a senior civilian or military official. But the following day a senior police officer and five junior officers are acquitted, gravely disappointing human-rights groups.

15: The leader of a gang of rapists that terrorised western Sydney is sentenced to 55 years in jail, the harshest fixed sentence recorded in Australia for rape. Howard says the sentence is a matter for the courts but adds, 'I'm certainly not condemning it.'

18: Iraq suddenly reverses its ban on Australian wheat and agrees to pay higher prices under the UN 'food for oil' scheme after AWB chairman Trevor Flugge leads a delegation to Baghdad. Trade Minister Mark Vaile congratulates the AWB team.

21: Natasha Stott Despoja resigns and Aden Ridgeway takes over as interim leader of the Democrats. The next day Brian Greig becomes interim leader.

September 2002

5: Three High court judges lash out at the Howard Government's post-*Tampa* laws, passed with the support of Labor, which specify that decisions of the minister, department or tribunals 'must not be challenged, appealed against, reviewed, quashed or called in[to] question in any court'.

8: As President Bush meets British Prime Minister Tony Blair at Camp David, US National Security Adviser Condoleezza Rice says of Saddam Hussein, 'If we aren't prepared to deal with his defiance now, will we be more prepared to deal with his violence when he is capable of delivering a [*sic*] nuclear weapons against either the United States or Britain?'

11: Howard says it will not be necessary to bring down Saddam if Iraq fully disarms, although many people and nations would welcome that outcome. Howard says: 'people who've been so quick to criticise the US—and there have been too many, in my view—are missing the point. America's not in the dock—it's Iraq's failure to comply with the United Nations resolutions, and the failure so far of the United Nations to do anything about that failure, which is the main issue.'

12: Bush puts to the Security Council his case for UN action, broadening it beyond the development of weapons of mass destruction to accusation of widespread human-rights abuses.

19: Singapore reveals that Jemaah Islamiah (JI) operatives arrested in August were planning to bomb the US embassy and the Australian and British High Commissions.

26: The US claims that Saddam's regime trained al-Qa'ida terrorists in the development of chemical weapons.

October 2002

12: A car bomb explodes outside the Sari Club in Kuta, Bali, and a second bomb explodes at Paddy's Bar, killing 202 people, including 89 Australians, and injuring a further 209. Howard orders a national security review and warns that the bombings are a 'terrible reminder that terrorism can touch anybody, any time and in any country'.

14: The Indonesian Government says, 'The Bali bomb blast is related to al-Qa'ida with the co-operation of local terrorists'. Addressing parliament, Howard says: 'We are living in different circumstances and different times. That has been the case since 11 September last year; it is dramatically more so … now.' Downer identifies JI as the most likely perpetrator. The US Government names Abu Bakar Bashir as the spiritual leader of JI. Bashir says, 'All the allegations against me are groundless.'

15: Howard is confronted with accusations that he was to blame for the Bali bombings because of his hard line on Iraq. He replies, 'I would say to those people that they are wrong. Terrorists murdered Australians in Bali, nobody else.'

16: After meetings between President Sukarnoputri and Foreign Minister Downer, Indonesia agrees to a joint police and intelligence investigation into the bombings.

17: At a memorial service for family and friends of the victims, Howard says: 'Australia has been affected deeply, but the Australian spirit has not been broken. The Australian spirit will remain strong and free and open and tolerant.'

18: Howard visits the Bail bomb site and says he cannot adequately explain the compassion he felt for the families, or his anger that so many young Australians had lost their lives.

21: Polls show that Australians overwhelmingly endorse Howard on the key issues of leadership and security.

Two students are killed and another five wounded when a fellow student fires indiscriminately into a tutorial at Monash University.

24: A national ban on almost all handguns could be in place by Christmas following agreement between Howard and the premiers.

27: Tension erupts between Australia and Indonesia as Howard refuses to lift hardline travel warnings which Sukarnoputri says are damaging the Indonesian economy. JI is listed as a terrorist organisation in Australia.

November 2002

5: Indonesian police believe they have a strong enough case to take Muslim cleric Abu Bakar Bashir to trial on charges that he sponsored a number of terrorist attacks and plots in Indonesia in the last three years.

6: In the US Republicans gain control of the Senate as well as Congress.

A man arrested in connection with the Bali bombings, Amrozi bin Nurhasyim, admits to being part of the conspiracy and to knowing both Abu Bakar Bashir and Hambali.

8: Amrozi confesses to buying the chemicals and building the bombs used in Bali. He says he hates Americans and wants 'to kill as many Americans as possible'.

13: Osama bin Laden warns Australia in a video-recorded message to pull out of the war on terror 'if you don't like looking at your dead'. Howard responds, 'I'm quite sure that I speak for all Australians in saying that we will not be intimidated in relation to the policies we pursue by threats from terrorists.'

14: Formal talks on a Free Trade Agreement with the US begin after US Trade Representative Robert Zoellick meets Howard in Canberra.

20: Australian troops in Afghanistan will come home by Christmas, Howard says as the Government prepares to introduce tighter security measures. 'The ultimate nightmare must surely be the possibility of weapons of mass destruction falling into the hands of terrorist groups,' Howard says.

28: Howard and Costello confirm that they have privately discussed the Liberal leadership. 'We have private discussions about a lot of things,' says Howard. Asked whether he wants to succeed Howard, Costello says, 'Let's see what happens next year.'

2003—Regime change

'I just pose the simple question: if what the coalition did was wrong according to these people, how else do they think Saddam Hussein would have been removed? By somebody issuing a press statement?'
—John Howard, 14 April 2003

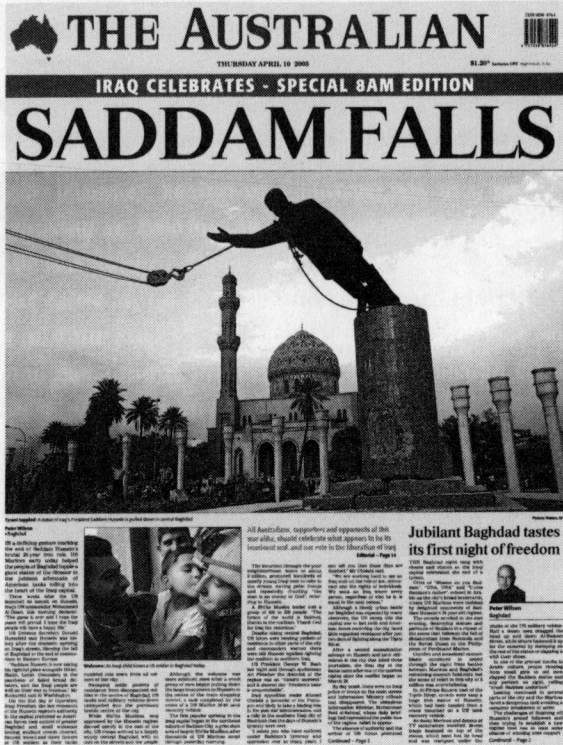

January 2003

2: Howard is under pressure from Coalition MPs to stay on as Prime Minister until after the 2004 election because of concern over marginal seats, *The Australian* reports.

3: Howard interrupts his holiday to defend Costello against criticism from former Treasury secretary John Stone that he is a weak political leader.

9: Opposition leader Simon Crean accuses Howard of 'itching for war' on the eve of a cabinet meeting to discuss the prospect of a US-led invasion of Iraq.

10: Howard gives the green light for deployment of Australian forces in Iraq but cautions: 'the weapons inspectors should be given a proper opportunity to succeed'.

Former UN chief inspector Richard Butler insists that Iraq is hiding weapons of mass destruction. 'For Iraq to say they don't exist is simply not true,' he says.

18: Bushfires strike Canberra, killing four people and destroying hundreds of homes. Howard says the national capital has been 'under attack' from 'the summer terror of bushfires'.

23: HMAS *Kinimbla* leaves Sydney for the Gulf. Howard warns that if the international community 'gives up because it is too hard, Iraq will not oblige by giving up its weapons of mass destruction'.

28: Chief UN weapons inspector Hans Blix says Saddam has failed to genuinely accept the need to disarm.

February 2003

3: Iraq's envoy in Australia, Saad Al-Samarai, warns that Australia will suffer 'horrible casualties' if it takes part in the invasion.

4: Howard tells parliament: 'The Australian Government knows that Iraq still has chemical and biological weapons and that Iraq wants to develop nuclear weapons.'

6: Labor frontbencher Mark Latham calls US President George W Bush 'the most incompetent and dangerous president in living memory'.

11: Howard meets Bush at the Whitehouse. Asked whether he considers Australia part of his coalition of the willing, Bush replies, 'Yes, I do.'

13: Blair welcomes Howard to London, declaring that the two governments are in 'total agreement' on Iraq.

16: Hundreds of thousands of marchers in Australian capital cities protest against the war in Iraq.

21: Howard will remain Prime Minister until at least the end of year, beyond his 64th birthday on 26 July, *The Australian* reports. Speaking of Iraq, Howard says he is 'going to see this issue through'.

27: Toppling Saddam could start a domino effect of democracy in the Middle East, Bush says.

March 2003

1: Howard virtually rules out taxpayer-funded maternity leave, saying the Government will improve opportunities for mothers to work part-time instead.

3: Howard defends the public's lack of access to free doctors, saying Medicare was never intended 'to guarantee bulk-billing for everybody, including people on very high incomes'.

13: Howard tells the National Press Club that peace in the Gulf would be a 'miracle'. 'If the world fails to deal once and for all with the problem of Iraq and its possession of weapons of mass destruction, it will … undo 30 years of hard international work … to enforce not only conventions on chemical weapons but also the Nuclear Non-Proliferation Treaty,' Howard says.

16: Crean toughens his anti-war rhetoric, saying 'John Howard should be bringing home the troops that have been pre-deployed'.

17: As Bush declares that the 'moment of truth' has arrived, Howard warns 'there will be civilian casualties', adding 'I accept that but I don't like it'.

18: Bush sets a 48-hour deadline for Saddam to flee Iraq or face war. 'The tyrant will soon be gone,' he says.

20: US Secretary of State Colin Powell rings Howard to tell him that military action is about to start. The war begins with a pre-dawn missile strike on Baghdad.

21: Howard says: 'I want to make it clear our primary goal has always been the disarmament of Iraq, but if military action now having become necessary, when that is concluded, axiomatically it's going to lead to the removal of the regime.'

22: Australian TV cameraman Paul Moran is killed by a suicide bomber in Kurdish Iraq while working for the ABC.

Bob Carr is re-elected for a third term in NSW, confirming Labor's dominance of every state and territory. Howard says that while the war did not affect the result it may have helped the Green vote and 'it probably would have ironically been at the expense of Labor'.

28: Bush calls up 100,000 more troops as the siege of Baghdad begins. British Defence Secretary Geoff Hoon claims British troops have found evidence that shows 'categorically' that Saddam planned to use chemical and biological weapons against the allies.

31: Asked about the death of children from American fire, Howard tells ABC television's Kerry O'Brien: 'For 30 years there have been images we haven't seen of children lying dead in ditches as a result of poison attacks by Saddam Hussein's regime on Kurdish parts of Iraq, that people had been tortured and starved and battered to death by the Iraqi secret police.'

April 2003

2: The battle for Baghdad intensifies as a daring US mission frees Private Jessica Lynch who was being held as a prisoner of war.

5: Health officers are stationed at Australian international airports as precautions are stepped up against Severe Acute Respiratory Syndrome (SARS).

6: The first US troops enter parts of Baghdad after two weeks of surgical strikes against Saddam's Republican Guard. Howard refuses to speculate when the war might end but says the first 17 days had been 'remarkable'.

8: US troops roll into the heart of Baghdad and are greeted by jubilant crowds. Asked about the progress in the search for WMD, Howard says: 'There aren't signs along the road to Baghdad saying WMD five kilometres from here. They've been obviously passed around and hidden, and some of them may have been taken out of Iraq.'

9: In a defining gesture, the people of Baghdad topple a giant statue of Saddam Hussein with the help of US marines. Asked whether he feels vindicated, Howard replies: 'I'm not going to employ the "v" word, I'm not, either of the "v" words.'

14: Howard backs a federal system for Iraq modelled on Australia with a semi-autonomous Kurdish area in the north.

15: Pressure mounts on Crean's leadership as internal party polling shows that his public support has nose-dived.

23: Beazley declares his ambition to reclaim the leadership of the Labor Party.

28: Howard and Health Minister Kay Patterson launch a $900 million Medicare package to stem the crisis in bulk-billing. Howard says he rejected lifting the rebate to doctors because 'It wouldn't have been as targeted and it would have ended up being a lot more expensive.'

May 2003

1: Howard rejects a call to sack Governor-General Peter Hollingworth despite a 471-page report finding that he let a known paedophile continue to work as a priest in his former role as Brisbane archbishop. 'I do not regret the appointment,' Mr Howard said.

2: Bush declares victory in the 'Battle of Iraq'.

3: An effusive Bush meets Howard in Washington, thanks him for Australia's participation in Iraq and sets a deadline for the Free Trade Agreement by the end of the year. 'I believe we can get it done, and I think it'll be an important step in our relationship,' he says.

6: Latham warns Beazley not to challenge Crean. 'We had two massive opinion polls about Kim: they were called general elections,' he says.

Workplace Relations Minister Tony Abbott says Hollingworth should not be 'hounded out of office' for a 'simple lack of judgment'.

7: Howard discusses the Hollingworth issue with the Queen during a scheduled meeting in London. The Queen says she would not object if the Governor-General stood down.

After a meeting with Howard, Blair says: 'In some of those very difficult times you come to judge whether you can depend on a fellow leader or not, and I did depend on John Howard and he did not let us down.'

8: In a taped address to the nation on television, Hollingworth denies allegations that he raped and assaulted Rosemarie 'Annie' Jarmyn in the 1960s, claiming it was a case of mistaken identity.

11: Hollingworth agrees to stand aside to focus on clearing his name. 'There is no question of this being a resignation,' Howard says.

13: Costello's 8th budget, includes a tax cut averaging a modest $4 a week, which is later dubbed the 'sandwich and milkshake' tax cut after comments from Senator Amanda Vanstone.

15: The Senate passes a historic motion calling for Hollingworth to resign.

23: The Victorian Supreme Court throws out Jarmyn's 'foolish' rape claim, but Hollingworth is reported to be on the brink of resigning.

25: Hollingworth resigns while insisting he did not cover up paedophilia. Howard accepts responsibility for the appointment. 'I'm sorry it turned out the way it did,' he says. 'I'm getting the blame. That's politics.'

June 2003

3: Howard tells Liberal MPs he will continue as Prime Minister as long as the party wants him. Costello later confesses: 'It wasn't my happiest day.'

4: Beazley's supporters say the former Labor leader is close to securing enough votes to oust Crean. They dismiss the comments of Crean supporter Mark Latham, who has ridiculed the challenge.

16: Crean beats Beazley 54 to 38 in a Caucus ballot for leadership. Beazley rules out another challenge. Latham is rewarded for his loyalty to Crean with a promotion to manager of Opposition business.

18: An independent review finds the Aboriginal and Torres Strait Islander Commission (ATSIC) is a 'corruption-riddled shambles'.

19: The Family Court rules that the federal Government is acting illegally by holding children indefinitely in immigration detention camps.

22: Howard announces that former Western Australian governor and SAS commander Michael Jeffrey will be the next Governor-General.

July 2003

2: Crean promotes Latham to Opposition Treasury spokesman.

14: JI explosives expert Rohman Al-Ghozi escapes from a Manila jail just hours after Howard signed an anti-terrorism accord with the Philippines. 'Plainly it's a big setback and nobody is happy about it,' Howard said.

16: In an ultimatum from Aboriginal Affairs Minister Phillip Ruddock, ATSIC chairman Geoff Clark is given seven days to explain why he should not be sacked.

22: Newspoll, published in *The Australian*, finds two-thirds of voters believe they were misled about the reasons for going to war with Iraq but Howard improves his lead over Crean.

Howard unveils plans for a South Pacific economic union to head off terrorism and corruption.

23: Howard commits himself to tackle endemic family violence in indigenous communities at a landmark summit with Aboriginal leaders in Canberra.

Howard talks Deputy Prime Minister John Anderson out of resigning before the next election in an attempt to stabilise the National Party.

26: Howard celebrates his 64th birthday, the age at which he said he would consider his future.

29: The federal Government agrees to accept most of the remaining 51 refugees on Nauru and Manus islands, including 26 from the *Tampa*.

August 2003

1: Aboriginal leader Pat Dodson describes the new direction of Aboriginal policy as 'a virulent form of assimilation'.

3: Vanstone opposes a plan for the federal Government's 'baby bonus', saying most women would rather have a guaranteed childcare place than 'a limited amount of cash in the hand now'.

5: JI explodes a bomb outside the Marriott Hotel in Jakarta, killing 10 and injuring almost 150. Howard says the victims were mostly ordinary Indonesian workers. 'They were not in any way the instruments of oppression,' he says.

6: Howard visits the Aboriginal community in Arukun, Cape York, with Aboriginal leader Noel Pearson. 'As a community you're entitled to say your position is more disadvantaged than others, that's a fact I can't argue with,' Howard said. 'You have the responsibility of doing something about it yourselves and we have the responsibility of working with you.'

7: Amrozi is sentenced to death for his part in the Bali bombing. Howard says he hopes the sentence will be 'some sort of comfort' to those who have lost loved ones. 'It will not be the intention of the Australian Government to make any representations to the Government of Indonesia that that penalty not be carried out,' he says.

13: Ruddock suspends Geoff Clark as ATSIC chairman, citing Clark's conviction five months earlier for obstructing police and behaving in a riotous manner during a pub brawl.

15: Hambali, the terrorist described as the Osama bin Laden of the east, is captured in Thailand. 'This is a huge breakthrough. This man is a big fish, he's the main link between al-Qa'ida and JI,' Howard says.

19: Howard comes under pressure to sack government minister Wilson Tuckey for pressuring South Australian Police Minister Patrick Conlon to quash a $183 fine handed out to his son. Howard later admonishes Tuckey for being 'very foolish' but keeps him on the frontbench.

20: Hanson is jailed, sentenced to three years for fraudulently registering the One Nation party and dishonestly obtaining funds.

22: Howard criticises Hanson's sentence. 'Like many, many other people I find the sentence certainly very long and very severe,' he says.

24: Disgraced former senator Mal Colston dies more than four years after 28 travel rort charges were dropped because of terminal cancer. Howard and other senior politicians decline to comment.

25: The Family Court orders five children to be released from Baxter Detention Centre. Their lawyer says it could set a precedent for more than a hundred other children still behind bars.

26: Abbott is forced to deny that the Liberal Party paid for legal action against Hanson and says there was nothing secret about the $100,000 Australians for Honest Politics trust fund he set up in 1998 to combat Hanson.

September 2003

2: Abu Bakar Bashir, is jailed for four years. Downer says: 'Many would feel it should be a good deal longer.'

5: Senior ALP figures are pressing NSW Premier Bob Carr to move to federal politics as a potential leader of the party, *The Australian* reports. Carr says: 'If some time in the future there was a chance to be part of a team, but not as leader, then I could be drawn to it.'

7: Australia would consider extraditing suspected terrorists Bilal and Maher Khazal to Lebanon where they are wanted for a series of bombings, Justice Minister Chris Ellison says.

8: Anderson ends speculation by telling colleagues he will remain as Deputy Prime Minister and National Party Leader until the next election. The decision saves Howard from making forced changes to his ministry.

15: Howard says he will defy a ruling by the International Rugby Board by singing *Waltzing Matilda* at the Rugby World Cup. The board has ruled that *Waltzing Matilda* will be permitted to be played only before the Wallabies take the field, because it's not the national anthem. 'Try and stop us,' Howard tells 2GB. 'This is just ridiculous. I think I'll start a campaign for every single Australian to learn all the verses of *Waltzing Matilda*.'

16: Crean tells wavering Labor MPs he will lead the Opposition to the next election. Meanwhile Howard all but rules out an early election, telling Coalition MPs that he intended the Government to serve a full three-year term.

22: Crean confirms that Labor will drop plans to roll back the GST at next year's election. Acting Treasurer Nick Minchin says, 'the Labor Party has been mugged by [the] reality that the GST was a critical piece of economic reform'.

24: Beazley lays out his leadership credentials by advocating that Labor be bold at a 'time of war' by opposing personal tax cuts, raising the Medicare levy and investing in national unity through health and education. Harking back to legendary Labor leaders John Curtin and Ben Chifley, World War II and the Great Depression, the former ALP leader has declared that for the war against terror to be won 'national unity is essential'.

25: Howard insists that evidence of Iraq's pre-war WMD program will emerge despite an interim report by the Iraq Survey Group that found no trace of chemical or biological weapons. 'I certainly believe that there will be evidence found that [Iraq] had programs,' he says.

29: Howard undertakes his biggest ministerial overhaul, warning his supporters not to imagine they were 'unbeatable or unbackable favourites at the next election'. Tony Abbott, Philip Ruddock and Amanda Vanstone are promoted into key portfolios. 'Eight seats is all that stands between us and electoral oblivion,' Howard says.

October 2003

1: One Nation Senator Len Evans blocks the Government's university reform package in the Senate, creating a trigger for a double-dissolution election.

7: Abbott and Defence Minister Robert Hill speak out against Malcolm Turnbull's bid for Liberal pre-selection in the seat of Wentworth, saying incumbent MP Peter King doesn't deserve to be defeated.

10: An independent panel set up to investigate 68 complaints from former communications minister Richard Alston accuses the ABC of 'serious bias' in its Iraq war coverage.

14: Crean orders Labor MPs to stand and applaud when President Bush addresses parliament next week. Several MPs say they will ignore the instruction.

17: Howard says the forthcoming visits of President Bush and Chinese President Hu Jintao are a measure of Australia's standing in the region. 'I think it goes beyond symbolism, although symbolism is very important,' he says.

23: President Bush's historic address to parliament is interrupted by heckling from Greens senators Bob Brown and Kerry Nettle. Liberals Ross Lightfoot and Bill Heffernan form a scrum around Brown and Nettle to keep them from Bush as he leaves the chamber.

24: President Hu addresses parliament to polite applause from assembled MPs and senators. Howard and Hu sign a Trade and Economic Framework, the first step towards a Free Trade Agreement.

27: al-Qa'ida suspect Willie Virgile Brigitte is deported to France after entering Australia in May on a tourist visa.

30: Costello declares that workers should not have to pay the top tax rate unless they earned more than $75,000 a year.

31: Howard says allegations against stockbroker Rene Rivkin, former Labor minister Graham Richardson and Qantas director Trevor Richardson are 'substantial'. The three are accused of share trading through a secret Swiss bank account. 'I have no doubt that ASIC and the ATO will have a very careful look at them,' Howard says.

November 2003

4: Crean writes to Howard supporting moves to list the military wing of Hamas and Lashkar-e-Taiba as terrorist organisations.

6: Hanson walks free from prison after appeals judges overturn her conviction.

18: Howard increases his Medicare package to $2.4 billion, lifting the Medicare payment to doctors and strengthening the safety net.

27: Supporters abandon Crean, setting the stage for a leadership ballot between Beazley and Latham in four days' time.

28: Crean announces his intention to step down from the leadership. Former Labor prime minister Gough Whitlam predicts: 'I think we will see a generational change … Latham is good, I think he's good on television.'

December 2003

1: *The Australian* reports that a late swing to Latham makes the vote too close to call.

2: Latham wins the caucus vote 47 to 45 and declares: 'I see this as a line in the sand for the Labor Party: a chance to move forward together.' *The Australian*'s Paul Kelly says it is 'the bravest, riskiest and most daring leadership choice made by Labor for several decades' in putting their faith in a man who is Howard's junior by 22 years.

3: Howard says Latham is 'dangerous' to Australia's alliance with the US. 'The Leader of the Opposition has allowed his tribal dislike... of the current American President to overwhelm his concern for the national interest,' Howard tells parliament.

Latham's first wife Gabrielle Gwyther said he had grown up thinking 'he was God's gift to the universe'. 'He was using me, he uses everyone. He uses his children, if you hadn't noticed,' she says.

4: Latham holds a press conference in front of the Star Spangled Banner saying he's a strong supporter of the American alliance. However he says: 'I'm not wrapping myself in the American flag.'

Universities win the right to set HECS levels and to accept one in three students on full fees as the Government's higher education reforms win approval in the Senate.

7: Andrew Bartlett stands aside from the Democrats leadership and issues an unconditional apology after a drunken confrontation with Liberal senator Jeannie Feris in parliament in which he called her a 'fucking bitch'. Bartlett had earlier removed five bottles of wine from a Liberal Party Christmas function.

11: Latham apologises after calling Turnbull 'unfit for public office'. Howard says: 'The truth is that Mr Latham, before he became leader, abused parliamentary privilege and used it to attack people, including female journalists, in a most objectionable fashion.'

14: Saddam Hussein is captured by US troops hiding in secret hole in the ground. Howard says the arrest 'will lift a huge burden and remove a great fear from the people of Iraq'.

17: Latham floats plan to slash superannuation payouts for MPs, judges and the governor-general. 'Let's get fair dinkum and bring it to the community standard for the future,' he says.

22: Indigenous Affairs Minister Amanda Vanstone flags sweeping reforms to indigenous policy in the new year including a major shake-up of indigenous governance and a push to curb family violence.

2004—Young pretenders

'It's what you can deliver and how able you are, not your age.'
—John Howard, 24 August 2004

January 2004

5: Electoral analyst Malcolm Mackerras predicts anything between 'a landslide to Howard and a landslide to Latham' in an October or November election

6: Howard pays tribute to 'a great Australian sporting identity' as Australian cricket captain Steve Waugh ends his career at the Sydney Cricket Ground.

11: Disabled pensioners encouraged to return to work under pilot scheme announced by the Government

15: Pauline Hanson declares her political career over saying it is time for others to 'shake up the political system'.

16: First train leaves Alice Springs for Darwin. 'If you're wanting to build something that captures a nation's imagination, you have to back your own judgment,' says Howard in response to criticism the project would lose money.

18: David Hookes is killed in a brawl outside a Melbourne hotel. Howard mourns 'an exciting and accomplished Test cricketer, a talented broadcaster and an immensely likeable person'.

26: Germaine Greer's description of Australia as too suburban, 'too relaxed to give a damn' is attacked as 'pathetic' by Howard. 'That was a particularly patronising, condescending, dare I say elitist article,' he says.

29: Howard demands an apology from his critics after the Hutton report in Britain finds no evidence that British Prime Minister Tony Blair manipulated pre-Iraq war intelligence on WMD.

February 2004

2: Howard passes the buck on the failure to find weapons of mass destruction in Iraq saying 'almost all the intelligence that came our way in relation to the invasion of Iraq pertained from British and American sources'.

3: Howard concedes WMD intelligence reports were inaccurate but insists he had no doubts Australia had done the right thing by going to war.

7: Peter Beattie wins by a landslide for Labor in the Queensland state election but Howard claims 'it has no federal implications'.

9: The Howard Government signs a Free Trade Agreement with the United States removing tariffs for 99 per cent of manufactured goods but leaving out sugar.

10: Howard meets canegrower lobbyists promising more government assistance.

Latham says a Labor government would slash retirement incomes for MPs.

12: An angry Coalition party room meeting is told by Howard he will adopt Latham's plan to cut superannuation for future MPs. 'I'd decided to act immediately to get it off the agenda as a partisan political issue,' he says.

28: Malcolm Turnbull beats incumbent MP Peter King in bitter preselection battle for Wentworth. Howard joins him at party fundraiser.

March 2004

2: Howard makes the first dip into the election war chest promising $267 million extra for retired service personnel.

4: Former diplomat Philip Flood is appointed to head an inquiry into pre-Iraq war intelligence.

9: Newspoll puts Latham in front with Labor attracting 55 per cent of the two-party-preferred vote. Howard plays down leadership speculation saying: 'I'll remain leader of the Liberal Party for as long as the party wants me.'

11: Suicide bombers strike in Madrid. Howard announces national student testing will be introduced in return for extra school funding.

14: Australian Federal Police Commissioner Mick Keelty tells Channel Nine the Madrid bombings were likely to be linked to Spain's participation in the Iraq war. He is immediately rebuked in a phone call from Howard's chief of staff Arthur Sinodinis.

15: As the death toll in the Madrid attacks rises to 201, Howard is adamant that Australia's participation in the Iraq war does not make it more of a terrorist target. 'The idea that by adjusting your foreign policy you can buy yourself immunity from terrorism is false,' he says.

16: Keelty issues a statement regretting that his remarks had been taken out of context. 'As I have said before, we cannot allow terrorism to dictate national policy,' he says.

19: Howard denies any improper contact between his office and the police commissioner.

20: Australian citizen Nguyen Tuong Van is sentenced to death in Singapore for heroin trafficking.

23: Latham says a Labor government would bring Australia's troops in Iraq home by Christmas. 'If a federal election is held this year, say the election was in September and there was a change of government, we would be hoping to have [the troops] back by Christmas, certainly,' Latham tells a radio audience.

25: Howard criticises Labor's 'cut and run' strategy after Latham hardens his commitment to pulling Australian troops out of Iraq.

30: Latham steals a march on Howard by proposing to abolish ATSIC.

31: Howard says ATSIC should be abolished and not replaced.

April 2004

7: In a major policy speech, Latham says the Iraq war is one of the 'great debacles' of Australian foreign policy.

14: US Secretary of State Richard Armitage repudiates Latham's criticisms of US–Australian relations.

15: Howard announces the abolition of ATSIC saying 'the experiment in separate elected representation for indigenous people has been a failure'.

21: Test cricketer Stuart MacGill's refusal to tour Zimbabwe is backed by Howard.

23: Kim Beazley returns from sick leave after being diagnosed with Schaltenbrand's syndrome saying he is not ready for retirement.

25: Howard makes a surprise Anzac Day trip to Baghdad and says Australian troops will not be home quickly. 'If we were to up stumps and go, it would certainly damage the US alliance,' he says. He denies the visit is a political act.

28: Howard offers sugar farmers $100,000 to quit the industry.

29: The High Court unanimously overrules a family court decision to free five asylum-seeker children in August 2003.

May 2004

7: Peter Costello supporters raise the prospect of a leadership handover after the election. 'I think most people expect that if we win the next federal election there will be a peaceful, harmonious transition from Howard to Costello,' Senator George Brandis says.

9: Costello declines to commit to handing down the 2006 budget. 'Ask me at the end of the year,' he tells Nine Network's *Sunday* program.

11: A big-spending budget includes tax cuts, child payments, a $5000 baby bonus and a cut in the superannuation surcharge. Costello calls it 'the largest package of measures ever to assist families who are juggling work and child rearing'.

20: More than 1200 guests celebrate the 30th anniversary of Howard's election to parliament at a gala dinner in Sydney. Howard says: 'There are a lot of things to finish and there are a lot of other milestones to pass.'

23: Howard vows to revise MP's travel entitlements after Liberal backbencher Trish Draper is criticised for taking her lover on an overseas trip.

26: Cabinet agrees to define marriage as an exclusive relationship between a man and a woman and not to recognise foreign gay unions. But gay couples will win the right to nominate their partner as a superannuation beneficiary.

June 2004

1: Howard apologises for misleading the public over what officials knew about abuse of prisoners in Iraq's Abu Ghraib prison.

4: President Bush attacks Latham's promise to withdraw Australian troops from Iraq by Christmas. 'It would embolden the enemy to believe that they could shake our will,' he tells *The Australian.*

5: Latham refuses to back down saying 'nothing President Bush has said changes our hopes and expectations about the future'.

6: Ronald Reagan dies in California aged 93. Howard pays tribute to 'the greatest of the post-World War II American presidents'. After a meeting in London, Howard and British Prime Minister Tony Blair agree to 'go the distance' in Iraq.

7: Latham says he would be 'tickled pink' if former rock star Peter Garrett ran as Labor candidate for Kingsford Smith.

9: News breaks that Garrett has not been on the electoral roll since 1994. He later blames a 'glitch'.

16: Howard attacks Latham's 'nanny state' proposal to ban junk food advertising on children's television.

18: In a major foreign policy speech Howard says Latham put at risk Australia's ability to 'speak openly and frankly with the United States' with 'intemperate, personal abuse.'

26: As the new Senate prepares to sit, Howard tells the Liberal Party's Federal Council: 'We will use the majority we have soberly, wisely and sensibly. We won't use it capriciously or wantonly or indiscriminately, and I make that solemn promise on your behalf to all of the Australian people.'

28: Independent Senator Brian Harradine announces he will quit the Senate when his term expires in June 2005.

July 2004

2: The Business Council of Australia predicts that a Latham victory will cost 100,000 jobs.

4: The Nine Network's *Sunday* program airs allegations that Latham 'king hit' an older constituent 15 years ago.

5: Latham calls an extraordinary press conference 'to clear the air' about his personal life. He blames the Government 'dirt machine' and 'Labor rats' for spreading damaging allegations about his fidelity and his temper.

Howard signs a Free Trade Agreement with Thailand.

6: Latham denies more unpublished allegations about his personal life, accusing the Government and his first wife Gabrielle Gwyther of a smear campaign. Howard says he is not interested in Latham's private life but observes that 'Mr Latham himself has never been a person reluctant to use parliamentary privilege to say outrageous things about other people in a very vitriolic and wounding fashion'.

7: US Secretary of State Richard Armitage claims Latham has divided the ALP with his push for an early withdrawal of Australian troops from Iraq.

8: The death of David Hookes and increased road rage mark a 'coarsening' of our culture, Howard tells an audience in Adelaide.

12: Latham recalls Beazley to his front bench as Defence spokesman in a move interpreted as an attempt to restore the Opposition's relations with the US.

13: With three marginal seats under threat in South Australia, Howard drops plans for a radioactive waste dump in the state.

14: In a surprise reshuffle, Howard dumps retiring ministers Daryl Williams and David Kemp from his cabinet, replacing them with fresh bloods Fran Bailey and Jim Lloyd.

19: Latham declares he will fight the federal election on social issues rather than the economy. Costello says the declaration is 'a poor excuse for the fact that he doesn't understand economic policy'.

22: The Flood inquiry finds that Australian spy agencies failed over WMD in Iraq but clears Howard of political pressure.

Latham attacks the 'lopsided market power' of big retailers.

26: Australia and Malaysia agree to investigate a joint Free Trade Agreement.

August 2004

2: After months of stalling, the ALP finally backs the FTA with the US but insists on a series of 'safeguard' measures.

13: Howard accepts Latham's FTA amendment to protect cheap medicines. 'The truth is the Labor Party has nailed this government flat to the floor,' Latham says.

16: Senior defence advisor Mike Scrafton tells *The Australian* he told the Prime Minister the children overboard claim was inaccurate in three telephone conversations on 7 November 2001. In a National Press Club speech the following day and subsequent interviews Howard had continued to claim children had been thrown overboard.

17: Howard claims Scrafton had told him a video recording of the children overboard incident was 'inconclusive' but Scrafton stands by his account.

Foreign Minister Alexander Downer says Australia would not necessarily take the US side against China in the event of an attack on Taiwan.

18: Latham is taken to hospital with stomach cramps and is diagnosed with pancreatitis. Howard wishes him 'a full and speedy recovery'.

19: US rebukes Downer for his Taiwan remarks. Downer backs away, saying the prospect of a dispute between China and Taiwan was 'hypothetical'.

22: Howard makes a pitch for the aged vote by lifting the health insurance rebate for over-65s.

23: Costello outlines his social agenda, including an end to children in immigration detention, higher levels of immigration and a republic.

24: Howard hints at political longevity, telling an audience of retirees: 'I think people should continue in the workforce for as long as they want to and as long as they're making a contribution and age is irrelevant.'

29: Howard announces a 9 October election. Howard says the campaign is about the economy and the fight against terrorism while Latham nominates 'building a ladder of opportunity and restoring trust in our national government'.

30: A senior Queensland Liberal accuses Liberal Senator George Brandis of describing Howard as 'a lying rodent'. Brandis denies using the words, but does not deny subsequent claims from other senior Liberals that he had referred to the Prime Minister as 'the rodent'.

September 2004

3: Howard tries to outflank Labor and the Greens by declaring there would have to be an end to old-growth logging.

6: The election bidding war hots up, with Howard trumping Latham's $180 million health announcement with a $1.8 billion injection into Medicare.

7: Latham promises to 'ease the squeeze' on middle Australia with an $11 billion tax and family package.

9: A massive truck bomb explodes outside the Australian Embassy in Jakarta, killing nine people and injuring 119. Howard says it won't change his policy on Iraq. 'The day any country surrenders decisions on those things to the dictates of barbarism and terrorism is the day a country loses control over its future,' he says.

10: Costello proposes to invest budget surpluses in a 'future fund' to meet the costs of an ageing population.

14: Latham is accused of playing the politics of envy as he threatens to cut or freeze grants to 178 private schools.

15: Hanson emerges from retirement to declare that she will run for the Senate under the slogan 'give the girl a fair go'. Queensland National Party President Terry Bolger rules out a preference deal.

19: Latham loses his cool in an interview with Nine Network's Laurie Oakes, attacking the media's 'smart-alec commentary'. 'Mate, if you don't get it, I can assure you that 1.4 million Australian families do,' he says.

20: Susilo Bambang Yudihoyono wins an Indonesian presidential election by a landslide.

24: Howard brokers a preference deal with the Family First party.

26: The Liberal Party campaign is officially launched with a $5.9 billion spending promise, including $1 billion for public schools, $2 billion for child rearing and $393 million for 24-hour GP access. 'There is a golden thread that runs through so many Coalition policies and that is that great principle of choice. Greater choice for families to choose how they will balance their work and their family responsibilities ... greater choice for young Australians to develop their talents to the full, and importantly greater choice for Australian parents to decide how and where their children will be educated,' Howard says.

28: Catholic and Anglican leaders jointly condemn Latham's 'potentially divisive' schools policy.

29: Latham targets the grey vote by launching 'Medicare Gold' policy with free healthcare for the over 75s and an $8 age pension increase.

October 2004

1: Howard counters Latham's grey vote pitch with a $100-a-year bonus for pensioners and $200 for self-funded retirees.

4: Latham makes a pledge to save old-growth forests in Tasmania, provoking an angry backlash from unions, the timber industry and senior ALP MPs.

6: Howard snookers Latham with a less-ambitious plan for saving trees, earning him a hero's welcome at a meeting of timber workers in Launceston where one burly logger tells him 'you're the best fucking prime minister we've ever had'.

8: Schappelle Corby is arrested at Denpasar airport carrying 4.2 kilograms of marijuana in a boogie board bag.

9: The Coalition is returned with an increased majority and control of both chambers. Howard hails 'a truly historic achievement'. 'We have to reach back to the 1960s to find an occasion when an incumbent government has increased its majority on two separate occasions,' he tells the party faithful.

10: Howard foreshadows further industrial relations changes but says: 'We're not going to allow this enhanced mandate to go our heads.'

16: Beazley retreats to the backbench, prompting leadership speculation.

Labor's John Stanhope is elected Australian Capital Territory chief minister, giving the ALP a clear majority in every state and territory government.

18: Frontbencher Bob McMullan declares he can no longer work with Latham as Labor's recriminations intensify.

19: Labor's Lindsay Tanner takes the path to the backbench.

20: Howard joins Asian leaders at the inauguration of President Yudhoyono in Jakarta.

28: As his seat in the Senate is confirmed, Queensland National Barnaby Joyce insists he will not be obliged to toe the party line. 'I will be a senator for the Queensland National Party first and foremost,' he says. Howard promises: 'The Government will use its majority in the new Senate very carefully, very wisely and not provocatively.'

29: Howard outlines a reform agenda for federal–state relations in a letter to premiers.

November 2004

4: George W Bush is elected for a second term as US President. Howard describes it as 'a wonderful victory for a person who has given strong leadership to his country, the anti-terrorist cause and the cause of freedom around the world'.

5: The 14-member National Indigenous Council is announced to replace ATSIC. Football star Adam Goodes and Labor stalwart Warren Mundine are appointed.

10: Vanstone reveals plans to introduce 'behavioural contracts' in Aboriginal communities in return for welfare. She tells *The Australian*: 'Passive welfare is over'.

Howard supports a parliamentary debate on abortion as Health Minister Tony Abbott tells mums to adopt out, not abort.

11: Howard says his proposed welfare reforms will drag unemployment below 5 per cent.

17: Deputy Prime Minister John Anderson fights allegations that he attempted to bribe independent MP Tony Windsor by offering him a diplomatic post to quit parliament.

18: The case against Anderson weakens as the businessman at the centre of the claim, Greg Maguire, denies acting as intermediary.

23: At an electoral post-mortem, Latham blames Labor premiers, a failure to engage business and problems in his office for the defeat. 'Latham's fucking mad; he's in complete denial,' a senior Labor figure tells *The Australian*.

26: Writing in *The Australian*, former Beazley advisor Michael Costello describes Latham as 'a dead parrot'. Beazley rejects suggestions that he could return for a third tilt at the prime ministership.

30: In a surprise diplomatic coup, Howard is invited to attend the 2005 Association of South-East Nations summit.

December 2004

4: Australia's two most influential Aboriginal leaders, Pat Dodson and Noel Pearson, make a joint appeal for a new dialogue with Howard based on the principle of mutual obligation. 'There is no argument with the principle of mutual obligation if we can get things fixed,' Pearson tells *The Australian*.

8: The first meeting of the National Indigenous Council considers behavioural contracts, including an offer of a petrol bowser for

Mulan community in West Australia in return for a commitment to wash children's faces twice a day.

9: Veterans Affairs Minister De-Anne Kelly keeps her job despite admitting breaching Howard's ministerial code of conduct.

12: Mundine challenges Labor to drop its 'politically correct' and 'touchy–feely' approach to Aboriginal affairs.

21: Howard becomes Australia's second-longest serving Prime Minister.

23: Twenty-five Coalition MPs form a ginger group lobbying Howard to overhaul tax and welfare.

26: A massive earthquake off the coast of Aceh triggers a devastating tsunami.

27: As the tsunami death toll rises across nine countries, Howard announces an initial aid package. Two RAAF C-130s laden with bottled water and emergency shelter are sent to the region.

28: Howard defends the Government's handling of the disaster. 'I think it's inevitable when something of this magnitude happens there is criticism ... but I guess that's the case whatever is done, but I hope the public understands that there was just total chaos,' he says.

29: A core group of Australia, the US, Japan and India forms to co-ordinate tsunami relief efforts. 'When something like this happens there is no standing international apparatus for dealing with it,' Howard says.

2005—A Majority of One

'The last thing that any political leader or party in this country should ever do is to assume that they have a licence from the Australian people to indulge in any kind of overzealous way their ideology or their enjoyment of power.'
—John Howard, 25 June 2005

January 2005

3: Australia prepares to take the leading international role in the long-term reconstruction of tsunami-ravaged Indonesia with an aid package worth more than $500 million.

THE AUSTRALIAN

Lib MPs bash bush dissenters

Howard's enforcer roughs up rebel Nat

Senator onside over uni foes

Trujillo will be read the act on T3

Top cop 'teamed up with gangsters'

Safe landing for Discovery

Vizard accountant steps aside as firm's chairman

Learning is the key to community growth

Adult Learners' Week

5: The Prime Minister agrees to fund one of the biggest peacetime aid operations in the nation's history. Australian officials prepare a long-term package of direct aid for Indonesia worth more than \$1 billion in cash and services-in-kind to rebuild roads, hospitals and schools.

6: 'You were the first to phone. You were the first to have aircraft on the ground,' an emotional President Yudhoyono tells Howard at the start of their meeting at the presidential palace in Jakarta. 'That is a gesture I will never forget.'

9: Two weeks after the tsunami Latham has made no public comment on the tragedy. His office says he is suffering a recurrence of pancreatitis. 'The doctors have told him he has to have complete rest and not work. He is obeying doctors' orders and his office is respecting that,' a spokesman says.

10: Latham's silence is increasingly disturbing his parliamentary colleagues. Acting Labor leader Chris Evans admits he has not spoken to Latham since Christmas.

Latham finally issues a statement declaring he will return to lead the ALP on Australia Day, despite mounting disquiet about his behaviour.

16: Kevin Rudd refuses to rule out a leadership challenge.

17: Carr and Beattie urge Latham to put an end to speculation about his leadership. Beattie goes further, endorsing Beazley as his replacement.

Janette Howard is admitted to hospital with chest pains.

18: Latham calls a snap press conference in a western-Sydney park to announce his resignation.

Janette Howard is discharged after tests.

24: Rudd withdraws from the leadership contest, sealing Beazley's return as Opposition Leader.

30: Howard lashes out at 'old Europe', describing criticism of the US in a BBC TV panel debate as 'unfair and irrational'. 'It's a sign of parochialism and it is disturbingly intense,' he says.

31: Former RAAF Flight Lieutenant Paul Pardoel, serving with the RAF, is the first Australian serviceman to be killed in Iraq.

February 2005

3: A mentally ill Australian woman is released from South Australia's Baxter detention centre after spending 10 months in immigration custody. Cornelia Rau, a 39-year-old former Qantas flight attendant, is admitted to Glenside psychiatric hospital.

6: Howard describes Rau's detention as 'regrettable' but says he would seek legal advice on whether the German-born woman should receive a formal apology.

9: Howard hints at a 2007 election run while announcing that the Asia Pacific Economic Co-operation summit will be held in Sydney late that year.

11: Howard defies the US by refusing to lobby European nations against arms sales to China.

17: An Israeli diplomat asked to leave Australia tells the Israeli Foreign Ministry he had been invited to Christmas lunch at Attorney-General

Phillip Ruddock's home as a guest of Ruddock's daughter Caitlin. Ruddock declines to comment.

22: Howard announces that he will double Australia's military strength in Iraq with a contingent of 450 troops to be sent to guard Japanese engineers. 'Iraq is very much at a turning point and it's very important that the opportunity of democracy, not only in Iraq but also in other parts of the Middle East, be seized and consolidated,' he says.

March 2005

1: Costello defends his handling of the economy as Australia's deficit rises to $15.2 billion, higher than the level that prompted Paul Keating's 'banana republic' warning.

2: Immigration Minister Amanda Vanstone prepares a plan to admit an extra 20,000 skilled workers a year, pushing the annual intake in 2005–06 to 140,000, the highest level for 20 years.

6: As the skills shortage grows, Howard urges young people to consider quitting school in Year 10 to pursue a trade vocation. 'We went through a generation where parents discouraged their children from trades,' he said. 'Higher Year 12 retention rates became the goal instead of us as a nation recognising there are some people who should not go to university.'

17: Liberal Senator Ross Lightfoot is accused of smuggling US$20,000 hidden in his jacket lining into Iraq on behalf of oil giant Woodside as a donation to a local hospital. Lightfoot says the money was delivered by someone else on the trip. Howard accepts his 'credible response'.

19: Labor's Chris Hayes wins Latham's old seat of Werriwa with a primary vote swing of almost 3 per cent.

22: Howard eases his tough stance on immigration detention, agreeing to release up to 100 asylum seekers following intense lobbying by some Coalition MPs.

26: The Business Council of Australia warns of an infrastructure crisis, urging Howard and state premiers to produce reforms needed to unleash investment.

29: An 8.7 magnitude quake hits Sumatra, killing hundreds. Indonesian President Yudhoyono postpones a three-day visit to Australia as Howard commits aid, aircraft and medical support.

30: Howard outlines his vision for a 'big Australia' with a global role in a foreign policy speech to the Lowy Institute. 'We can choose to turn inward or we can lend a hand for freedom at a moment when voices of democratic hope are being heard right across the Middle East,' he says.

Costello outlines plans to force single mothers to look for work once their children reach school age.

April 2005

1: Malaysian Prime Minister Abdullah Badawi criticises Howard for saying Australia could consider pre-emptive military strikes in South-East Asia against terrorist threats.

2: Pope John Paul II dies peacefully in Rome. Howard pays tribute to 'one of the great dominant personal influences' of his generation. 'It was his commitment to the dignity of the individual and the essential spirituality of man that was the source of his opposition to Soviet communism,' he says.

3: Nine Australians are killed when an ageing naval Sea King helicopter crashes while on an earthquake relief mission in Nias, Indonesia. 'They died living out the essential decency and compassion and mateship of the Australian people,' Howard says.

4: Howard signs an historic pact with visiting President Yudhoyono who declares his nation is 'looking south' for the first time towards a confident, dynamic and multicultural Australia.

6: Aborigines should be able to 'share in the bounty of this country' and own their own homes, Howard says during a visit to a remote NT community. 'I believe there is a case for reviewing the whole issue of Aboriginal land title in the sense of looking more towards private recognition,' Howard says.

11: Howard proposes a more centralist approach to federal–state relations in which Canberra would take a greater role in areas where the states are failing. In a major speech to the Menzies Research Centre he says: 'For some this is yet another terrible incursion into states' rights. In reality, it is the federal Government stepping in where eight different state systems are failing to deliver.'

12: Faced with losing $16 billion in GST revenue, state premiers cave in to Costello, agreeing to abolish up to $8.8 billion worth of business taxes.

Thousands of extra out-of-school-hour child care places will be provided to encourage parents to move from welfare to work, *The Australian* reveals.

17: Nine Australians arrested in Bali are accused of taking part in a heroin-smuggling operation after Indonesian police were tipped off by the Australian Federal Police.

18: Howard visits China where he signs an historic bilateral trade pact.

20: German-born Joseph Ratzinger is anointed Pope Benedict XVI. 'On behalf of the Government and the people of Australia, Janette and I wish Pope Benedict XVI well as he guides the Church in the years ahead,' Howard says.

23: Former Queensland premier Joh Bjelke-Peterson, who derailed Howard's bid for the Lodge in 1987 with his 'Joh for PM' campaign, dies age 94. 'I don't bear any grudges. There's no point in bearing grudges. Life moves on,' Howard says.

30: In an interview published in *The Australian*, Howard squashes Costello's immediate leadership hopes by declaring 'I'm not going anywhere'. Speaking in Athens he says: 'I still have got plenty of ideas and there are lots of things I want to do. I am not planning my post–prime-ministerial life.'

31: Australian businessman Douglas Wood is kidnapped in Baghdad.

May 2005

1: Costello refuses to rule out a leadership challenge. 'I don't think the events of the last 24 hours have helped the Government or the Liberal Party,' he says, referring to the coverage of Howard's so-called 'Athens declaration'.

2: Wood appears in a video recording released by his captors, pleading for his life. 'President Bush, Prime Minister Howard, Governor Schwarzenegger, family, friends, please help take the American troops, the Australian troops, the British troops out of here and let Iraq look after itself,' he says. Howard takes 'total responsibility' for any harm that might occur to Wood as a consequence of his government's decisions.

5: Tony Blair is re-elected as British Prime Minister. Howard is the first world leader to phone to congratulate him.

9: The Government deals with another Immigration Department bungle when it emerges that a mentally ill Australian woman, Vivian Alvarez, was wrongfully deported to the Philippines in 2001.

10: Costello's 10th budget raises the threshold for the top tax rate, offers incentives for single mothers to return to work and restricts disability pensions to those incapable of working more than 15 hours a week. Howard calls it Costello's 'best budget' but declines to say whether it's his last.

11: Beazley comes under fire from his own party for his decision to oppose Costello's $21.7 million tax cuts. 'We've blown our brains out,' one Labor MP tells *The Australian*.

19: Tax Commissioner Michael Carmody warns that workers will have to wait a year for their tax cuts if Labor blocks them in the Senate.

20: Howard promises a 'fair and effective' relief package for drought-stricken farmers.

26: Howard will exempt businesses with up to a hundred employees from unfair dismissal legislation under changes to IR laws, *The Australian* reveals.

27: Schappelle Corby is sentenced to 20 years in jail. 'Guilty or innocent, I feel for this woman,' Howard says.

29: Victorian premier Steve Bracks breaks ranks with other Labor state leaders to offer Howard bipartisan support for a new round of reforms including training, infrastructure and personal tax.

30: Howard tells the Reconciliation Australia conference he will meet indigenous people 'more than half way' to unite blacks and whites. The warm welcome he receives is in sharp contrast with that of 1997 when conference delegates turned their backs on him.

June 2005

2: Howard reverses a plan to penalise single parents who refuse a job because they can't find appropriate child care.

3: Chinese diplomat Chen Yonglin seeks political asylum in Australia.

9: The Democrats agree to deliver the Government's tax cuts in the Senate, thwarting Labor tactics.

12: Beazley promises to roll back Howard's IR reforms after the next federal election.

Douglas Wood is freed in a military raid in a Baghdad suburb.

13: Howard agrees to release parents and children from immigration detention and fast-track applications for temporary protection visas after eight hours of negotiations with dissident MPs.

20: Arriving back on Australian soil, Wood apologises to Howard and Bush for pleading at gunpoint for them to give in to his kidnappers' demands. 'I'm very committed to the policy of the two governments,' he says.

23: Deputy Prime Minister John Anderson announces his resignation. 'I haven't met a person with greater integrity in public life,' Howard says.

29: Latham describes Beazley as a 'stand-for-nothing type of leader' and the Labor Party as 'A-grade arseholes' in an e-mail to writer Bernard Lagan which is quoted in Lagan's new book, *Loner: Inside a Labor Tragedy*.

July 2005

1: Australian politics enter a new era as the Coalition officially gains control of the Senate with a slender one-seat majority.

5: The ACTU cranks up its campaign against Howard's IR legislation, warning that paid holidays are at risk.

7: Four bombs explode in the London peak hour, killing 56 people and injuring hundreds. Howard expresses 'shock and disgust'.

12: Howard identifies a new breed of 'enterprise workers' in a speech to the Sydney Institute. 'They recognise the economic logic and fairness of workplaces where initiative, performance and reward are linked together,' he says.

14: Howard issues an apology to Cornelia Rau and Vivian Alvarez after the release of a damning official report.

20: Howard meets President Bush in Washington and commits to staying the course in Iraq. Bush says of Howard: 'He's got backbone, he's not afraid to make the hard decision, he's not afraid to lead.'

21: Suicide bombers bungle a second series of bombs on London transport as Howard is about to meet Tony Blair. Later, at a joint press conference, Howard says: 'The determination of the British people to continue with their daily lives is something we have always seen as one of the defining characteristics of this remarkable country.'

Malaysia agrees to allow Australia to be present at the inaugural meeting of the ASEAN-sponsored East Asia Economic Summit in December after Foreign Minister Alexander Downer agrees to sign a non-aggression pact.

27: Australia agrees to a climate change pact with the US, China, India and South Korea following talks between Howard and Bush in Washington.

Bob Carr resigns as NSW Premier.

August 2005

2: Maurice Iemma is the surprise successor to Carr.

4: The federal Government seizes control of Northern Territory uranium mining to give 'certainty' to the industry.

5: Howard announces sweeping changes to anti-terror legislation, dismissing concerns about encroachment on civil liberties. 'The most important civil liberty I have, you have, is to stay alive,' he says.

Labor state governments vow to fight IR legislation in the High Court.

9: As the new-look Senate sits for the first time, Coalition unity splinters. The Nationals demand extra cash for regional universities which they claim will suffer if student union membership is made voluntary.

17: The Government plans to launch the biggest overseas recruiting drive since the days of the 'ten pound pom' in search of an extra 20,000 skilled workers.

18: Howard seals the full sale of Telstra with a $3.2 billion package for the bush to appease National Party MPs.

19: Underwear model Michelle Leslie is arrested in Bali carrying two ecstasy pills.

23: Howard warns that Australians found with drugs in Asia, where the laws are 'black and white', can expect 'no mercy'.

26: Liberal MP Malcolm Turnbull outlines a plan to reduce the top tax rate to 35 to 40 cents in the dollar as business leaders urge Howard to make tax reform his legacy.

30: Costello adds momentum to his leadership push when he tells the Nine Network: 'I feel in a sense that I do lead in this country.'

September 2005

1: Beazley commits Labor to review all tax rates as part of fundamental reform of the tax and welfare system.

12: Howard challenges the US to adopt a less hostile view of China, saying 'China's progress is good for China and good for the world.'

15: Extracts from *The Latham Diaries* are printed in *The Australian*. They contain damning criticism of Beazley and other senior Labor figures, with Latham calling his successor as Labor leader 'one of the most indecent politicians I have ever come across'.

17: More extracts from *The Latham Diaries* show Latham believed the US alliance should be ditched as 'the last manifestation of the White Australia mentality'. Labor Treasury spokesman Wayne Swan says the book shows that voters made the right decision.

18: Beazley's daughters Jessica and Hannah issue a statement. 'Mark Latham's bitter and hateful rantings will not destroy Dad's legacy,' they say.

23: Federal Education Minister Brendan Nelson confirms plans to introduce a national report card for key subjects to stop 'dumbed down' curriculums.

27: At a summit in Canberra state and territory leaders agree in principle to back Howard's tough anti-terror laws. 'We've done that because we live in unusual circumstances,' Howard says.

28: Howard abandons plans to reform the media landscape restricting changes to cross-media and foreign ownership laws.

29: The Government considers holding a referendum on four-year federal parliamentary terms as part of electoral reforms. 'I remain in principle in favour of four-year terms,' Howard says.

October 2005

1: Three suicide bombers attack Bali restaurants, killing 22 people, including four Australians. Howard says he is sickened by the 'cowardly, wanton, indiscriminate, horrific attacks'.

4: China overtakes the US to become Australia's biggest source of imports, ABS figures reveal.

7: The Government softens IR reforms to protect workers who want to remain in the award system after a campaign by union gains traction.

Two days before the anniversary of his fourth election victory, Howard denies he is thinking of retiring.

9: Howard releases his proposed IR reforms, revealing that the right to strike will be curtailed in a direct assault on union power. Howard says he is unable to guarantee that no worker will be worse off.

10: Costello savages Turnbull's tax plan, claiming it would cost up to $14 billion to implement.

14: ACT Chief Minister John Stanhope angers Howard by releasing the federal Government's draft anti-terror legislation online.

26: 'Sit-down' money for Aborigines stops flowing as Centrelink tells indigenous claimants they must look for work or lose their hand-outs.

27: A report by UN chief investigator Paul Volker into the United Nation's oil-for-food scandal finds that Australian wheat sales to Iraq were used to funnel US$222 million to Saddam Hussein's regime.

28: Lawyers for condemned Australian Nguyen Tuong Van urge Howard to do more to stop the convicted drug runner being hung in Singapore. Howard later rules out 'megaphone diplomacy', saying 'I have done what I can do and my personal views are very well known to the Prime Minister of Singapore'.

31: Howard orders an independent inquiry into the AWB kickback scandal as fresh evidence emerges that AWB officials played an intimate role in setting up the deal which channelled money to Saddam through a Jordanian trucking company.

November 2005

2: The Government rushes through emergency amendments to anti-terror laws as Howard tells of a 'specific intelligence' received this week 'which gives cause for serious concern about a potential terrorist threat'. Beazley is given a confidential briefing and agrees to support the legislation.

4: Police express private concern that Howard's dramatic announcement may have jeopardised a long-running operation against a suspected terrorist cell.

8: Police swoop in Sydney and Melbourne, arresting 17 suspected members of a terrorist cell. Chemicals, computers and other evidence are seized. Howard says: 'I'm not interested in vindication. I've only ever set out to do everything I can to protect the security of the Australian public.'

9: The mastermind of the Bali and Jakarta Embassy bombings, Azahari bin Husin, is shot dead in a house in East Java. Howard describes it as 'very good news' but warns 'it doesn't mean that JI is crippled'.

10: Howard says that the AWB kickbacks inquiry will have the powers of a royal commission but won't investigate the role of the Government.

11: Beazley tells Labor to 'stop navel-gazing', warning that Howard's fourth-term agenda has raised the stakes so high that the ALP 'must win' the next election.

15: Hundreds of thousands of protestors take to the streets around the country to rally against IR laws. Howard dismisses the unions' campaign, saying 'the sky would not fall in' under the new laws.

17: Howard meets with Singapore Prime Minister Lee Hsien Loong at an APEC summit in Seoul but is embarrassed when he later learns Lee had not told him a date had been set for the execution of Nguyen Tuong Van. Lee later apologises.

18: Michelle Leslie wins her freedom at a Denpasar court hearing.

20: Howard warns Singapore that Nguyen's execution would 'not go unnoticed in Australia'.

29: Costello is forced to defend his 2003 appointment of Rob Gerard to the Reserve Bank board after details are revealed of a tax investigation into a 'sham' insurance transaction by Gerard Industries.

December 2005

2: Gerard quits the RBA board.

Nguyen is executed in Singapore. Howard denies that it was hypocritical to seek clemency for Nguyen but not oppose it for Saddam.

4: Leadership tensions are fuelled when Howard tells the Nine Network it was Costello who first raised the idea of appointing Gerard to the RBA board.

7: Costello publicly rejects challenging Howard and commits himself to delivering the 2006 budget.

9: Voluntary Student Union legislation is passed by the Senate after Howard strikes a deal with Family First Senator Steve Fielding to outflank rebel National Barnaby Joyce. But Howard faces criticism for using his Senate power to steamroll through IR and anti-terror legislation.

11: Race violence erupts in the Sydney beach suburb of Cronulla. Howard condemns the 'sickening mob violence' but says 'I do not accept that there is underlying racism in this country'.

13: Howard offers to help state governments fix the hospital crisis.

14: Howard is welcomed at an ASEAN gathering in Malaysia by Malaysian president Badawi, who makes a point of sitting next to Howard at the formal gathering.

27: Media magnate Kerry Packer dies at the age of 68. Howard pays tribute to a person who, 'despite his wealth and his business power, had a great capacity to talk the language of the common man and to understand what that person thought'. 'He is a person whose company I liked. I regarded him as a friend,' he says.

23

HOWARD BY NUMBERS

Compiled by George Megalogenis

'I haven't met anybody yet who's stopped me in the street and shaken their fist and said: "Howard, I'm angry with you, my house has got more valuable."'
—John Howard, 21 July 2004

SINCE John Howard took office in 1996, property prices have more than doubled across the nation. While this has allowed most households to feel wealthier than ever before, the transaction has come at a cost. Households have never been more exposed on their borrowings. The interest repayment burden crossed 9 per cent of disposable income for the first time under Howard in 2003 and was heading to 10 per cent at the end of 2005. The worst Paul Keating ever achieved as Treasurer in the late 1980s was 8.9 per cent, and that was with mortgage rates of 17 per cent.

The paradox is that, while households are carrying record debts, the nation's foreign borrowings have become significantly easier to service. In fact, the amount of export income required to cover our international obligations is at a 20-year low. The foreign debt bill is now less in real terms than household debt. The only drawback is the current account deficit: the difference between what we buy and borrow and sell and lend to the world is at a record high.

The tables presented below are a real-world snapshot of the Howard era, from bricks and mortar to work and family and the balance of payments. The report card, while mixed, is generally very good. The Howard years have been recession-free, which is a boast no other long-term prime minister can make, not even Howard's hero Robert Menzies.

But if you look closely enough, you can see the seeds for the next slowdown. They are the imbalances in the household debt and the current account. Sooner or later, our borrowing binge will have to end, and with it the warm buzz of the nation's longest boom.

Bricks and mortar

Proportion of taxpayers with investment properties
  1995–96: 11.2 per cent
  2002–03: 13.1 per cent

Debt burden on households

Interest bill as a share of disposable income
  Mar qtr 1996: 7.6 per cent (housing 5.8, credit 1.8)
  Jun qtr 2005: 9.8 per cent (7.9 housing, 1.9 credit)

Household savings
  Mar qtr 1996: 6.8 per cent
  Sep qtr 2005: –2.1 per cent

* * *

GDP

Average annual growth
  Howard years, 1996–2005: 4.2 per cent, with no recession,
  Hawke–Keating years, 1983–96: 4.7 per cent, but with the recession
    'we had to have' in 1990–91.

CPI

Jun 1996 to Jun 2005: 2.7 per cent per annum
(Keating's prime ministership had inflation at 2.6 per cent, Jun 1991 to Jun 1996)

* * *

Work

Employment rate
Mar 1996
  Male 67.2 per cent
  Female 46.6 per cent
Nov 2005
  Male 68.3 per cent
  Female 54.1 per cent

Unemployment rate
Mar 1996
  Male 8.6 per cent
  Female 7.6 per cent
Nov 2005
  Male 5.1 per cent
  Female 5.0 per cent

The jobs cake

	Mar 1996	Nov 2005
Full-time male:	50.4 per cent	47 per cent
Full-time female:	24.9 per cent	24.2 per cent
Part-time male:	6.3 per cent	8 per cent
Part-time female:	18.4 per cent	20.8 per cent

Full-time average weekly earnings

Aug 1996
  Male: $776.60
  Female: $615.50

Aug 2005
  Male: $1148.20
  Female: $926.70

Wages as a share of non-farm GDP
  Mar 1996: 56.7 per cent   Sep 2005: 54.3 per cent

Share of jobs going to …
Highest skilled workers:
  1996: 24.8 per cent
  2004: 26.4 per cent

Lowest skilled workers
  1996: 21.8 per cent
  2004: 19.3 per cent

* * *

Family

Families with children under 5 as a share of all families with dependent children
   1996: 47.7 per cent
   2004: 45.1 per cent

Families with dependent children, both parents working
   1996: 54.5 per cent
   2004: 57.3 per cent
One parent working
   1996: 37.6 per cent
   2004: 36.3 per cent
Neither parent working
   1996: 7.9 per cent
   2004: 6.4 per cent

* * *

Overseas students as a share of all students in higher education
   1996: 8.4 per cent
   2003: 22.6 per cent

* * *

Current account deficit as share of GDP
   1995–96:   4.1 per cent
   2004–05:   6.4 per cent (worst ever)

Net foreign debt
   Mar 1996: $193.258 bn
   Sep 2005: $449.696 bn

But it is easier to service foreign debt interest as share of export income
   Mar 1996:   11.4 per cent
   Sep 2005:   9.4 per cent

* * *

Immigration

Top four new arrivals of the Howard years, 1996–2004
New Zealand: 127,000
China: 60,800
South Africa: 47,400
India: 43,800

* * *

Hip pocket

Personal tax scales
Keating's at March 1996

$ 0–5400	00c
$ 5401–$20,700	20c
$20,701–$38,000	34c
$38,001–$50,000	43c
$50,001+	47c

Howard's from 1 July 2006, based on the 2005 budget

$ 0–6000	00c
$ 6001–$21,600	15c
$21,601–$70,000	30c
$63,001–$125,000	42c
$125,001+	47c

24

10 YEARS IN 25 PICTURES

Compiled by Paul Burston

John Howard, with his wife Janette, flanked by sons Tim (left) and Richard (right) on election night, claims victory at the Wentworth Hotel, Sydney, 2 March 1996. Daughter Melanie is obscured by a camera (far right). Photo: News Limited

Howard at The Lodge, 7 June 1996. Photo: Lyndon Mechielsen,
The Australian

Howard wears a bullet-proof vest at a pro-gun rally in Sale, Victoria,
16 June 1996. Photo: Ray Strange, News Limited

Howard withdraws money from an ATM in Phillip St, Sydney,
23 June 1996. Photo: Milan Scepanovic, News Limited

US president Bill Clinton and Howard at Mrs Macquarie's Chair, Sydney, 21 November 1996. Photo: Paul Burston, The Australian

Allan Border, Howard and Courtney Walsh spin the toss at Manuka Oval, Canberra, at the start of the Prime Ministers' Eleven (XI) v West Indies match, 10 December 1996. Photo: Trent Parke, The Australian

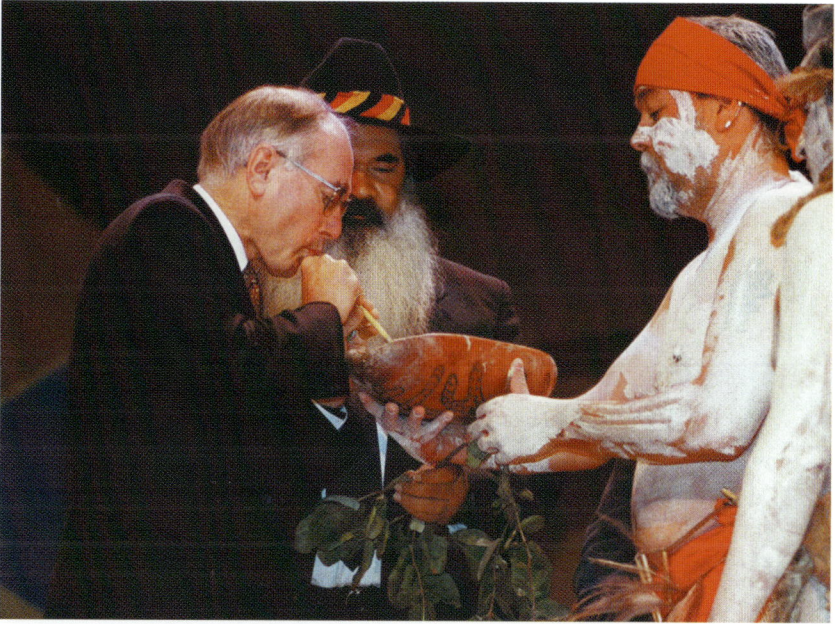

Council for Aboriginal Reconciliation chairman Pat Dodson watches as Howard drinks water from a traditional container at the Aboriginal Reconciliation Convention in Melbourne, 26 May 1997. Photo: News Limited

Howard celebrates with Brisbane Broncos player Kevin Walters after the team's NRL grand final victory against Canterbury Bulldogs, 27 September 1998. Photo: David Crossling, News Limited

MPs Jackie Kelly (left) and Danna Vale (right) celebrate retaining their marginal seats with Howard at Kirribilli House, Sydney, 5 October 1998.
Photo: Jeff Darmanin, News Limited

Howard cheers on Pat Rafter during a Davis Cup quarter-final in Brookline, Massachusetts, 17 July 1999. Photo: David Crosling, News Limited

Howard with Palestine Liberation Organisation chairman Yasser Arafat in Gaza City, 1 May 2000. Photo: John Feder, News Limited

International Olympic Committee president Juan Antonio Samaranch watches the swimming competition with Howard at the Sydney 2000 Olympic Games, 22 September 2000. Photo: Gregg Porteous, News Limited

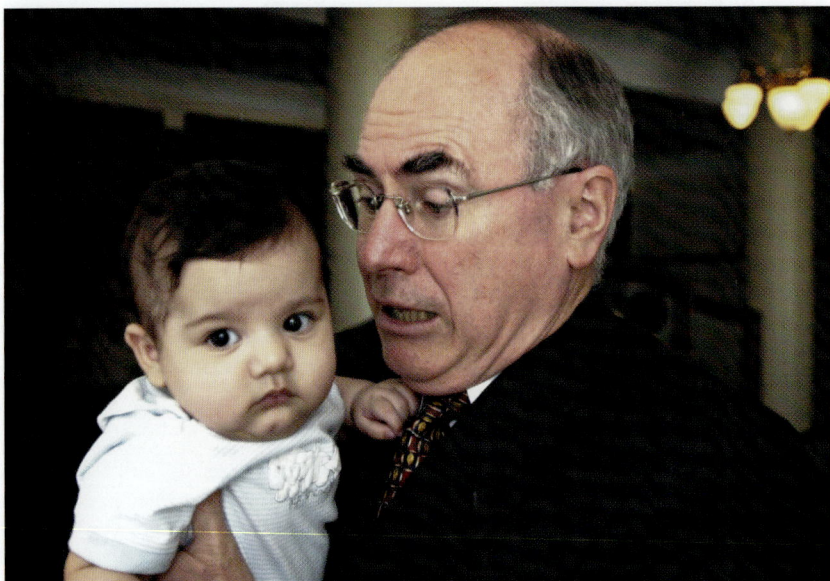

Baby Salim Osman with Howard at a ceremony to present millennium baby certificates at the Epping Club, Sydney, 6 April 2001. Photo: Renee Nowytarger, The Australian

*Howard with Indonesian president Abdurrahman Wahid in Parliament House,
Canberra, 26 June 2001. Photo: Reuters*

*Howard greets the Queen as she arrives at the Adelaide Festival Centre for a
state dinner, 27 February 2002. Photo: Chris Crerar,* The Australian

Howard visits John Paul II at the Vatican, 6 July 2002. Photo: Reuters

US President George W Bush looks down at his dog Barney as Howard speaks to a press conference at the Bush ranch in Crawford, Texas, 3 May 2003. Photo: Reuters

Howard escorts his daughter Melanie at her wedding to Rowan McDonald, Christ Church, Lavender Bay, Sydney, 27 September 2003. Photo: Brett Costello

Howard comforts a relative at a memorial ceremony for victims of the first Bali bombing, 12 October 2003. Photo: Renee Nowytarger, The Australian

Howard makes a Christmas visit to Honiara to meet Australian Federal Police officers on duty in the Solomon Islands, 22 December 2003. Photo: John Feder, News Limited

Timber workers give Howard a warm welcome at Albert Hall, Launceston, 6 October 2004. Photo: Chris Crerar, The Australian

Opposition leader Mark Latham shakes hands with Howard outside an ABC radio studio in Sydney while campaigning, 8 October 2004. Photo: David Geraghty, The Australian

British Prime Minister Tony Blair and Howard outside Number 10, Downing St, 21 July 2005. Photo: AFP

Howard dressed in protective vest and helmet on board an RAAF Hercules C-130 as he prepares to visit Baghdad, Iraq, 25 July 2005. Photo: Andrew Taylor, Pool

Howard and Treasurer Peter Costello during question time in the House of Representatives as Minister for Local Government Jim Lloyd looks on, 6 December 2005. Photo: John Feder, News Limited

NOTES

1   How Howard Governs

1   This article draws heavily on my 2005 Cunningham Lecture to the Academy of the Social Sciences in Australia.

2   John Howard, 8 September 2005.

3   John Howard, 'Reflections on Australian Federalism', address to the Menzies Research Centre, 11 April 2005.

4   ibid.

5   This draws on the main idea in Julian Disney and J R Nethercote (eds), *The House on Capital Hill*, The Federation Press, Sydney, 1996.

6   *The Spectator*, 11 December 2004.

7   Professor Peter Hennessy, University of London, 'Rulers and Servants of the State: The Blair Style of Government, 1997–2004', Public Management Foundation speech, 11 June 2004.

8   Paul Kelly, interview with John Howard, *The Australian Magazine*, 11–12 December 2004.

9   ibid.

10   Material provided by the Department of Prime Minister and Cabinet.

11   Refer Patrick Weller, *Malcolm Fraser PM*, Penguin Books, Ringwood, Victoria, 1989.

12   John Howard, Sir Robert Garran Oration, 19 November 1997.

13   ibid.

14   Patrick Weller, *Australia's Mandarins*, Allen & Unwin, Sydney, 2001, p. 193.

15   ibid.

16   Vince Fitzgerald, 'Advice on Public Policy', in Julian Disney and J R Nethercote (eds), *The House on Capital Hill*, The Federation Press, 1996.

17   The Senate Select Committee on A Certain Maritime Incident Report, October 2002.

18   Inquiry into the Circumstances of the Immigration Detention of Cornelia Rau Report, July 2005, by Mick Palmer, Commonwealth of Australia, and Inquiry into the Circumstances of the Vivian Alvarez Matter, Commonwealth Ombudsman, Report no. 03/2005.

19   John Howard, 'Strategic Leadership for Australia—Policy Directions in a Complex World', 20 November 2002.

20 For Howard's attitude to the media see Michelle Grattan, 'Gatekeepers and Gatecrashers: The Relationship between politics and the media', 38th Alfred Deakin Lecture, 2 May 2005.
21 John Faulkner, 'Address to RSSS roundtable on the politics of opposition', 7 October 2005.
22 The departing ministers were Assistant Treasurer Jim Short, Minister for Small Business and Consumer Affairs Geoffrey Prosser, Minister for Administrative Services David Jull, Minister for Transport John Sharp, and Minister for Science and Technology Peter McGuaran.
23 John Howard, press conference, 14 July 2005.
24 House of Representatives Hansard, 12 September 2005.
25 John Howard, Ministerial Conversations Lunch Seminar, 12 August 2005.
26 Paul Kelly, *The Australian*, 20–30 October 2005; Peter Jennings, 'The Policy Shift the Media Missed', The Centre for Independent Studies, *Policy*, vol. 20, no. 2, Winter 2004.
27 ibid.
28 Paul Kelly and Patrick Walters, *The Weekend Australian*, 25 June 2005.
29 Erika Feller, the *Georgetown Journal of International Affairs*, winter/spring 2002; refer www.unhcr.ch
30 See Matthew J Gibney, *The Ethics and Politics of Asylum*, Cambridge University Press, Cambridge, 2004.
31 John Howard, interview with John Laws, 8 March 2004.

3 Two Howards

1 Howard's Big Regret, *The Weekend Australian*, 7 January 1995.
2 Keating's second address as UNSW visiting professor, 11 November 1996.
3 On Nine Network's *A Current Affair*, 29 November 1996.
4 John Howard, unpublished speech, 25 June 2005, Liberal Party Federal Council.
5 John Howard, interview with the author, December 2005.

5 Getting Personal

1 *Enough Rope* with Andrew Denton, ABC television, 12 July 2004.
2 Conversation on 21 March 1987 as reported in *Sun News Pictorial* ('Sun sent secret phone talks', 23 March 1997) and *The Australian* ('Kennett asks for probe in phone tap', 24 March 1987).
3 David Barnett and Pru Goward, *John Howard: Prime Minister*, Viking Press, Melbourne, 1997.
4 Anthony Albanese, grievance debate, House of Representatives, 6 April 1998.
5 'So ordinary, this man's extraordinary', *The Australian*, 14 December 2002.
6 Graham Richardson, in *Quarterly Essay*, Black Inc., December 2005.
7 Howard valedictory, House of Representatives, 8 December 2005.
8 ibid.

6 The Golden Years

1 Address to the Business Council of Australia, 1 October 2003.

2 Under the linked structure of wage awards, a wage increase gained in one sector spread rapidly to other 'comparable' award classifications and hence through the whole economy.

3 See Ian Macfarlane, Governor of the Reserve Bank of Australia, Some Observations on Recent Economic Developments, 13 December 2005.

4 Ken Henry, Secretary to the Treasury, in Peter Dawkins and Michael Stutchbury (eds), *Sustaining Prosperity*, Melbourne University Publishing, Melbourne, 2005.

5 See note 45.

6 Three important reforms are missing from this list: reform of the commonwealth debt market between 1979 and 1982 under Howard as Treasurer; competition policy reform, initiated by Paul Keating and implemented, somewhat unenthusiastically, under Howard as Prime Minister; and Reserve Bank independence, an initiative of Treasurer Peter Costello.

7 However, it is equally true that labour market reform, at least in its legislative form, was initiated under Keating, with the introduction of enterprise bargaining. It was, in fact, the private sector that was the catalyst, through individuals such as Charles Copeman at Robe River, and by the Business Council of Australia, which advocated enterprise bargaining.

8 J Quiggin, 'Economic Policy', in Robert Manne (ed.), *The Howard Years*, Black Inc., Melbourne, 2004.

9 Peter Costello, address to the National Press Club, Canberra, 17 May 1995.

10 Fiscal Policy in Australia, 2 October 2003.

11 Keating once unwisely boasted that he had the Reserve Bank in his pocket.

12 Transcript of questions and answers, Australian Business Economists Dinner, 13 December 2005.

13 Quiggin, op. cit.

7 The Carrot and the Stick

1 Figures from budget statements 1996–97, Budget Paper No. 1, Commonwealth of Australia, 1996, pp. 1–24, and Budget Strategy and Outlook 2005–06, Budget Paper No. 1, Commonwealth of Australia, 2005, pp. 13–14. The figure for 2006 includes 2.5 per cent for GST, collected by the Commonwealth but not included in the budget paper figure.

2 ibid., calculated from various pages.

3 Welfare to Work, Budget Paper, Commonwealth of Australia, 2005, p. 2.

4 Budget Strategy and Outlook 2005–06, op. cit., pp. 6–12.

5   Quoted in *Australia's Welfare 2005*, Australian Institute of Health and Welfare, 2005, p. 75.
6   Participation support for a More Equitable Society, final report of the reference group on welfare reform, July 2000.
7   Quoted in Peter Dawkins and Mike Steketee (eds), *Reforming Australia— New policies for a new generation*, Melbourne University Press, Melbourne, 2004, p. 30.
8   Rosanna Scutella and Paul Smyth, The Brotherhood's Social Barometer, Brotherhood of St Laurence, December 2005, pp. 28–9.

8   Taxing Times
1   John Howard, interview with the author, December 2005.
2   ibid.

9   Unfinished Business
1   A total of 337 amendments were made to the bill, mostly minor ones to fix drafting errors and eliminate unintended consequences. Several last-minute amendments were included to pacify maverick Queensland Nationals' Senator Barnaby Joyce, who raised concerns about public holidays and the capacity of large businesses to split into corporate units with fewer than a hundred employees as a means of escaping unfair dismissal laws.
2   John Howard, statement on workplace relations reform, House of Representatives, 26 May 2005, Hansard, p. 39.
3   John Howard, interview with the author, December 2005.
4   Paul Kelly, *The End of Certainty: The story of the 1980s*, Allen & Unwin, Sydney, 1992, p. 115.
5   Milton Cockburn, 'What makes Johnny run', *The Sydney Morning Herald*, 7 January 1989.
6   John Howard, interview with the author, December 2005.
7   Milton Cockburn, op. cit.
8   David Barnett, *John Howard, Prime Minister*, Viking, Melbourne, 1997, p. 5.
9   Milton Cockburn, op. cit.
10   ibid.
11   John Howard, interview with the author, December 2005.
12   Paul Kelly, op. cit., p. 115.
13   John Howard, speech to the National Press Club, 31 August 1983; Paul Kelly, op. cit., p. 114.
14   Gerard Henderson, 'The Industrial Relations Club', *Quadrant*, September 1983.
15   Des Keegan, 'A peek inside the IR club', *The Australian*, 31 August 1983; Kelly, op. cit., p. 114.
16   The Mudginberri, Dollar Sweets, SEQEB and Robe River disputes, as well as later ones involving domestic airline pilots and Weipa bauxite miners, proved that employers could tackle union muscle head-on. Jay Pendarvis,

the Mudginberri abattoir owner, became a potent symbol of the changing attitude as the result of a campaign by *The Australian*.

17   Brad Norington, *Sky Pirates: The Pilots' Strike that Grounded Australia*, ABC Books, Sydney, 1990, pp. 184–5.

18   John Howard, interview with the author, December 2005.

19   ibid.

20   Gerard Henderson, *Australian Answers*, Random House Australia, Sydney, 1990, pp. 158–9.

21   Jobsback! The federal Coalition's industrial relations policy, 20 October 1992.

22   Paul Keating, speech to Institute of Company Directors, 21 April 1993; Brad Norington, *Jennie George*, Allen & Unwin, Sydney, 1998, pp. 211–13. Labor had embraced economic reform by floating the dollar, opening up financial markets and removing trade barriers, but was limited in how far it would go on labour market reform considering the historical relationship with unions.

23   Brad Norington, op. cit., p. 285; Pamela Williams, *The Victory*, Allen & Unwin, Sydney, 1997, p. 166. As Williams points out, Reith worked hard to change the Coalition's 'anti-worker' image. Howard's guarantee that no worker would be worse off was Reith's idea.

24   John Howard, industrial relations policy speech, address to the 28th Annual Convention of the Young Liberal Movement, 8 January 1996.

25   John Howard, statement on workplace relations, Hansard, House of Representatives, 26 May 2005, p. 43.

26   Workplace Relations Amendment (Work Choices) Bill 2005.

27   Howard and Treasurer Peter Costello believed increases in minimum wage rises granted by the AIRC were too high, so they created a new 'Fair Pay Commission' with orders to consider the unemployed first. The new tribunal's chairman, economist Ian Harper, was on record criticising increases in the basic wage that did not take into account productivity or an employer's capacity to pay. The Government's intent was clear, yet publicly it predicted higher wages. Under Freedom of Information laws, *The Australian* obtained Treasury advice to Costello on the workplace changes that confirmed the view that 'increases in minimum wages are likely to be lower'. Michael McKinnon, Steve Lewis, 'IR laws: what Costello was told', *The Australian*, 19 December 2005; Brad Norington, Steve Lewis, 'Costello hiding Treasury IR report', *The Australian*, 5 November 2005.

28   John Howard, 'Workplace relations reform: The next logical step', speech to the Sydney Institute, 11 July 2005.

29   Mark Wooden, 'Australia's industrial relations reform agenda', Melbourne Institute of Applied Economic and Social Research, University of Melbourne, paper to the 34th Conference of Economists, University of Melbourne, 26–28 September 2005.

30   Brad Norington, 'A "far cry" from the NZ workplace', *The Australian*,
      4 November 2005.
31   John Howard, interview with the author, December 2005.
32   ibid.
33   ibid.

11 Mixed Race, Mixed Messages
1   ibid.
2   John Howard, interview with the author, December 2005.
3   ibid.
4   ibid.
5   9 December 2005.

12 Beyond Sorry
1   Warren Mundine, interview with the author, December 2005.
2   Pat Dodson, interview with the author, *The Weekend Australian*, 2–3 August
      2003.
3   Herbert Cole Coombs (1906–97), a former governor of the Reserve
      Bank, was one of Australia's most influential public servants, serving and
      advising seven prime ministers over a 30-year period. As chairman of the
      Australian Council for Aboriginal Affairs (1968–76) he was a principal
      architect of indigenous self-determination. Interviewed in 1992 by Robin
      Hughes for *Australian Biography*, Coombs reflected that Aboriginal people
      had refused to become an 'unpaid or a poorly paid proletariat working
      for our industries in our enterprises. They have never been willing to
      accept that. They will starve rather than do that. So that, if we want
      anything to come out of this, what we have to do is to accept the fact that
      Aborigines are different. They do have a different way of seeing the world
      and understanding it, they have a different vision of what the place
      should be like.' During the Howard years, Coombs's legacy came under
      increasing criticism from ideological conservatives who argued that the
      communal land ownership implicit in Aboriginal land rights was keeping
      Aboriginal people poor and dependent on welfare. For an understanding
      of this criticism, see 'Hasluck v Coombs' (1996), by Geoffrey Partington.
      This was commissioned by Peter Howson and Ray Evans, former
      executive officer at Western Mining Corporation (WMC), who was
      instrumental in the establishment of several conservative societies
      including the HR Nicholls Society, the Bennelong Society and the
      Samuel Griffith Society.
4   See Patrick West, 'Conspicuous Compassion: why sometimes it really is
      cruel to be kind', first published February 2004 by Civitas, the Institute
      for the Study of Civil Society, London, and reprinted with an Australian
      introduction December 2004 by the Centre for Independent Studies.
5   Vanstone, address to Australia and New Zealand School of Government,
      Australian National University, Canberra, 7 December 2005.

6   In 'Pointing the Bone—Reflections on the Passing of ATSIC', April 2004, republished in *Quadrant,* June 2004, Howson wrote: 'The people who live in these former ration depots, if they are to escape from the horror of these places, will need to move to places where civilisation exists, where labour markets are operating, where effective schools are teaching literacy, numeracy and the other skills that will enable the rising generation to take its place in mainstream Australian life. Ideally, these ration depots should be shut down but as a second-best every conceivable effort must be made to persuade the people there, especially the children and teenagers, to move. This should at least include the cessation of provision of infrastructure and other assistance to the 900 or so communities which have average populations of only fifteen.'

7   Assimilation was government policy for part-Aborigines from 1933. In 1965, at a welfare conference in Adelaide, the policy shifted slightly to 'integration', described as seeking 'that all persons of Aboriginal descent will choose to attain a similar manner of living to that of other Australians and live as members of a single community, enjoying the same rights and privileges, accepting the same responsibilities and influenced by the same hopes and loyalties [as] other Australians.' Opponents said assimilation would result in the destruction of Aboriginal culture and identity.

8   Paul Keating, 10 December 1992, at the Australian launch of the International Year for World indigenous people.

9   The expression 'black-armband view of history' was first used by historian Geoffrey Blainey in April 1993, in his Latham Memorial Lecture in Sydney. The lecture was subsequently edited and published in the *Weekend Australian* 1–2 May 1993, p. 16, as 'Goodbye to All That?' Blainey said that what he called the 'Black-Armband View' was a rival to the old way Australian history was taught, which he called the 'Three-Cheers View of History' and which 'viewed Australian history as largely a success'.

10 See Joshua Foa Dienstag, 'The Pozsgay Affair: Historical Memory and Political Legitimacy', *History and Memory,* vol. 8, no. 1, Spring 1996, pp. 51–65; and Sean Brawley, 'A Comfortable and Relaxed Past: John Howard and the Battle of History', The Electronic Journal of Australian and New Zealand History, http://www.jcu.edu.au/aff/history/articles/brawley. htm

11 Influential conservative texts during this period included Roger Sandall's *The Culture Cult: Designer Tribalism and Other Essays* (Westview Press, 2001), which warned against sentimentalising tribal cultures, and Keith Windschuttle's *The Fabrication of Aboriginal History: Volume One, Van Diemen's Land 1803–1847* (Macleay Press, Sydney, 2002). Many attacks were carried in the conservative journal *Quadrant,* edited by P P (Paddy) McGuinness. By October 2000, *Quadrant* was in full roar, with several incendiary articles in the one edition: Keith Windschuttle on 'The Myths of Frontier Massacres', Roger Sandall on 'The Middle-Class Culture Cult',

Reginald Marsh on the great mistake of land rights in the Northern Territory and Geoffrey Partington on the woeful state of Aboriginal education that consigned children to a 'sub-culture'. Michael Connor—in 'The Invention of Terra Nullius: Historical and Legal Fictions on the Foundation of Australia' (Macleay Press, Sydney, 2005)—suggested that the concept of 'terra nullius', raised by the High Court in Mabo, was also a myth.

12   John Howard, 'The Role of Government: A Modern Liberal Approach', Menzies Research Centre, 6 June 1995.

13   John Howard, 'The Liberal Tradition: The Beliefs and Values Which Guide the Federal Government', Sir Robert Menzies Lecture, Melbourne, 18 November 1996.

14   The National Inquiry into the Separation of Aboriginal and Torres Strait Islander Children from Their Families, Bringing Them Home [Bringing Them Home], Human Rights and Equal Opportunity Commission, p. 275. The inquiry was commissioned by the Keating Government but was delivered to the Howard Government, which rejected the finding of genocide.

15   In July 2001, *The Age* newspaper in Melbourne, under the headline 'Geoff Clark: Power and Rape', published allegations that Clark had raped four women in the 1970s and 1980s. In December 2002, Clark and ATSIC deputy chairman 'Sugar' Ray Robinson, who was also facing serious allegations of financial irregularities, were re-elected to their positions. ATSIC was finally abolished in March 2005 and replaced by a small hand-picked advisory body, the National Indigenous Council, which functioned along the lines of a Senate estimates committee.

16   Sutton, 'The Politics of Suffering: Indigenous Policy in Australia since the 1970s', Inaugural Berndt Foundation Biennial Lecture, September 2000, published in various places, including *Anthropological Forum*, vol. 11, no. 2, 2001, pp. 125–73.

17   Peter Sutton to the author, early 2001.

18   Robertson, The Aboriginal and Torres Strait Islander Women's Task Force on Violence Report, 1999.

19   Pearson brought together these ideas in a booklet, 'Our Right to Take Responsibility' (self-published, 2000).

13   The Doctrine of Choice

1   Address to the Enterprise Forum, Hilton Hotel, Adelaide, 8 July 2004.

2   Andrew Robb, interview with the author, December 2005.

3   'Howard slams public schools', *The Australian*, 20 January 2004.

4   Vanstone in an after-dinner speech to an Adelaide conference, as reported by Catherine Armitage, 'Vanstone lectures don't impress VCs', *The Australian*, 25 May 1996.

5   Amanda Vanstone, interview with the author, December 2005.

6   David Kemp, interview with the author, December 2005.

7   Address to the Australian Industry Group, 15 August 2005.
8   Michael Wooldridge, interview with the author, December 2005.

14 Jumping the White Picket Fence

1   This term was coined by Howard himself when being interviewed on ABC television's *7.30 Report*, on 9 May 1989 after losing a ballot for Liberal Party leader to Andrew Peacock.
     KERRY O'BRIEN: Do you see yourself as having another chance at the leadership at some future time?
     JOHN HOWARD: I mean, that's Lazarus with a triple bypass, I mean ...
     O'BRIEN: Aren't you a political corpse now? Why don't you just toss it in completely?
     HOWARD: Oh, I ... pass
2   Pru Goward, interview with the author, December 2005.
3   ibid.
4   Grahame Morris, interview with the author, December 2005.
5   ibid.

16 At War with Terror

1   Interview with John Laws, Radio 2UE, 3 November 2005.
2   Press conference, Washington, 11 September 2001.
3   Interview with Alan Jones, Radio 2GB, 3 October 2001.
4   Newspoll, December 2005.
5   COAG joint press conference, Canberra, 27 September 2005.
6   Australia's National Security, A Defence Update 2005, p. 3.
7   Launch of the Defence Update 2005, Victoria Barracks, Sydney, 15 December 2005.
8   Defence 2000—Our Future Defence Force, December 2000, www.defence.gov.au/whitepaper

17 Team America

1   *The Los Angeles Times*, 7 September 2001.
2   White House news transcript, 3 May 2003.
3   Paul Kelly, 'Bush pins a sheriff badge on Australia', *The Australian*, 16 October 2003.
4   Australian Associated Press, 17 October 2003.
5   Cameron Forbes, 'Reality bites after the barbecue', *The Australian*, 14 July 1999.
6   Robert Garran and Christopher Dore, *The Australian*, 'Call for US troops tests alliance', 8 September 1999.
7   John Howard, press conference, Canberra, 8 September 1999.
8   John Howard, press conference, Sydney, 9 September 1999, official transcript.

9   Former Clinton National Security Council official Eric Schwartz, 'The Intervention in East Timor', report for the National Intelligence Council, December 2001.

10   Dennis Shanahan, 'US fury at our failing', *The Australian*, 17 September 1999.

11   'Don't forget we're on our own', *The Australian*, 14 September 1999.

12   Governor George W Bush, 'A Distinctly American Internationalism', Ronald Reagan Presidential Library, Simi Valley, California, 19 November 1999.

13   White House press conference, 13 September 2001.

14   Paul Kelly, 'Phoenix rising', *The Australian*, 29 September 2001.

15   John Howard's National Press Club Address, 11 September 2002.

16   Interview with Neil Mitchell, Radio 3AW, 20 August 2004.

17   Mike Steketee, 'Beneficiaries of an obsequious foreign policy', *The Australian*, 26 November 2005.

18   John Kerin and Roy Eccleston, 'Any strike on our soil spells war', *The Australian*, 4 December 2002.

19   John Howard, doorstop interview, Penrith, 19 September 2004, transcript.

20   Bob Woodward, *Plan of Attack*, Simon & Schuster, New York, 2004, p. 150.

21   Bob Hawke launching *The Power of Speech—Australian Prime Ministers Defining the National Image* by James Curran (Melbourne University Press, Melbourne), Sydney, 6 May 2004.

22   Kevin Rudd, 'My old boss is wrong about the US alliance', *The Australian*, 23 September 2005.

23   House of Representatives, 5 February 2003.

24   Mark Latham, *The Latham Diaries*, Melbourne University Publishing, Melbourne, 2005.

25   George W Bush with John Howard, Rose Garden, White House, 3 June 2004.

26   George W Bush, political rally, Waterloo, Iowa, 9 October 2004.

27   Roy Eccleston, 'US trade supremo boasts of "Con Job"', *The Australian*, 11 March 2004.

28   Alexander Downer, official transcript of media conference, Beijing, 17 August 2004.

29   US ambassador Bob Schieffer and John Howard, quoted on *Lateline*, ABC TV, 20 August 2004.

18 Losing the Plot

1   Kim Beazley, interview with the author, December 2005.

2   Evan Thornley's essay 'To My Friends on the Occasion of an Election Defeat', published by The Fabian Society, December 2004.

3   ibid.

4   ibid.

19 Read My Lips

1   From *The Snake Has all the Lines*, Doubleday & Co., New York, 1960.
2   Keating's election night concession speech, 2 March 1996.

20 The Howard Idiom

1   I would like to thank Rod Kemp, Christopher Pearson and Gregory
     Melleuish for their kind help with this chapter. Unless otherwise
     attributed, all views expressed are my own.
2   Judith Brett, 'The New Liberalism', in Robert Manne (ed.), *The Howard
     Years*, Black Inc., Melbourne, 2004, pp. 74–5.
3   Delivered 6 June 1995 and available at www.australianpolitics.com
4   Unpublished address to Liberal Party National Convention, Adelaide,
     8 June 2003.
5   House of Representatives, 20 September 1990.
6   *The Australian*, 29 October 2004, p. 1.
7   *The Australian*, 19 October 2004, p. 1.
8   See Sally Warhaft (ed.), *Well May We Say: The Speeches that Made Australia*,
     Black Inc., Melbourne, 2004, pp. 551–2.
9   Op. cit., p. 157.
10   *The Australian*, 23 July 2005, p. 1.
11   John Howard, joint press conference with Tony Blair, London,
     21 July 2005.
12   'The New Liberalism', p. 75.

21 Howard's South Park Conservatives

1   Bean et al., *Australian Election Study 2004* (AES 2004), 2005.
2   *The Australian*, 28 June 1999, p. 1.
3   'Youth deserted Labor at last poll', *The Australian*, 9 September 2005.
4   *South Park Conservatives*, Brian C Anderson, Regnery Publishing,
     Washington, 2005.
5   'Mum's so young', *The Australian*, 21 November 2005.
6   Interview with the author, December 2005.
7   Interview with the author, December 2005.

ACKNOWLEDGEMENTS

No newspaper is better equipped for the task of producing a work of this nature than *The Australian*. The newspaper's Canberra bureau is the strongest news team in the press gallery, with a depth of experience, knowledge and analytical skill that our rivals do not come close to matching. The newspaper's Canberra-based political editor, Dennis Shanahan, came up with the idea for this book, persevered with his proposal until he got the answer he wanted, then worked tirelessly to ensure that it became a reality.

With due respect to Dennis and his colleagues, however, no book on John Howard would be complete if it were written entirely from Capital Hill. *The Australian*'s unique network of bureaus harbours a wealth of talented journalists who are well qualified to assess Howard's impact on the nation's society and culture. I was fortunate to be able to draw on writers based in Melbourne, Sydney, Adelaide and in Darwin who were able to give the book a genuinely national perspective.

My thanks go to the contributors who responded above the call of duty to meet the impossible deadlines I gave them. I acknowledge that my balance sheet of favours is now firmly in the red.

I owe a huge debt to *The Australian*'s editor in chief, Chris Mitchell, who gave me the opportunity to work on *The Australian* in 2004 and entrusted me with this absorbing project a year later. The intellectual rigour Chris injects is evident in the pages of *The Australian* every day of the week and also, I trust, in the pages of this book.

The enthusiasm, knowledge and eye for detail shown by *The Australian*'s editor, Michael Stutchbury, were gratefully appreciated, as was his grasp of the economic agenda that helped shape that side of the book. Canberra bureau chief Sid Marris helped frame the structure of the book and marshalled the bureau's resources to ensure that it happened.

Night editor Helen McCabe was generous with her support and suggested many improvements after reading early drafts. Managing editor Deborah Jones, national chief of staff Paul Whittaker and Melbourne Editor Chris Dore went out of their way to ensure that I was able to meet deadlines. Thanks to Ian Gunn for checking proofs.

Louise Adler at Melbourne University Publishing recognised the importance of this project from the start. She was brave enough to take it on despite the tight timetable and her support has been invaluable. Thanks, too, to the staff at MUP, especially Felicity Edge, Wendy Skilbeck and copyeditor Sally Moss.

Finally, my thanks to my partner, Rebecca Weisser, who spent weeks in News Limited's basement library trawling through a decade of bound volumes of *The Australian* to chronicle the critical events and issues that have defined the Howard years. From that endeavour sprung many lively discussions that enabled us to distil the essence of the Howard factor and crystallised the ideas that form the basis for this book.

Nick Cater
January 2006

One Brief Interval
A Memoir by

Sir Edward Woodward
The Miegunyah Press

'This is an interesting read on a life lived to the full. It will be fascinating for those interested in politics, law and some of the big issues of the 1970s, 80s and 90s.'

—*Herald Sun*

In these long-awaited memoirs, Sir Edward Woodward reflects on his life, both public and private, from his childhood before World War II to the present day. He recounts his rise to prominent QC, then judge of four different courts, and his involvement in some seventeen Royal Commissions or Boards of Inquiry, of which the best known is his Royal Commission into Aboriginal Land Rights in the Northern Territory in 1973–74.

Sir Edward takes the reader through the corridors of power in Canberra, the opposing forces of politics and the famous dismissal of Gough Whitlam. Reflecting on his time as head of ASIO from 1976 to 1981, he talks openly about the rumours, conspiracy theories and intrigue that are synonymous with intelligence organisations such as ASIO, and indeed the CIA and KGB. He includes his views on current political issues, such as police corruption and Australia's involvement in the Iraq War.

The Beginner's Guide to Winning the Nobel Prize

Peter Doherty
The Miegunyah Press

'A great tale from a great Australian—and he writes like an angel!'

—Robyn Williams, ABC Radio National Science Show

Is it possible to be passionate about politics or football and still be a creative scientist? In this witty and passionate account of life as one of the world's leading scientists, Nobel Prize winner and Australian of the Year Professor Peter Doherty offers an insider's guide into just what research scientists do all day.

Starting with the story of his own career—its improbable origins in the outer suburbs of Brisbane, and its progression to a breakthrough discovery about how human immunity works—Doherty explores the realities of a life in science. He argues the case for integrity, creativity, engaged science and the principle of working for the common good. Along the way he answers some of the great questions of our age. Are Nobel Prize winners exceptional human beings or just lucky? Are GMO crops really dangerous? Why can't scientists and born-again Christians get along?

Forged by War
Edited by Gina Lennox

'This book goes to the heart of how war affects individuals and changes lives.'

—*The Mercury Magazine*

These stark first-hand accounts from Australian veterans and their families describe the reality of military action and its personal consequences, in every major conflict and peacekeeping mission since World War II, including the invasion of Iraq. Sometimes the reader is in lockstep with a soldier on patrol, watching as a land mine explodes, or a local militiaman points an AK-47 at Australian peacemakers. Other times, the reader is inside a returned veteran's head, feeling their superfluous adrenaline, their need to control their environment, even at home.

Underpinning Gina Lennox's compelling investigation is the question: where does family fit in a veteran's life?